American Language Hub

LEVEL 3A
Student's Book

JEREMY DAY
GARETH REES

macmillan education

Contents

Welcome

GRAMMAR
Verb tenses and structures

A Choose the correct verb forms to complete the conversation.

A: Excuse me. I [1]*look* / *'m looking* for room 14. I have an English class today, but I [2]*don't know* / *'m not knowing* where to go.

B: Room 14? It's right here. It looks like we're [3]*being* / *going to be* in the same group. My name's Diego, by the way.

A: Hi, Diego. I'm Yulia. So [4]*did* / *have* you studied at this school before?

B: Yes. I [5]*was* / *'ve been* in the same group last year. The teacher, Helena, is really nice. [6]*You* / *You'll* like her, I'm sure. So … why [7]*did you decide* / *were you deciding* to join this school, Yulia?

A: Well, about two weeks ago, I [8]*'ve tried* / *was trying* to help my son with his English homework, but I couldn't remember anything! So I decided to come back to school, after all these years!

B Find and correct the mistakes in the sentences or questions.The first one has been completed as an example.

1 How ~~many~~ *much* time do you spend doing homework every day?
2 It's an online course, so all the answers are check by a computer.
3 Everybody make mistakes when they speak English – even English speakers!
4 It's important to learn a lot of new words, but I don't really enjoy to study vocabulary.

C SPEAK Work in pairs and discuss the questions.

1 Why did you decide to join this class? Use the ideas from the conversation in Exercise A to help you.
2 What is the best way to learn English? Use the ideas in Exercise B to help you.

VOCABULARY
Describing places, illnesses and transportation

A Complete the table with the words in the box.

attractive bus ~~cold~~ ~~dirty~~ headache helicopter modern noisy ~~plane~~ temperature toothache trolley

Describing places	Illnesses	Transportation
dirty	a *cold*	a *plane*
	a	a
	a	a
	a	a

Collocations

B Choose the correct words to complete the collocations.

1 Is it better if somebody helps you *by* / *for* / *to* / *with* your homework, or should you always work alone?
2 When was the last time you *did* / *made* / *took* / *went* a day off from school or work?
3 Are you good *at* / *in* / *from* / *on* cooking?
4 Is it better to *borrow* / *earn* / *lend* / *pay* money from your friends or from the bank?
5 Is it possible to *have* / *stay* / *make* / *play* in shape without spending a lot of time or money?
6 Do you prefer to pay *by* / *on* / *for* / *with* your shopping by card or in cash?
7 What is the best way to *fall* / *get* / *meet* / *win* a good job in your country?

C SPEAK Work in pairs. Ask and answer the questions in Exercise B. Ask your partner to explain his/her answers.

A: I think it's better to do your homework with someone.
B: Really? Why do you think so?

PRONUNCIATION

0.1 **Listen and choose the words you hear.**

1 *where* / *were*
2 *can* / *can't*
3 *work* / *walk*
4 *mouth* / *mouse*
5 *have* / *of*
6 *this* / *these*
7 *cap* / *cup*

FUNCTIONAL LANGUAGE

Match the sentences (1–9) with the responses (a–i).

1 My name's Adam, by the way.
2 What a nice surprise. Long time, no see!
3 What do you think I should do?
4 Would you like me to check it for you?
5 Are you doing anything this evening?
6 Do you feel like watching a movie this weekend?
7 I feel really sick today … and I have an exam later.
8 In my opinion, young people these days are incredibly rude.
9 It was really nice to see you again.

a Why don't you try to find a new job?
b Sounds great. I'll just check that I'm free.
c You, too. See you later. Take care.
d Nice to meet you.
e Some are, but then some adults are, too.
f No. Why? Should we go out?
g Oh, no! Poor you! That sounds terrible.
h Yeah, I know! What are you doing these days?
i Yes, please. That would be really helpful.

1 COMMUNICATION

> Wise men speak because they have something to say; fools because they have to say something.
>
> Plato

A young woman enjoys her walk outdoors.

OBJECTIVES

- update your status on social media
- make a short podcast
- plan and conduct an interview
- use rhetorical questions in a presentation
- ask for, offer and respond to help
- write a report about trends

Work with a partner. Discuss the questions.

1. How does 21st century technology make it easier or harder to communicate with other people?
2. Read the quote. To what extent do you agree with Plato?
3. Which forms of communication do you use most often: face-to-face or electronic; written or spoken communication? Which do you prefer and why?

1.1 Communication today

- Update your status on social media
- Make a short podcast

G simple present and present progressive **V** seeing and hearing **P** schwa /ə/ **S** listening to check predictions

READING

A SPEAK Work in groups and discuss the questions.

1. Do you ever use social media sites? Which ones?
2. What sort of information do people usually post on social media?

B PREDICT Match the pictures (1–3) with the social media status updates (a–c). How do you think the people in the pictures are feeling? What can you guess about their lives?

a. On my way to the top! Looking forward to an amazing view!
b. Can't believe we're on vacation again! We're having a wonderful time!
c. Our beautiful new kitchen! Looks good, doesn't it?

C READ FOR GIST Read the social media posts quickly to check your predictions from Exercise B. Write about the true stories behind the pictures.

D READ FOR DETAIL Read again and answer the questions.

1. How do Katia and Elisa know each other?
2. Why was Katia confused?
3. When did Katia go to the top of the mountain?
4. How does Katia feel about her new kitchen?
5. How does Katia feel about her 'boring' life?
6. Why doesn't Elisa post pictures when she isn't on vacation?

1

2

My ***perfect*** *online life*

@Katia … is feeling confused
6 hours ago

Had a very strange experience today. I met my old school friend **@Elisa** for the first time in eight years. 'You're so lucky!' she said. 'You have such a perfect life! I'm so jealous!'

A perfect life? Me? I have a very normal life: I get up early every day, take the bus to work, watch TV … and that's all. In fact, Elisa seems to have a perfect life: her pictures always show her wonderful family relaxing in the sunshine on a beautiful beach.

But now that I'm writing this post, I think I understand what happened: on social media, our lives look perfect, but the reality is very different.

For example, last week I posted a selfie from the top of a mountain. In the picture, you can see I'm smiling. But in fact, I felt absolutely exhausted and just wanted to go home as quickly as possible! But you can't see that in the picture!

And did you see the picture of our new kitchen a few weeks ago? Well, yes, it's beautiful, but I didn't mention that it took six months to finish. Six months without a kitchen! And it cost us twice as much as we expected, so now we're getting worried about money. But no one ever talks about money problems on social media, do they?

I'm not complaining, though. I'm very happy with my life! I love being normal … and I don't mind that my life is becoming a little boring! In fact, I'm thinking of staying at home this evening – just me, my husband and a takeout pizza! Perfect!

Reply from **@Elisa**
4 hours ago

Hey, **@Katia**! Great to see you this morning. I know what you mean about our 'perfect lives'. I guess I need to explain about all those beach pictures. You see, I work really hard all year, and the only time I use social media is when I'm on vacation. That's why I'm sitting on the beach in all my pictures! It usually rains for most of the week we're on vacation, but of course we only take pictures when the sun's shining!

Glossary

jealous (adj) unhappy because someone has something that you would like or can do something that you would like to do

E SPEAK Work in pairs and discuss the questions.

1 Does your life look perfect on social media? What about your friends' lives?

2 Do you ever feel jealous when you see other people's status updates?

GRAMMAR

Simple present and present progressive

A Look at the underlined verbs in the social media posts. Which verbs are in the simple present? Which are in the present progressive?

B WORK IT OUT Match the sentences (a–f) with the rules (2–5).

a In the picture, you can see I'm smiling.

b I know what you mean about our 'perfect lives'.

c But now I'm writing this post, …

d You have such a perfect life!

e I get up early every day.

f So now we're getting worried about money.

Simple present and present progressive

1 Dynamic verbs (*talk*, *go*) usually describe actions.

2 We use the simple present with dynamic verbs to talk about actions that always, usually or never happen.

3 We use the present progressive with dynamic verbs:

- a to talk about actions that are in progress at the moment of speaking or writing.
- b to describe actions in a picture, video, etc.
- c to describe trends (e.g. something is happening more and more these days).

4 Stative verbs (*want*, *seem*) frequently describe feelings and ideas. We use the simple present with stative verbs.

5 A few verbs (*have*, *look*, *speak*, *think*) have two or more meanings. They are sometimes dynamic verbs and sometimes stative verbs.

C Find at least one more example of each rule (2–5) in the posts.

D Go to the Grammar Hub on page VI.

E Are the verbs stative verbs (S) or dynamic verbs (D)?

1 contain	S	7 include	___
2 cost	___	8 mean	___
3 depend	___	9 own	___
4 deserve	___	10 relax	___
5 enjoy	___	11 seem	___
6 happen	___	12 shine	___

F SPEAK Work in groups and discuss the questions.

1 Why are you studying English? Why do you need English?

2 How is this week different from your normal weekly routine? What are you doing differently this week? What do you normally do?

3 What are people doing more and more these days? What are some trends in your own life?

SPEAKING

A Work in groups. If you have some pictures on your phone, choose two or three to discuss with your group. If you do not, think about some of your favorite pictures of you and your friends or family.

B Tell your group:

- What's happening in the pictures?
- Does your life seem perfect or exciting in the pictures? What's the real story behind the pictures?
- Do you have any pictures of you doing normal things, e.g. watching TV? Why/Why not?

C Write a short social media status update for one or two of your pictures. Decide whether to make your life seem perfect or normal.

Writing a status

We frequently leave out the subject and *be* from the beginning of status updates when it's easy for the reader to guess the missing words.

- *(It) Looks good, doesn't it?*
- *(I) Had a very strange experience today.*
- *(It was) Great to see you this morning.*

D Read some of your classmates' social media status updates. Do their lives look perfect or normal?

LISTENING

A SPEAK **Work in pairs and discuss the questions.**

1 What do you use your cell phone for?

2 How did people do those things before they had cell phones? What problems did they have?

B PREDICT **Work in pairs. You are going to listen to** ***A week without phones!*** **Look at the pictures and discuss the questions. Use the strategies in the box to help you.**

Listening to check predictions

Before you listen to something in English, it's always a good idea to predict what you will hear.

If there's a title and pictures, you can try to predict the connection between them. Then you can listen to check your predictions.

1 Who are the people in picture a? What are they doing?

2 What is the device in picture b?

3 What does the title mean? What's the connection with the people and the device?

C LISTEN FOR GIST **Listen to Part 1 of the podcast and check your answers to Exercise B.** 1.1

D PREDICT **Work in pairs and discuss the questions. Then listen to Part 2 and check your answers.** 1.2

1 What went wrong when Olivia and Jackson tried to meet up on Monday?

2 How did they solve the problem?

E PREDICT **Work in pairs and discuss what you think Olivia and Jackson did differently on Tuesday when they met. Then listen to Part 3 and check your answer.** 1.3

F PREDICT **Work in pairs and discuss the questions. Then listen to Part 4 and check your answers.** 1.4

1 Do you think Olivia and Jackson are enjoying the experiment?

2 What do you think they're doing more or less of than usual?

G LISTEN FOR DETAIL **Listen again. Choose the correct answers, a, b or c.** 1.5

1 When is the last day of the experiment?
   a Tuesday
   b Thursday
   c Sunday

2 Why does Olivia decide to stop waiting outside on Monday?
   a She doesn't want to get wet.
   b She thinks Jackson isn't coming.
   c She knows the university closes at four o'clock.

3 How does Sebastian know Jackson and Olivia?
   a They study together at the university.
   b Olivia met Sebastian outside the bakery.
   c Sebastian has seen them before in pictures and videos.

4 Why is Olivia enjoying the concert more than usual on Tuesday?
   a She isn't recording it on her phone.
   b The audience isn't having as much fun.
   c Jackson isn't there with her.

5 On Thursday, why is Olivia surprised at the end of the podcast?
   a The university buildings are amazing.
   b Jackson doesn't usually talk so much.
   c She can't believe Jackson forgot his camera.

H SPEAK **Work in groups and discuss the questions.**

1 What problems did Olivia and Jackson have during the experiment?

2 What good things happened as a result?

3 Do you think Olivia and Jackson's experiment was a good idea?

4 Would you like to try a similar experiment? Why/Why not?

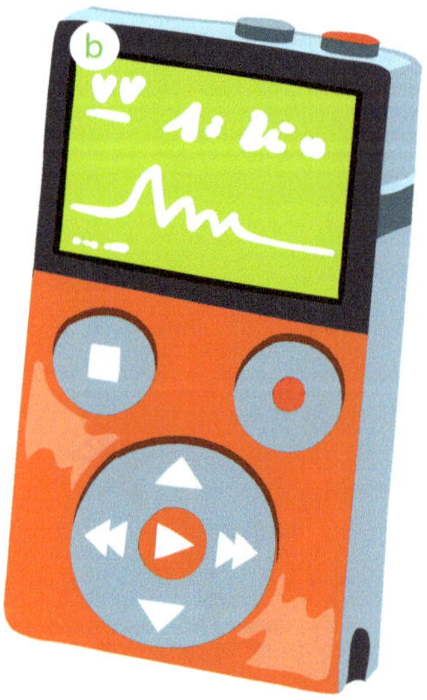

VOCABULARY
Seeing and hearing

1.6 **A** Choose the correct verbs to complete the sentences from *A week without phones!* Then listen again and check your answers.

1. In this week's podcast, we're ***looking at / seeing / watching*** phones.
2. It ***looks / sees / watches*** like he isn't coming, and I'm not sure what to do.
3. I'm ***looking / seeing / watching*** for Olivia, but I can't ***look at / see / watch*** her.
4. I ***hear / listen to / sound*** your podcast every week, and I ***look at / see / watch*** all your videos.
5. Yeah, that ***hears / listens / sounds*** like a great idea. Thanks a lot.
6. Maybe you can ***hear / listen to / sound*** the music in the background.
7. He plays the guitar in the band, and he ***hears / listens / sounds*** really good.
8. It doesn't ***look / see / watch*** great, but it's good for telling the time!

B WORK IT OUT Complete the rules with the correct form of *hear, listen, look, see, sound* or *watch*.

hear, listen, look, see, sound and watch

1. When you (eye) ____*see*____ or (ear) ________ something, it just happens, not because you're trying to do it.
2. When you (eye) ________ *at* or (ear) ________ *to* something, you do it because you decide to do it.
3. When you (eye) ________ something, you look at it for a period of time, perhaps because it's moving.
4. When something (eye) ________ good or (ear) ________ good, it probably is good, but you aren't sure.
5. When it (eye) ________ like or (ear) ________ like something is happening, it probably is happening, but you aren't sure.

C Go to the Vocabulary Hub on page XVI.

D Complete the questions with the verbs in the box. There are two extra verbs.

notice observe recognize spot stare

1. Do you ever sit in a café and ________ the people through the window? Why do people enjoy doing this?
2. Are you good at remembering people's faces? Do you always ________ people when you meet them the second time?
3. When you're traveling around (e.g. by bus), do you usually ________ the buildings around you?

E SPEAK Work in groups. Ask and answer the questions in Exercise D.

PRONUNCIATION
Schwa /ə/

Schwa /ə/

Schwa is the most common sound in English. We use it for most unstressed vowel sounds, especially in words like *a, the, of, to, and* and *but*.

1.7 **A** Listen to the sentences from *A week without phones!* Underline all schwas. The numbers in parentheses tell you how many schwas to find. The first one has been done for you.

1. We're not looking at our phones for a whole week! (3)
2. We arranged to meet here, outside the university, at four o'clock. (5)
3. It's Monday afternoon and I'm late meeting Olivia. (3)
4. I'll buy you a cupcake to say thank you, and you can tell us what you think of our podcasts. (7)
5. Yes, I'm wearing a watch today – an old one from when I was a teenager. (7)

B SPEAK Work in pairs. Practice saying the sentences. Listen and check your partner's pronunciation.

SPEAKING HUB

A Work in groups. You are going to make a short podcast about an experiment. Choose one of the ideas in the box or use your own ideas.

a week of doing something completely new every day
a week speaking only English
a week without complaining
a week without the internet/TV, etc.
a week without spending any money
a week of helping as many people as possible

B PLAN Plan a short podcast (about two minutes). Imagine you are in the middle of your experiment. Write notes on:

- what you can see and hear during your podcast.
- what's going well and/or badly with your experiment.
- what you're doing more or less as a result of your experiment.

C SPEAK Record your podcast and present it to the class.

D SHARE After listening to the podcasts, discuss the questions.

- Which group's experiment worked well?
- Which podcast did you enjoy most?

E REFLECT Work in new groups and discuss the questions.

- Will you try any of the experiments in real life? Why/Why not?
- Would you like to make a real podcast? What would your podcast be about?

— Update your status on social media
— Make a short podcast

1.2 Who owns English?

- Plan and conduct an interview
- Use rhetorical questions in a presentation

G subject and object questions   P pronouncing questions   V languages   S rhetorical questions

TOP 10 ENGLISH SPEAKING COUNTRIES

1. US 251,388,301
95.81% of population

2. India 125,226,449
11.38% of population

3. Philippines 89,800,000
92.58% of population

4. Nigeria 79,000,000
53.34% of population

5. UK 59,600,000
97.74% of population

6. Germany 46,272,000
56% of population

7. Canada 25,246,220
85.18% of population

8. France 23,000,000
36% of population

9. Australia 17,357,800
97.03% of population

10. Italy 17,000,000
29% of population

*The most amazing fact is that **only 11.38% of India's population** speaks English and yet it is the second largest English speaking nation in the world.*

USVisaTalk.com

LISTENING

A SPEAK Work in groups and discuss the questions.

1 Look at the infographic. What does it show? What do you know about the countries and the languages that people in those countries speak? Are you surprised by any of the numbers?
2 Who owns English? Who has the power to decide what's good and bad English?

B LISTEN FOR MAIN IDEA (1.8) Listen to an interview about different types of English and answer the questions.

1 Why does Mona want to interview Juan?
2 Why did Juan enjoy his journey?
3 Where did Juan have problems with English?
4 How is Multicultural London English (MLE) different from the English we learn at school?
5 What's the connection between 'Standard English' and 'standard class' on a train?
6 Why is Standard English useful?

C LISTEN FOR DETAIL (1.8) Listen again. Which person (Juan, Mona or Both) thinks …

1 traveling is a good way to practice your English? ______
2 it's difficult to understand people in England? ______
3 MLE grammar contains mistakes? ______
4 Standard English is boring but useful? ______
5 it's sometimes better when you don't sound like a native speaker? ______

D SPEAK Work in groups. Look at the sentences from the interview. For each one, discuss what Juan and Mona were talking about. Do you agree with their opinions?

1 'Millions of people speak like that, so how can it be wrong?'
2 'There are hundreds of other forms of English all over the world … They're all different, but I think that's really cool!'
3 'Surely Standard English is better, isn't it?'
4 'We don't need to speak like native speakers. In fact … it's usually better when we don't speak like native speakers.'

GRAMMAR

Subject and object questions

1.9 **A** Put the words in the correct order to make questions. Then listen to the interview again and check your answers.

1 you / I / a / questions / ask / can / few / ?

____

2 countries / did / which / visit / you / ?

____

3 England / happened / what / in / ?

____

4 changing / English / is / how / ?

____

5 MLE / uses / who / ?

____

6 mean / do / 'Standard English' / by / you / what / ?

____

7 to / you / need / non-standard English / saying / are / learn / we / so / ?

____

B WORK IT OUT Match the questions (1–7) in Exercise A with the rules (a–c).

Subject and object questions

a When we make questions in English, we usually put the auxiliary verb (*be*, *have*, *can*) before the subject. 1, ___, ___

b In sentences with no auxiliary verb, we add *do*, *does*, or *did* when we make a question. ___, ___

c When the question is about the subject, we use the same word order as in sentences. We don't add *do*, *does* or *did*. ___, ___

C PRACTICE Make questions about the missing information.

1 (Somebody) writes a blog for a website.
Who writes a blog for a website?

2 Juan visited (a number of countries).
How many ______________________________?

3 You (can/can't) give me an example.
______________________________?

4 (A form of English) is becoming popular in London.
Which ______________________________?

5 (A number of people) speak non-standard English.
How many ______________________________?

6 Most native speakers (speak/don't speak) Standard English.
______________________________?

D Go to the Grammar Hub on page VI.

E SPEAK Work in pairs. Student A – go to the Communication Hub on page XXIV. Student B – go to the Communication Hub on page XXII.

PRONUNCIATION

Pronouncing questions

1.10 **A** Listen to two people asking questions from the interview. What differences do you notice in the way they speak? Who is easier to understand?

1 *Why do you want to talk to me?*

2 *What do you want to talk about?*

a Which speaker joined the words together?

b Which speaker is easier to understand?

B SPEAK Work in pairs. Read the information in the box. Then practice saying the questions. First, try to say them by joining the words together. Then try to say them as clearly as possible.

- What do you think?
- Where did you go?
- Do you want to talk about it?
- Why did you say that?

Pronouncing questions

Many English speakers join words together when they speak quickly. In questions with *do/did* + *you*, it can be difficult to hear whether the speaker is saying *do* or *did*.

- *What do you want to do?* /wɒʤə wɒnə duː/
- *How did you travel?* /haʊʤə trævəl/

1.11 **C SPEAK** Work in pairs. Listen to two people asking the questions in Exercise B. Which version is better for you to use, the first or the second speaker? Why? Tell your partner.

SPEAKING

A Work in pairs. You are going to interview another student about their experiences of using English and communicating with English speakers. Write five questions. Use the prompts to help you. You can also use your own ideas.

- frequently communicate / English speakers?
- using English in the classroom / in real life?
- for work / while traveling?
- problems: speaking/understanding?
- Standard/non-standard English?
- advice for others?

B Work in new pairs. Use your questions to interview your partner. Listen carefully and ask follow-up questions.

Follow-up questions

Really? Why?
What happened? What went wrong?
Can you give me an example?

C Work in groups and discuss the questions.

1 What was the most interesting thing you learned from your interview?

2 What advice can you give to other people about using English in real life?

READING

A SPEAK Work in pairs and discuss the questions.

1 Look at the title of the magazine article. What do you think it means?

2 Think of some examples where you can lose something if you stop using it. Have you ever lost a skill or an ability because you didn't use it?

B READ FOR GIST Read *Use it or lose it?* quickly and answer the questions.

1 Is the writer generally positive or negative about learning languages?

2 What's the connection between the pictures, the word cloud and language learning?

Use it *or* lose it?

1 What's the worst thing about learning a language? Is it the hundreds of hours you need to spend studying and practicing? No, although that's bad enough. In fact, the worst thing is how easy it is to forget everything!

2 How do I know? From bitter experience! Many years ago, I lived in Spain for a year and studied Spanish for hours every day. By the end of that year, I spoke Spanish fluently (but not very accurately). But now, 20 years later, it's all gone. My only evidence that I ever spoke Spanish is an old certificate.

3 So is there any hope for me and my Spanish? Recent research suggests that there is. Imagine your brain is like a big library. As you keep adding new information to that library, the old information doesn't disappear; it just gets harder to find.

4 How does this work in practice? When I see a dog, my English-speaking brain thinks of the word *dog*. But when I lived in Spain, my brain had two words to choose from, *dog* and *perro* (and yes, that's *dog* in Spanish!). My brain learned to block the wrong word: it blocked *dog* when I was speaking Spanish and *perro* when I was speaking English. Over time, my brain got very good at blocking words.

5 And what happened when I left Spain? The word *perro* stayed blocked. And, like a door that's been closed for years is harder to open, it became harder to unblock the word! Now, 20 years later, all those Spanish words are still in my brain. But they're blocked behind heavy old doors.

6 How can I open those doors? Two things: I need to make an effort to push the doors open again; and I need to keep the doors open by practicing regularly.

7 Is there anything good to say about this 'blocking' process? In fact, there's lots of evidence that it makes your brain work better. For example, look at the words in the box. As quickly as possible, say what color they're written in. Try it now. Did you notice how hard it was to say the color when the word itself was a color? That's because 'bad information' (the word on the page) blocked the 'good information' (the color of the word).

8 What's the connection with language learning? It turns out that bilingual people are much better at activities like this than monolingual people, because their brains are trained to block 'bad information' quickly and accurately. And in the modern world, where we have to deal with too much information all the time, the ability to block 'bad information' is the key to success.

9 What's the best thing about learning a language? Is it the ability to communicate with different people around the world? No, although that's amazing enough. In fact, the best thing is that it makes our brains more powerful.

C SCAN Read again. How many rhetorical questions are there? Use the information in the box to help you.

Rhetorical questions

A rhetorical question is a question that you ask when you don't expect other people to answer it. You usually answer the question yourself. It's a useful way of presenting information because it makes the reader or listener think about the answer.

When you read a rhetorical question at the beginning of a paragraph, always pause to predict the answer first. Then read the rest of the paragraph to check.

D Work in pairs. Look at the rhetorical questions at the start of each paragraph. Discuss the answers. Then read the paragraph again to check.

E SPEAK Work in pairs and discuss the questions.

What does the writer mean by 'we have to deal with too much information all the time'? Can you think of any examples from your own life?

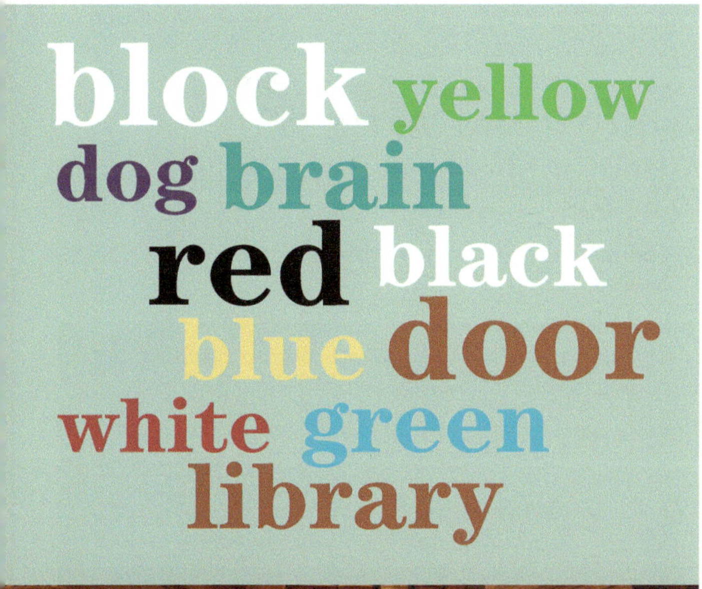

Glossary

block (v) to stop something from moving through something else

evidence (n) facts or physical signs that help to prove something

VOCABULARY

Languages

A WORK IT OUT Look at the sentences from the interview between Mona and Juan and from *Use it or lose it?* Then use the correct form of the underlined words to complete the definitions (1–5).

They used really strange words and phrases – lots of idioms that I've never heard before.

Plus, the people had very strong accents, so I couldn't understand very much at all!

By the end of that year, I spoke Spanish fluently (but not very accurately).

It turns out that bilingual people are much better at activities like this than monolingual people.

1 If you're ________________, you only speak one language; if you're ________________, you speak two languages.

2 A(n) ________________ is a group of two or more words that go together as a unit (e.g. heavy old doors).

3 Your ________________ is the way you pronounce words. It sometimes shows which part of a country you are from.

4 A(n) ________________ has its own meaning (e.g. 'Use it or lose it'). It's usually hard to figure out the meaning just by looking at the words.

5 If you speak ________________, you don't pause to think in the middle of sentences. If you speak ________________, you don't make mistakes.

B Go to the Vocabulary Hub on page XVI.

SPEAKING HUB

A Work in groups. You are going to give a short presentation about learning and using languages. Choose a topic from the list or use your own ideas. You can talk about English, your own language or both.

- accents
- standard and non-standard varieties
- advice on fluency and accuracy
- advice on how to practice
- how the language is changing
- why it's good to be bilingual

B PLAN Write three or four rhetorical questions about your topic. Then plan how you can answer those questions in a presentation. Write notes but do not write the answers down.

C PRESENT Give your presentation to the class. While you are listening to the other presentations, listen carefully and be ready to ask questions.

D REFLECT Work in groups and discuss the questions.

1 What did you learn from the presentations? What surprised you?

2 Will you use rhetorical questions again in your presentations or writing?

Plan and conduct an interview

Use rhetorical questions in a presentation

Café Hub

1.3 Welcome back

F – ask for, offer and respond to help   P – intonation and stress

COMPREHENSION

A Watch the video. Complete the sentences with the names in the box.

Gaby   Milly   Neena   Sam   Zac

1 ________________ owns a café.
2 ________________ runs a vintage clothing shop.
3 ________________ is Sam's best friend.
4 ________________ lives with Gaby and Zac.
5 ________________ is meeting Milly's mum tomorrow.
6 ________________ agrees to lend Zac some clothes.
7 ________________ falls over and hurts her arm.

B Work in pairs and discuss the questions.

1 Why is Gaby taking pictures?
2 Why does Sam say 'Oh no Zac, I'm so sorry …'?
3 Why does Zac need to borrow some clothes?
4 Why is Sam surprised when Zac asks for pants?
5 Why is Gaby worried about tomorrow?

C Imagine you wanted to borrow the items in the box. Who would you ask and why? Tell your partner.

$10 $500   a belt   a book   a ladder   a scarf   a suitcase or backpack   some shoes or boots

Glossary

flat **(n) (British)** = apartment **(n) (American)**
mum **(n) (British)** = mom **(n) (American)**
trousers **(n) (British)** = pants **(n) (American)**

FUNCTIONAL LANGUAGE

Asking for, offering and responding to help

A Complete the phrases with the correct form of *give*, *help* or *need*.

Asking for help

Could you [1] ________ me out?
Would you mind [2] ________ me a hand?
Do you think you could [3] ________ me out?
I [4] ________ a favor. Can you lend me some clothes? Please? ☐

Offering to help

I can [5] ________ you a hand with that. ☐
I'd be happy to [6] ________ you with that.
Can I [7] ________ you with that?
Shall I bring some stuff round to the flat later? ☐
Do you [8] ________ a hand? ☐
Do you need any [9] ________?

Responding to help

Thank you so much, that would be great. ☐
That would be awesome. ☐
If you wouldn't mind.
I can manage. I'm OK. ☐
It's OK – I can do it myself.
Listen, let me [10] ________ you. ☐

B 01:01–03:40 Watch the last part of the video. Mark the eight phrases you hear in the order in which you hear them.

MILLY

SAM

NEENA

ZAC

GABY

USEFUL PHRASES

A Match the useful phrases (1–6) with the phrases which show the meaning (a–f).

1 I'm really busy at the moment.
2 I don't know how to say this.
3 Good luck with that!
4 You're a legend!
5 I owe you one.
6 There you go.

a That isn't going to be easy.
b You are amazing!
c I must return the favor.
d I can't talk to you at the moment.
e I've finished.
f This is difficult for me to talk about.

B How do you say these useful phrases in your language?

PRONUNCIATION
Intonation and stress

1.12 **A** Listen and repeat the two questions in the table. Complete the headings with *falls* or *rises*.

1 Asking for help: intonation ______.	2 Offering help: intonation ______.
Can you lend me some clothes?	Can I help you with that?
______	______
______	______
______	______
______	______

1.13 **B** Listen, repeat and write down each question in the correct column. Practice the stress and intonation.

SPEAKING

A Work in pairs. You are going to write and perform a conversation where you ask a friend for help. Think about the following things:

- What sort of help do you need?
- Why do you need help?
- When do you need help?
- Who do you ask?

B PRESENT Write and practice your conversation. Then perform it for the rest of the class.

Ask for, offer and respond to help

➤ Turn to page XXV to learn how to write a report about trends.

Unit 1 Review

GRAMMAR

A Complete the social media update with the simple present or present progressive form of the verbs in parentheses.

I'm in Moscow! As you can see in the picture, I [1] *'m having* (*have*) coffee with some of my new friends. I [2] ________ (*study*) here on a two-week intensive language course. I [3] ________ (*really enjoy*) it so far. I [4] ________ (*not speak*) very much Russian at all, so it was really difficult on the first day, but now it [5] ________ (*get*) easier every day, and my teachers are excellent. Why Russian? Well, first, I [6] ________ (*think*) it's a beautiful language, and second, I [7] ________ (*consider*) studying at the university here next year.

B Read part of a report about social media trends. Then write questions about the underlined information in the report. Use the prompts to help you.

These days, more and more people [1]<u>are choosing to stop using social media completely</u>. I asked [2]<u>twelve people</u> about the way they use social media. [3]<u>Three people</u> said they never use social media, and [4]<u>two</u> are using it less and less. One student, Franek, believes social media is dangerous [5]<u>because it makes us feel jealous of other people's 'perfect' lives</u>. Another student, [6]<u>Lin</u>, thinks social media is useful for his work, but he never uses it with his real friends. He says his friends can speak to him face-to-face to find out his news!

1 What / more and more people / do / these days?
What are more and more people doing these days?

2 How many people / the writer / ask / about the way they use social media?
____

3 How many people / say / they never use social media?
____

4 How many people / use / social media less and less?
____

5 Why / Franek / believe / social media is dangerous?
____

6 Who / think / social media is useful for work?
____

VOCABULARY

A Complete the sentences with the correct form of the verbs in the box.

hear listen look see sound watch

1 **A:** 'I think we should go soon.'
B: 'Yes, that ________ like a good idea.'

2 I prefer normal phone calls to video calls – it's better when the other person can ________ you, but they can't ________ you!

3 Excuse me. I ________ for my dog. I can't find him anywhere. Have you seen him?

4 I usually ________ to podcasts while I'm traveling to work.

5 Can I call you back later? I ________ a TV show and I don't want to miss the end.

B Choose the correct words to complete the conversation.

A: Oh, this is nice, just sitting outside a café and relaxing. I think it's really interesting to [1]*observe / recognize / stare* all the people on the street.

B: Yes, but be careful. It looks like you're [2]*noticing / spotting / staring* at other people a little too much. It's pretty rude.

A: Don't worry! They're too busy to [3]*notice / observe / recognize* me! They're all looking at their phones, anyway!

C Read about five English-speaking friends. Then answer the questions.

Angela only speaks English and no other languages.

You can hear that **Brian** is from New Zealand because of the way he pronounces *ed*.

When **Eryk** is speaking English, he doesn't make many mistakes.

Francesca speaks English as well as Italian.

George loves using phrases like 'use it or lose it' and 'plan B'.

1 Who speaks accurately? ________
2 Who's monolingual? ________
3 Who likes idioms? ________
4 Who's bilingual? ________
5 Who has a strong accent? ________

FUNCTIONAL LANGUAGE

Complete the dialogues with the words in the box.

busy could favor hand help mind want

1 **A:** Hey, Gary, I need a ________. Do you have a few minutes?
B: Sorry, Paul, I'm really ________ right now.

2 **A:** Do you think you ________ help me write this?
B: Sure, I can give you a ________ with that.

3 **A:** Do you ________ me to take a look at that?
B: If you wouldn't ________.

4 **A:** Hi, Sam. If you aren't busy, I could use your ________ with my application letter.
B: Sure.

2 EXPERIENCES

Nothing is a waste of time if you use the experience wisely.
Auguste Rodin

Skydiver in mid-air over Southern Australia.

- talk about past experiences and things you want to do
- talk about a life-changing decision
- talk about an inspirational person
- talk about solving a problem
- ask for, give and refuse permission
- write an informal email

Work with a partner. Discuss the questions.

1 Look at the picture. What do you think of the activity the person is doing?

2 Read the quote. What do you think it means?

3 Tell your partner about experiences you have had that were:

- incredible
- unusual
- risky
- memorable
- eye-opening
- thrilling

2.1 Important decisions

- Talk about past experiences and things you want to do
- Talk about a life-changing decision

G – present perfect and simple past **P** – *'s* and *'ve* **V** – collocations: making big decisions
S – listening for the main idea

READING

A Match the different types of lists (1–5) with the examples (a–e).

1 list of favorite things, e.g. movies, songs
2 shopping list
3 everyday to-do list
4 list of pros and cons
5 bucket list

a
- bananas
- cheese
- yogurt

b
1 Call Mom
2 Email the bank
3 Pay rent

c
1 Toy Story
2 X-Men
3 Beauty and the Beast

d
1 Swim with dolphins
2 Learn to surf
3 Do a parachute jump

e
For: cheaper / easy to find
Against: poor quality / ordinary

B SPEAK Work in pairs. How often do you make lists? What types of lists do you make? Why?

C READ FOR GIST Read *Not yet? No more!* and answer the questions.

1 Which sentence summarizes the blogger's opinion?
  a A bucket list is a great idea, but remember that you probably can't do all those things in your lifetime.
  b Make a list of things that are possible to do, rather than a list of dreams.
  c People write bucket lists just for fun and to dream a little, not in order to actually do those things.
2 How many of the people commenting on the blog agree with the writer?

Not yet? No more!

About me | Recent posts | Archive

posted by Julia
November 16 | Leave a comment

Have you ever written a bucket list? If so, have you done many of those incredible things on your list? I certainly haven't.

I wrote mine on New Year's Day five years ago, and I chose 50 things, like swimming with dolphins and climbing Mount Everest. However, after all these years, I've only done one thing on that list. Last year, I watched the sun rise and set on the same day. I still haven't swum with dolphins. I still haven't climbed Everest. And, I think I never will!

The problem is that you need an infinite amount of time and money to do all those incredible things or to learn those skills. I've simply never had that time and money. What is the point in making an unachievable list? How does that improve your life?

So, this is my achievable bucket list blog. The aim is still to do unusual things that are positive and life-enhancing, but without needing to be a millionaire or to have all the time in the world to achieve these goals.

Here's the start of my list. I haven't done any of these things yet, but I think I can in the future. What do you think? Achievable? Life-enhancing?

- Plant a tree.
- Do a charity walk or run.
- Write a poem.
- Learn how to make a fire in the wild.
- Ride a horse.
- Eat nothing but fresh food for a week.
- Stop using social media for two weeks.
- Learn and perform a magic trick.

Comments:

Yuka W

Thanks! Before I read this, my bucket list was only expensive travel ideas. I just wrote a new list of interesting but doable things!

dream_catcher77

Actually, I think a bucket list should be about amazing things. I wrote mine last year and I've done half of it already. This year, I've seen lions in the wild and I've done a parachute jump. Next month, the Pyramids! All because they're on my list.

Robin Stannard

Also, sometimes those incredible things are not so great. I've swum with dolphins. It was garbage! I'd rather swim with my friends. Keep it simple – it's still special ;-)

D READ FOR DETAIL Read again. Answer the questions.

1. How many things on her first bucket list has the writer not done?
2. Why is it not possible to do all the things on a typical bucket list?
3. How is her new list similar to her original list?
4. How many outdoor activities are there on her new list?

E SPEAK Work in pairs. Read again and discuss the questions.

1. Are the writer's choices good ideas for an achievable bucket list?
2. Which choices do you like most and why?

GRAMMAR

Present perfect and simple past

A WORK IT OUT Look at the sentences (1–4) from *Not yet? No more!* Underline the verbs in the simple past and circle the verbs in the present perfect. Then match each sentence with a diagram (a–d).

1. I wrote mine on New Year's Day five years ago.
2. I've only done one thing on that list.
3. This year, I've seen lions in the wild.
4. Last year, I watched the sun rise and set on the same day.

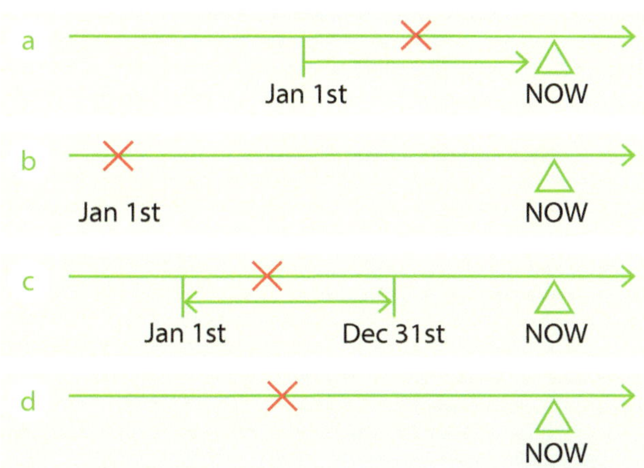

B Look at the adverbs of time in the box. Can you find them in the blog? Match the adverbs with the definitions (1–5).

already just never not yet still

1. at no time in the past ________
2. a short time ago ________
3. a situation has not changed or not completely ended ________
4. not happened before now, but will probably happen ________
5. happened before a point in time, perhaps sooner than expected ________

C Complete the rules with *present perfect* or *simple past*.

Present perfect and simple past

For actions that we completed:

during a finished period of time, we use the [1] ________.

during a period of time that continues to now, we use the [2] ________.

at a specific time in the past, we use the [3] ________.

before now, but we do not say exactly when, we use the [4] ________.

We frequently use adverbs of time with these tenses, but we do not use *yet* and *already* with actions in the [5] ________.

D Go to the **Grammar Hub** on **page VIII**.

PRONUNCIATION

's and 've

2.1 Listen to the pairs of sentences (1–6). Which sentence (*a* or *b*) is in the present perfect?

1 __ 3 __ 5 __
2 __ 4 __ 6 __

SPEAKING

A Work in pairs. You are going to write an achievable bucket list. Student A – go to the **Communication Hub** on **page XIX** and read the bucket list. Student B – go to the **Communication Hub** on **page XXI** and read the bucket list. Has your partner done any of the things on your list? If they have, find out more details.

B Work in pairs. Choose eight things to put on your achievable bucket list. Use the ideas on the lists and your own ideas. They should be positive, life-enhancing and achievable.

C Work in groups. Compare your lists and choose ten things for a group bucket list.

D Compare your list with another group. Are their ideas the same or different?

a

b

LISTENING

A Match the words and phrases in the box with the pictures (a–b).

cross oceans   cruise along canals
freshwater   houseboat   saltwater   yacht

B SPEAK Work in pairs and discuss the questions.

1 Have you ever been on a boat? If so, what kind?
2 Which of the two boats in the pictures would you prefer to travel on?

2.2 **C LISTEN FOR GIST** Look at the pictures (a and b) and listen to a podcast interview with Emma. Complete the sentences with *a* or *b*.

1 Picture ___ shows Emma's ultimate dream.
2 Picture ___ shows Emma's current reality.

2.2 **D** Listen again. Which of the phrases (1–8) from the podcast are the main ideas of Emma's story? Use the strategies in the box to help you.

1 I love swimming
2 yachts are very expensive
3 to make a decision to put a plan into action
4 it won't take me around the world
5 to stay motivated and not lose heart
6 learning to live in a small space
7 doing something similar to my dream, it's a start
8 the hardest part of any journey is the first step

Listening for the main idea

To help you catch the main ideas of a conversation, listen carefully for common expressions that we use to introduce a main idea.

- *The most important thing here …*
- *Well, it is important to note …*
- *And I stress the importance of …*

Listen carefully for common words and phrases that we use to talk about things generally.

- *in general, overall, on the whole*

We usually speak more slowly or loudly when we want to emphasize a main idea.

2.2 **E LISTEN FOR DETAIL** Listen again. Find and correct six mistakes in the summary of Emma's story.

Emma is 33 and she works in the sailing industry. She loves swimming and fishing. For the last few years, she's been learning how to sail. Her dream is to live on a yacht and sail around the world. She hasn't bought a yacht yet because she can't find one that she likes. She sold her house and bought a houseboat. The houseboat is an opportunity for Emma to learn to live on the sea and move from place to place. She is happy with her decision to buy a houseboat because it means that she has 'made the break' from the water to the land.

F SPEAK Work in groups and discuss the questions.

1 Do you agree that living on a houseboat will help Emma to achieve her ultimate dream? Give reasons.
2 What are the pros and cons of living on a houseboat compared to living on land?

VOCABULARY

Collocations: making big decisions

A Match the verbs (1–8) with the phrases (a–i) to make collocations that Emma used in her interview. One verb can be used twice. Use the audio script on page XXXII to help you.

1 lose	**a** a decision
2 make	**b** a plan into action
3 put	**c** short-term and long-term goals
4 set	**d** toward a goal
5 stay	**e** a dream into reality
6 take	**f** motivated
7 turn	**g** the break/change
8 work	**h** the next step
	i heart

B Read the information from the people (1–3) about a life-changing decision. Fill in the blanks with collocations from Exercise A in the correct form.

2.3 **C** Listen and check your answers.

D **SPEAK** Work in pairs. Which decision in Exercise C do you think is the most achievable? Which is the least achievable? Give reasons.

SPEAKING HUB

A Think about a life-changing decision that you have made. Use the ideas below to help you.

- moving (changing cities/countries)
- studying (a new course, retraining, learning a new skill)
- a lifestyle change (becoming healthier, in better shape, more relaxed)
- turning a dream into reality

B **PLAN** Write notes about your decision. Think about:

- why you made the decision.
- how you put it into action.
- short-term/long-term goals.
- how you feel about the decision now.
- any advice you can give related to your decision.

C **SPEAK** Work in pairs. Interview your partner about his/her life-changing decision. Use your ideas in Exercise B to help you. Take turns.

D **REFLECT** Work in groups. Tell the group about your partner's decision. Then discuss all of the decisions. Whose decision was the most life-changing?

1

Lee, 31

The biggest [1] ___decision___ I've ever made was when I decided to move out of my parents' house. I was pretty scared at first, to be honest. But I soon found an apartment in the same town with a couple of friends. Thinking about it now, it was the right time for me to [2] ______________ the change from living at home to living with friends.

2

Three years ago, I decided to climb El Capitan in Yosemite National Park. It was always one of those things on my bucket list. Since I started to put the [3] ______________ into action, I've learned a lot about climbing and myself. My advice? Never [4] ______________ heart! If you are [5] ______________ toward a goal, you'll achieve it in the end. I haven't gone to Yosemite yet, but I know I will!

Maki, 25

3

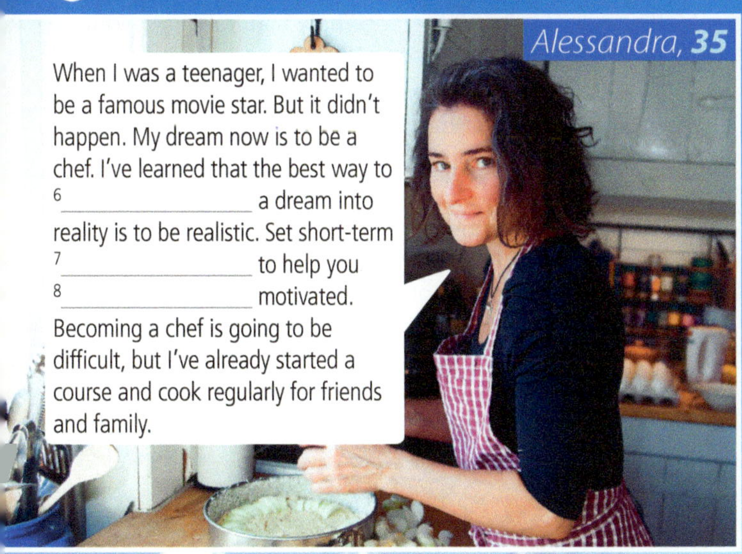

Alessandra, 35

When I was a teenager, I wanted to be a famous movie star. But it didn't happen. My dream now is to be a chef. I've learned that the best way to [6] ______________ a dream into reality is to be realistic. Set short-term [7] ______________ to help you [8] ______________ motivated. Becoming a chef is going to be difficult, but I've already started a course and cook regularly for friends and family.

- Talk about past experiences and things you want to do
- Talk about a life-changing decision

2.2 You can do it!

- Talk about an inspirational person
- Talk about solving a problem

V – dependent prepositions; problems and solutions
G – present and past ability
P – word stress: verbs with two syllables
S – deducing the meaning of unknown words from context

READING

A SPEAK Work in pairs and discuss the question.

How do retired people typically spend their time in your country?

B Read the ad taken from a local newspaper. Then answer the questions.

1 What is unusual about the ad?
2 Why do you think he has written the advertisement?
3 How do you think people reacted to the ad?

C READ FOR GIST Read *89-year-old seeks job* and check your answers to Exercise B.

D Look at the words in bold in the article. What do you think they mean? Use the strategies in the box to help you. Then work in pairs and compare your ideas.

1 seeks
2 snaps him up
3 spotted
4 enable him to
5 role
6 taking on

WORK WANTED

Senior citizen 89 seeks employment in Paignton area. 20hrs+ per week. Still able to clean, light gardening, DIY and anything.

I have references.
Old soldier, airborne forces.

Save me from dying of boredom!

89-year-old **seeks** job: café **snaps him up**

An 89-year-old has found a job after putting an ad in his local paper asking for part-time work to stop him from 'dying of boredom'. Joe Bartley, from Paignton, south Devon, is due to start working in a café next week in the town after the owners of the family-run business **spotted** his ad.

'Whatever your age or your background, you deserve a chance,' said Cantina Bar and Kitchen's co-owner Sarah Martin. 'Most people have something to offer, and Joe is someone who is eager, who is putting himself out there. What is not to like about that? A lot of people who come here don't just come for coffee – they come for a chat – so Joe is perfect.'

Bartley has lived alone since his wife, Cassandra, died a couple of years ago, and he has been lonely. 'I miss my wife dreadfully, when you live on your own there is no one to speak to. I like reading, and I'll watch a little television, but there's a lot of trash on these days. I just got bored stiff with nothing to do. I thought even though I am 89, I can still work. I can clean tables, do some gardening – anything really.'

Bartley put his advertisement in the *Herald Express* last month. 'The owner called me and she asked me to come in. So I arrived at the café, we had a little chat and shook hands.' He is now looking forward to earning his own money to **enable him to** pay his rent. 'I can't believe it really. I feel great about it,' he said.

Bartley told *The Guardian* that the media reaction has been incredible, adding that he is in danger of becoming a celebrity. 'When I first put in the ad, I thought it was just an old guy looking for work – I don't really see what is strange about that,' he said. 'But have I now reached celebrity status? That might worry some people, but it doesn't worry me.'

His new **role** in the café was not the only job offer he got. Glenn Rodgers, an independent baker in Barnstaple, north Devon, offered him a job, but the bakery was too far away for Bartley to travel.

Rodgers wanted to offer the senior citizen a job to put a 'smile on his face'. 'More employers should think about **taking on** older staff,' he added. 'Why not give him a chance? Also, it works both ways: employers are getting experienced reliable staff who really want to work.'

Bartley will get a ride to work with his new employer on Sundays, but will take a bus the rest of the week. 'He is delighted and we are looking forward to it,' said Martin. 'We think about these things all the time. We are never going to be rich, but we like to give something back to society.'

Deducing the meaning of unknown words from context

When you do not know the meaning of words and phrases, you can use their context to help you understand them.

Think about:

- What type of word or phrase is it (noun, adjective or verb)?
- Does it have a prefix (*un-*, *im-*) or suffix (*-ment*, *-ion*)?
- Where is it in the sentence and what other words are near it?
- How does the word relate to the paragraph?
- What possible meanings of the word suit the topic of the sentence, paragraph and text?

E **SPEAK** Work in pairs. Look at the readers' comments on the article. Do you agree or disagree with them? Why?

Comments

Smart1

Joe is an inspiration to us all! He should be very proud of himself for getting a job that some would say is more suitable for a younger person.

ID2

If no one had replied to the ad, Joe could have thought about volunteering. Mind you, even those roles are hard to find these days!

Jan1003

The government should be more aware of this problem and work with communities to help people like Joe. Loneliness is a big problem nowadays.

4Kent

Though fairly typical of this newspaper, it's great that this issue is in the news. We need to prepare for our retirement now, so we can retire comfortably, not serve coffee in our old age.

VOCABULARY

Dependent prepositions (verb/adjective + *for*/*of*)

A Look at the phrases from *89-year-old seeks job* and from the comments. Are the words in bold verbs or adjectives? Complete each phrase with *for* or *of*.

1. **look** ________ work
2. **prepare** ________ retirement
3. **typical** ________ this newspaper
4. **suitable** ________ a younger person
5. **proud** ________ himself
6. **aware** ________ this problem
7. **work** ________ a café
8. **ask** ________ part-time work

B Complete the questions with a verb or adjective from Exercise A.

1. What do you ______________ for in an ideal job?
2. Do you think age ever makes people more or less ______________ for some jobs?
3. Which of your achievements are you most ______________ of?
4. What big changes in your life are coming soon? How can you ______________ for them?

C **SPEAK** Work in pairs. Ask and answer the questions in Exercise B.

SPEAKING

A Think of three people who should receive an award for inspiring others because of their special or unusual achievements.

B Work in pairs. Discuss your choices and choose the most inspirational person. Write down some of your reasons for choosing that person.

C Work in groups. In pairs, give a short presentation about your inspirational person, explaining why the person should win the award. As a group, vote for who should win the award.

D Tell the class about your group's choice. Why did the group feel the person was special? Did everyone in the group agree with the vote?

1

2

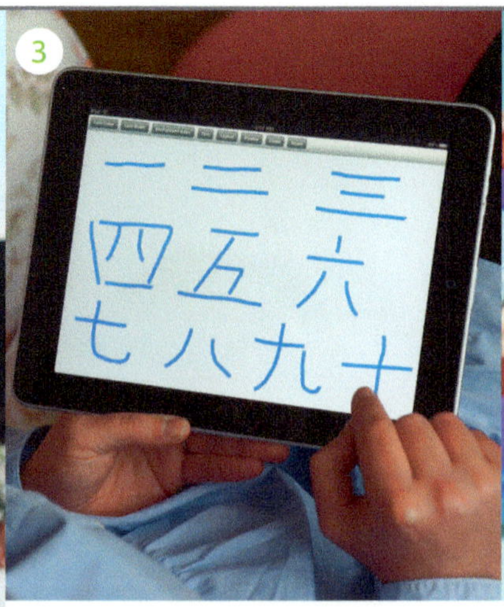

3

4

LISTENING

A SPEAK Work in pairs. Look at the pictures (1–4). What are the people doing? What problems could they have when they do these things?

2.4 **B LISTEN FOR MAIN IDEA** You are going to listen to four people talking about a challenge or problem. Complete the sentences (1–4) with the phrases in the box. There are four extra phrases.

> by pretending to be a different person
> by spending a lot of money by taking classes
> by using a different skill by using books during a vacation
> on his/her own with the help of his/her family

1 Matt solved a problem ______________.
2 Suzanna solved a problem ______________.
3 Nancy solved a problem ______________.
4 Roberto solved a problem ______________.

2.4 **C LISTEN FOR DETAIL** Listen again. Choose the correct words to complete the sentences.

1 Matt *knew* / *didn't know* how to cook simple hot food.
2 He found useful advice on *the internet* / *TV*.
3 Suzanna needed to give a speech at *work* / *a family event*.
4 She *read* / *didn't read* her speech aloud from a script.
5 Nancy *knew a little* / *didn't know any* Chinese.
6 She *made several* / *didn't make any* mistakes when she first sang to the children.
7 When Roberto was a child, he *tried* / *didn't try* to learn to swim.
8 He *has* / *still hasn't* swum in the ocean.

D SPEAK Work in pairs and discuss the questions.

1 Which of the four challenges do you think is the hardest?
2 What advice could you give to someone who can't do those things well?
3 Have you had any of these challenges yourself? What did you do to deal with them?
4 Is it more important to solve problems yourself or ask for help?

PRONUNCIATION

Word stress: verbs with two syllables

A Work in pairs. Look at the verbs from the listening below. Take turns saying the verbs and marking the stress.

1 achieve	3 complete	5 regret
2 arrive	4 create	6 study

B Does the stress normally come on the first or second syllable?

2.5 **C** Now listen to the verbs. Check and repeat.

GRAMMAR

Present and past ability

A WORK IT OUT Look at the sentences (1–9). Write *a* if they are about having (or not having) a general ability or skill in the past. Write *b* if they are about doing something (or not doing something) on a particular occasion in the past.

1 I was able to speak very basic Chinese. a
2 I managed to cook them a very tasty meal. b
3 I was able to complete the speech. ___
4 I couldn't boil an egg. ___
5 I could make a salad. ___
6 The first time, I didn't manage to make anything. ___
7 I wasn't able to swim. ___
8 I wasn't able to stop my hands shaking. ___
9 I couldn't say no to him. ___

B Choose the correct words to complete the rules.

Present and past ability

1 When we talk about ability or skills in general in the present, we **use** / **do not use** *can/can't* or *(not) be able to*.
2 When we talk about ability or skills in general in the past, we **use** / **do not use** *could, couldn't* or *(not) be able to*.
3 When we talk about ability to do a specific task on a particular occasion in the past, we **use** / **do not use** *(not) manage to, (not) be able to* or *couldn't*. We do not usually use *could*.

C Go to the Grammar Hub on page VIII.

D SPEAK Work in pairs. Play *True or false?* Follow the instructions.

1 Write two sentences for each idea (a–c). One sentence should be true and one should be false.
   - a something you can do now, but which you couldn't do five or ten years ago
   - b a problem you had because you weren't able to do something
   - c a particular time that you managed to do something that was difficult

2 Listen to your partner's sentences. Ask questions to find out more information, then guess which sentences are true. Take turns.

VOCABULARY
Problems and solutions

A SPEAK Work in pairs. How good are you at solving problems? Give yourself a score out of five. Explain your score to your partner.

B Look at the personality test. Complete the sentences with *problem(s)* or *solution(s)*.

How do you feel about difficult situations and problems?

Use this personality test to find out. How true are the following statements for you on a scale of 1–5?

1 = False
2 = Mostly false
3 = Sometimes true / Sometimes false
4 = Mostly true
5 = True

1 If I can't **solve** a difficult ____________, I don't give up. I keep trying until I find a ____________.
1 2 3 4 5

2 I always try to **deal with** ____________ because ignoring them only **causes** more ____________.
1 2 3 4 5

3 When working in groups, I **suggest** a lot of ____________ to any ____________.
1 2 3 4 5

4 When I have a ____________, I look at it from different angles to **come up with** the best ____________.
1 2 3 4 5

5 When I deal with a complicated ____________, I **analyze** the possible ____________ with lists of their pros and cons.
1 2 3 4 5

6 I prefer to discuss a ____________ with other people. Then we can **agree on** a ____________ together.
1 2 3 4 5

C WORK IT OUT Match the verbs in bold in the personality test with the definitions (1–7).

1 to think of something such as an idea or a plan
2 to study or examine something in detail in order to understand or explain it
3 to decide together what will be done and how it will be done
4 to offer an idea or plan for someone to consider
5 to take action to do something
6 to find a solution to something that is causing difficulties
7 to make something happen, usually something bad

D Go to the **Vocabulary Hub** on **page XVI**.

E SPEAK Take the personality test. Go to the **Communication Hub** on **page XXIII** to see what your answers may show about you. Then work in pairs and discuss your answers.

SPEAKING HUB

A You are going to answer a question that employers frequently ask in job interviews to find out about problem-solving skills.

> Can you tell us about a time when you faced a challenge or a difficult problem that you successfully dealt with?

B PLAN Write notes about:

- the situation.
- what action you took to deal with the situation.
- what you learned from trying to deal with the situation.

C SPEAK Work in pairs. Ask and answer the question. Write notes about your partner's answer.

D REFLECT Tell a classmate what your partner said. Think about what you both heard. Whose answer was best?

- Talk about an inspirational person
- Talk about solving a problem

Café Hub

2.3 Picture this

F – ask for, give and refuse permission
P – intonation and stress in questions

COMPREHENSION

A 00:00–00:50 Watch the first part of the video. What wakes Gaby up?

B Work in pairs. The actual photo shoot is not successful. Look at the stills and predict the difficulties that Gaby has.

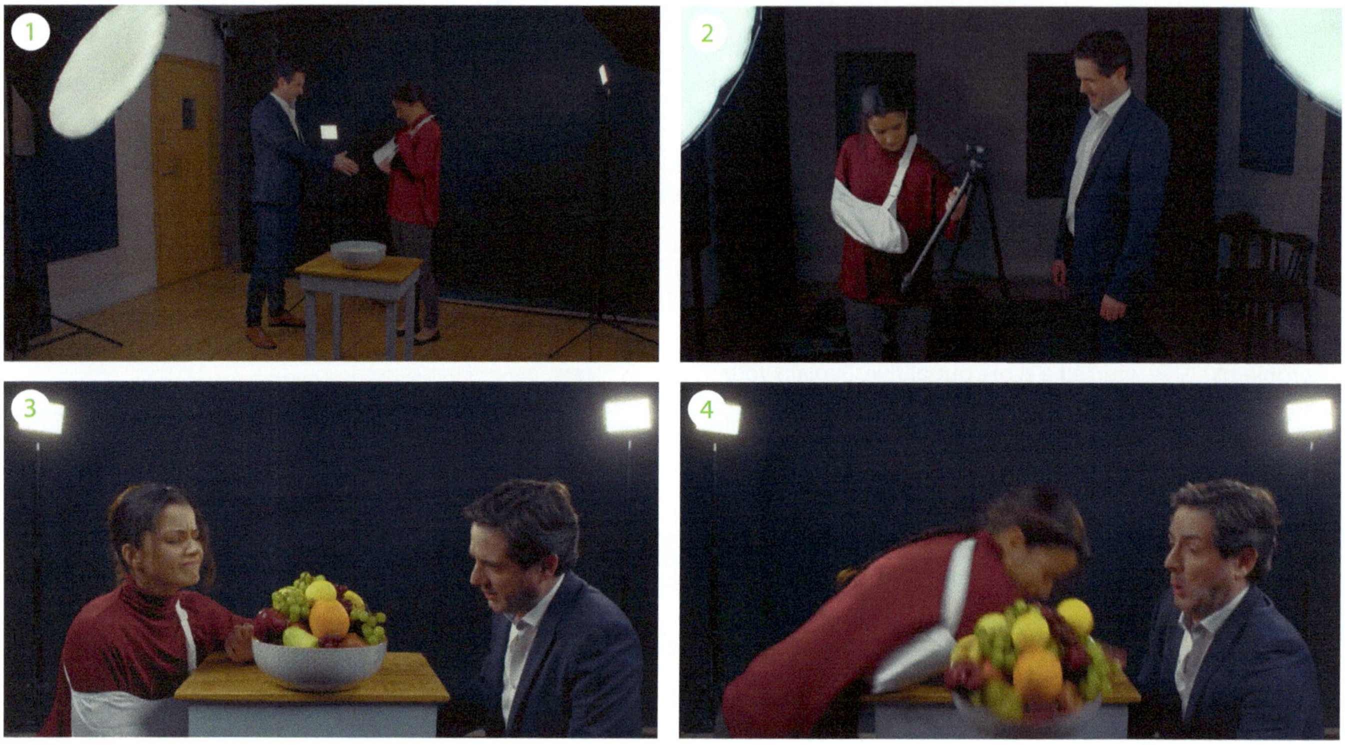

C 00:51–04:00 Watch the second part of the video and check your ideas. Then complete the sentences with *Gaby* or *Eric*.

1 ______ gets ______'s name wrong.
2 ______ is in a hurry.
3 ______ can't set up the tripod.
4 ______ gets ______'s name wrong again.
5 ______ drops the camera.
6 ______ fixes the camera onto the tripod.
7 ______ suggests more light on the bowl.
8 ______ suggests putting fruit in the bowl.

FUNCTIONAL LANGUAGE

Asking for, giving and refusing permission

A Eric was in a hurry and wanted to start the photo shoot right away. Check (✓) the phrase he used.

Asking for permission		
		Least formal
Can we start …	☐	↑
Could we start … right away?	☐	
May we start …	☐	
Is it all right if we start …	☐	
Would it be OK to …	☐	
Would you mind if we started …	☐	↓
		Most formal

Giving and refusing permission	
Sure, I don't see why not.	I'm sorry, but …
No problem.	I'd like to help, but …
Yes, of course.	I'm afraid that isn't possible.

MILLY

SAM

NEENA

ZAC

GABY

B **Write down phrases asking for permission in the following situations. Choose an appropriate level of formality.**

1 It's very hot in the classroom. You want to open a window. Ask your classmates.

____

2 You have a dental appointment tomorrow. You want to leave work early. Ask your boss.

____

3 You are chairing a business meeting. You want to start. Ask everyone in the meeting.

____

4 It's a beautiful day and you're in a park. You want to sit on the grass. Ask the park ranger.

____

5 You're in front of somebody's house. You want to park your car there. Ask the home owner.

____

6 You're in a lecture with 200 other people. You want to ask a question. Ask the lecturer.

____

USEFUL PHRASES

A **Choose the correct alternatives to complete the useful phrases. Watch the video again if necessary.**

1 ***Call / Name*** me Gaby. = Please use the name 'Gaby' when you talk to me.

2 I can't thank you ***enough / at all***. = I am very grateful to you.

3 You ***must / should*** be Derek. = I am sure your name is Derek.

4 I don't have ***this / that*** long. = I have very little time.

5 We're ***almost / fairly*** there. = We have nearly finished.

B **How do you say these useful phrases in your language?**

PRONUNCIATION

Intonation and stress in questions

2.6 **A** **Listen and repeat the questions. Does the intonation rise or fall after the main stress in the sentence?**

1 Could I open the window? _______________
2 Can I leave work early? _______________
3 Is it all right if we start now? _______________
4 Would it be OK to sit on the armchair? _______________
5 Would you mind if I parked my car here? _______________
6 May I ask you a question? _______________

B **Practice the stress and intonation in the questions in Exercise A.**

SPEAKING

A **Work in pairs. You are going to write a conversation in which you ask permission for something.**

- Decide on the situation: why do you need permission and who from?
- Decide on the level of formality.
- Write your conversation.

B **PRESENT** **Practice your conversation. Then act out your conversation for the class.**

Ask for, give and refuse permission

➤ Turn to page XXVI to learn how to write an informal email.

Unit 2 Review

GRAMMAR

A Complete the comments (1–2) about achievable bucket lists with the correct form of the verbs in parentheses.

Comments

1 Maybe the best bucket list is a mixture of easy and hard to achieve . I [1] ______________ (*do*) both simple activities and bigger adventures. Both [2] ______________ (*give*) me great memories. I once [3] ______________ (*learn*) to bake a cake in the morning, and then [4] ______________ (*do*) my first bungee jump in the afternoon. The cake [5] ______________ (*taste*) great after that! I [6] ______________ (*do*) a bungee jump since, but I [7] ______________ (*made*) plenty of cakes!

2 How about awesome adventures that also benefit other people or society? A few years ago, I [1] ______________ (*want*) to ride an elephant, so I [2] ______________ (*find*) a position as an international volunteer at an elephant conservation park. I [3] ______________ (*stay*) there for two months. It [4] ______________ (*be*) great to help a charity and do something on my bucket list. Since then, I [5] ______________ (*do*) loads of similar things.

B Find and correct the mistakes in five of the sentences.

1. When I was a kid, I could to swim. I learned as a baby.
2. They wasn't able to score a goal. What a boring game.
3. I managed to finish everything.
4. I couldn't to ride a bike until I was 19.
5. I am able dance fairly well.
6. I'm afraid you didn't managed to pass. You'll have to retake it.

VOCABULARY

A Match the sentence beginnings (1–5) and endings (a–e).

1. I don't believe in setting ___
2. It's easy to stay ___
3. I'm sorry you didn't get the job, but don't lose ___
4. When I moved to the countryside, I ___
5. I was nervous about taking ___

a. the next step, but I knew it was the right time to make the change.
b. motivated when you really enjoy what you do.
c. turned my dream into reality!
d. long-terms goals – I prefer to focus on my weekly plans.
e. heart – there will be other opportunities.

B Complete the sentences with the correct form of the words in the box and *for* or *of*.

ask	aware	look	prepare
proud	suitable	typical	work

1. We're lost. We need to ______________ help and get directions.
2. I ______________ a new job. I check a few online agencies each week.
3. This behavior is ______________ Jane. She has always been difficult.
4. She's giving a presentation tomorrow. She needs to ______________ that tonight.
5. Is this movie ______________ young children? I'd like to watch it with my niece.
6. We have both ______________ the same company all our lives. That's very unusual.
7. Is your boss ______________ all the problems with the project?
8. I'm very ______________ my achievements. It's never too late to learn something new.

C Choose the correct words to complete the results of a personality quiz about problem solving.

The results show that when you try and [1]***deal / solve*** a problem, you like to make quick decisions. This can be helpful, but sometimes you should take more time to [2]***analyze / come up with*** the problem first. This will help when you have to [3]***deal with / suggest*** complicated situations and need to [4]***come up with / cause*** many different solutions.

The results also show that when you work on a team, you expect to [5]***solve / agree on*** solutions quickly, and if you don't, you usually lose interest. However, if you don't take the time to look at the pros and cons of your solutions, this might [6]***cause / suggest*** more problems.

FUNCTIONAL LANGUAGE

Put the dialogue in the correct order.

A: Alright, no problem. In that case could you lend me your phone? ___
A: Hey there, Pete. Would you mind if I borrowed your laptop? ___
B: I'm afraid I can't do that either – I'm expecting an important call. ___
B: I'm not sure to be honest – I have a lot of work to do today and I need it. ___
A: Yes, Arsenal is playing and I want to check the score! ___
A: OK, never mind. ___
B: Is it for something urgent? ___

3 ON THE MOVE

I never travel without my diary. One should always have something sensational to read in the train.

Oscar Wilde

View from Nelson's Column in Trafalgar Square towards Westminster, England.

OBJECTIVES

- talk about a difficult trip or travel experience
- talk about behavior on public transportation
- evaluate suggestions and justify a choice
- talk about why a plan didn't work
- tell a story
- write an email of complaint

Work with a partner. Discuss the questions.

1 Look at the picture. What different types of transportation can you see? How does the city's transportation compare to that in your own city?

2 Read the quote. How do you pass the time on public transportation?

3 Which types of transportation would you describe with the adjectives in the box?

convenient dangerous essential exciting expensive free fun noisy relaxing safe stressful tiring

3.1 Travel experiences

- Talk about a difficult trip or travel experience
- Talk about behavior on public transportation

G narrative tenses
P word stress in nouns ending in *-ion*
V collocations: travel information; nouns ending in *-ion*
S skim-reading to build a map of a text

LISTENING

A SPEAK Work in pairs and discuss the questions.

1. What types of transportation do you use? How often do you use them?
2. Which do you prefer and why? Which is your least favorite?
3. What problems might there be for each one?

3.1 **B LISTEN FOR GIST** Listen to a call-in radio show. What is the topic of today's discussion?

a. bad or unusual trips to work
b. bad or unusual trips in general
c. bad or unusual trips on national holidays

3.1 **C LISTEN FOR DETAIL** Are the sentences true (T) or false (F)? Correct the false sentences. Then listen again and check your answers.

Junko's experience

1. There were no trains because of the bad weather. ___
2. She didn't sit at the bus stop for a long time. ___
3. She stopped a police car to ask for help. ___
4. The police found a taxi for her. ___
5. She arrived at her friend's house in time for dinner. ___

Alan's experience

6. He missed the first train because the taxi was slow. ___
7. The second train stopped moving after half an hour. ___
8. When the train reached its destination, he was already two hours late for the interview. ___
9. Because the traffic was heavy, he walked from the station to the office. ___
10. Another job candidate was late because of the train problems. ___

D SPEAK Work in pairs and discuss the questions.

1. What mistakes did Junko and Alan make? Who made the worst ones?
2. Who had the worst or most unusual trip? Why?

GRAMMAR

Narrative tenses

A Look at the pairs of sentences from the call-in radio show. In each pair, who is the speaker? Write J (Junko) or A (Alan). What tenses are the underlined verbs?

1. **A:** It was raining when I left. ___
   B: It was snowing. ___
2. **A:** I took the next train, but after about 30 minutes, that train broke down. ___
   B: I found a bus stop and sat down. ___
3. **A:** A police car was driving by, when it suddenly stopped. ___
   B: We were still not moving, so I got out and walked. ___
4. **A:** We arrived about two hours late, and that meant I'd already missed the interview. ___
   B: I'd arranged to go to a classmate's house for dinner. ___

B WORK IT OUT Complete the rules with *simple past, past progressive* or *past perfect*.

Narrative tenses

When we tell a story, we use a range of past tenses.

1. We use the ______________ to describe the main events in a story, in the order that they happened.
2. We use the ______________ to describe a longer action that is interrupted by a shorter event. We also use it to describe a longer action that is not a main event in the story, such as the weather.
3. We use the ______________ to describe an event that happened before the main events in the story.

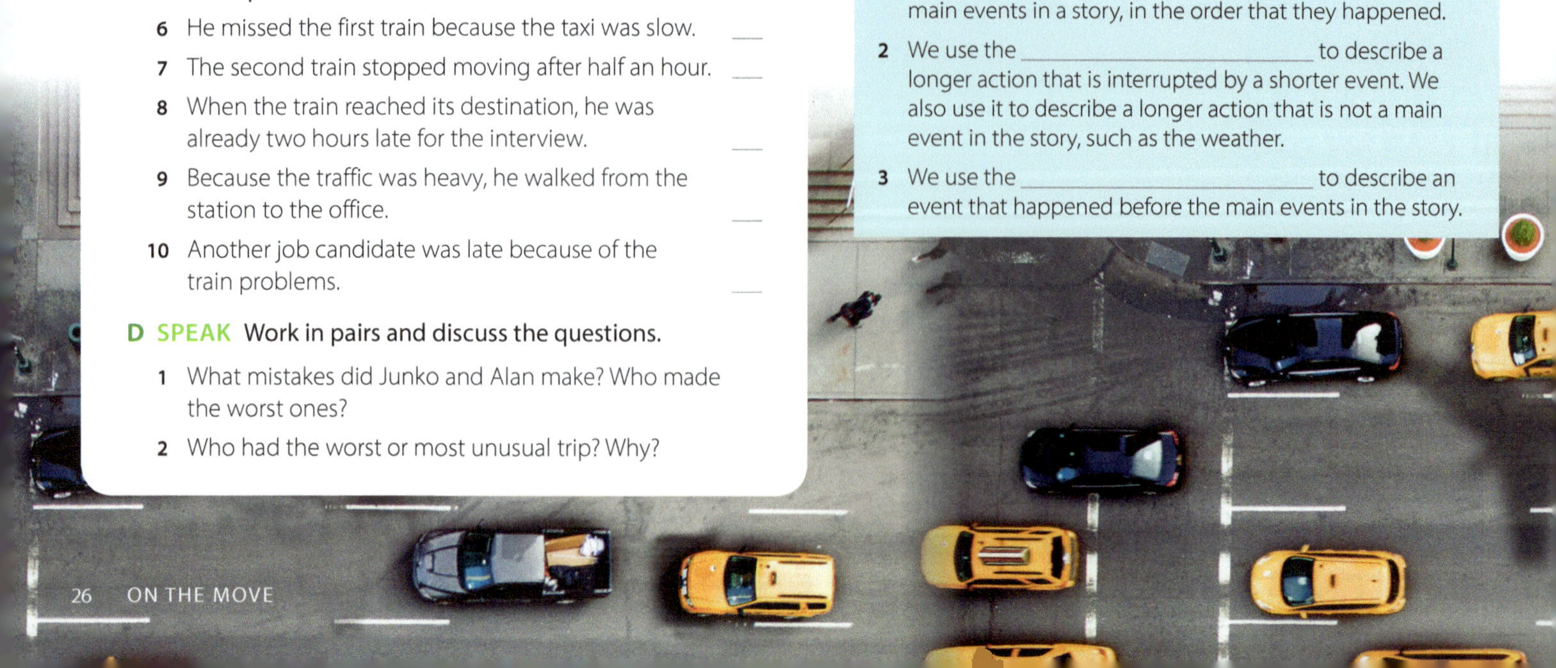

C Match the timelines (a–d) with the rules (1–3) in Exercise B.

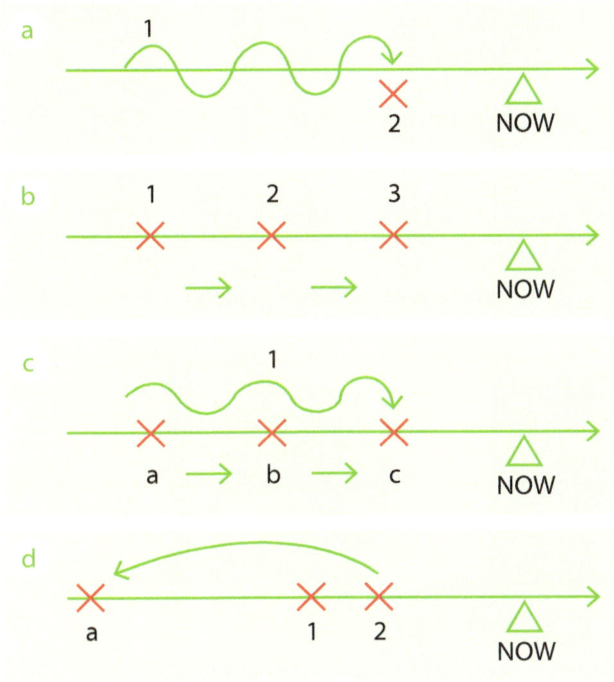

D **PRACTICE** Complete the stories with the correct form of the verbs in parentheses.

It [1] ________________ (*rain*), and I [2] ________________ (*drive*) at night in the countryside when a wild animal suddenly [3] ________________ (*jump*) in front of me. I [4] ________________ (*manage*) to avoid hitting the animal, but I [5] ________________ (*go*) off the road into a field and I couldn't move the car. Unfortunately, I [6] ________________ (*forget*) to charge my phone, so I couldn't call for help. That was a long walk home!

I [7] ________________ (*travel*) to work on the train when a ticket inspector [8] ________________ (*ask*) to see my ticket. I [9] ________________ (*look*) everywhere, but I had no idea where I [10] ________________ (*put*) it. I emptied out my pockets but it [11] ________________ (*disappear*) completely. There were two kids across from me, and while I [12] ________________ (*pay*) the inspector, I [13] ________________ (*notice*) they [14] ________________ (*smile and laugh*). They got off at the next station, and my ticket [15] ________________ (*be*) on their seat. They [16] ________________ (*find and hide*) it.

E Go to the Grammar Hub on page X.

F Work in pairs. Go to the Communication Hub on page XXIV.

VOCABULARY

Collocations: travel information

A (3.2) Listen to a traffic news and travel update on a radio show. Answer the questions.

1 How many types of transportation do they mention?
2 Which has the fewest problems?

B (3.2) **LISTEN FOR KEY WORDS** Listen again. Choose the correct words to make the collocations used in the travel update.

1 rush *hour* / *job*
2 traffic *lights* / *jam*
3 road *sign* / *work*
4 severe *delay* / *problem*
5 slight *delay* / *interest*
6 good *conditions* / *service*
7 subway *station* / *line*
8 cancel *a train* / *an event*
9 heavy *rain* / *traffic*
10 overcrowded *trains* / *buses*

C Go to the Vocabulary Hub on page XVI.

D **SPEAK** Work in pairs and discuss the questions.

1 When was the last time you were stuck in heavy traffic?
2 What do you think about traveling during rush hour?
3 Which is worse: being on an overcrowded train or in a traffic jam?

SPEAKING

A You are going to tell a story for a radio show. Think of either an interesting or a difficult trip that you have made. Write notes to help you plan your story. Think about:

- Background information (When? Where? Why?)
- What was the weather like?
- What happened on the trip?
- How did it finish?

B Work in groups. Share your stories. Ask and answer questions about the stories.

C Which story do you think would be best for the radio show? Which was the most interesting, unusual or difficult trip? Which was the funniest story?

READING

A SPEAK Work in pairs. Look at the pictures (a–c) and discuss the questions.

1 What are the people doing?
2 Which activities do you like / not like doing when you are traveling?

B SKIM Read the article quickly and answer the questions. Use the strategies in the box to help you build a map of the text.

Skim-reading to build a map of a text

You can build a map of a text by identifying the main topic and the paragraph topics.

Read the title and the first paragraph to find out what the main topic is.

Read the first sentence of each paragraph to find out what the paragraph's topic is. Make a note of the paragraph topics.

1 What is the main topic or idea in this text?
2 Match the headings (a–f) with the paragraphs (1–6).
   a The details of what the research discovered
   b Epley's conclusions regarding the research
   c How the research changed Epley's life
   d Avoiding conversations and reasons not to
   e How the research was carried out
   f The reason why Epley and Schroeder did the research

a

b

DAY2DAY SCIENCE Your source of science news

Is it time to start talking to strangers?

1 Using your cell phone. Putting on your headphones. Staring out of the window. Those are all classic ways to avoid talking to strangers on public transportation. However, this may not be the best thing to do for your well-being. Recent research by Nicholas Epley, a professor of behavioral science at the University of Chicago, and Juliana Schroeder, a PhD student, reveals that people are happier when they talk with other passengers rather than ignoring them.

2 The inspiration for the research came from Epley's own daily commute. Humans are, by nature, social animals, and being social is key to our happiness. However, the commuters that Epley saw every day were behaving in very antisocial ways, avoiding all communication as if they were sitting next to a rock. He wondered why nearly everyone acted against their social nature in this situation. Is talking to a stranger on a train truly less pleasant than sitting in silence? Or is everybody wrong?

3 To find out, Epley and Schroeder designed two experiments. In the first, Epley simply asked people to imagine starting a conversation with another passenger. Would it be a pleasant thing to do? Would they feel happy afterward? In the second study, they asked commuters to actually start conversations with strangers on their trip, and then to complete a survey about the experience.

4 His studies revealed a difference between people's expectations of talking to strangers and the reality. In the first study, people generally said it would neither be a pleasant thing to do nor increase their happiness. In addition, they felt that most strangers would not want to talk.
In contrast, the second experiment showed that people enjoyed their commute more when they talked to a stranger and their general level of happiness increased. It also revealed that the reaction was positive because they all took part in the conversations, even though they were not aware it was an experiment.

5 Based on the findings, Epley feels that passenger cars filled with silence, blank expressions and little eye contact are the result of basic misunderstandings and false expectations. Despite what everyone thinks, strangers are happy to talk and talking makes you happier. Once people make the decision to start a conversation, they find this connection to others improves their own lives.

6 Since publishing the research, Epley has put his findings into action and changed his own commuting behavior. He no longer uses his cell phone and he starts conversations with opening lines as simple as 'I like your hat'. He regularly finds himself sitting next to someone he has talked to before, which 'just makes it more pleasant'.'

C Work in pairs. Compare your answers to Exercise B. What other information can you remember from your skim-reading?

D SPEAK Work in groups. What do you think of the results of the research?

VOCABULARY

Nouns ending in *-ion*

A WORK IT OUT Look at *Is it time to start talking to strangers?* again. Find and underline nouns that end with *-ion*.

B Complete the definitions with nouns from Exercise A.

1 to have an ________________: to have a belief about what something will be like or what will happen
2 to have a positive ________________: to feel good as a result of something that happens
3 to make a ________________: to choose something after thinking carefully
4 to have a ________________: to have a relationship to something
5 to have a confused ________________: to look like you don't understand something
6 to be in a difficult ________________: to be doing something that is not easy
7 to be in ________________: to be sharing information, ideas and feelings
8 to be an ________________: to give you new ideas or the enthusiasm to create something with them

C Go to the Vocabulary Hub on page XVII.

D SPEAK Work in pairs. Do you agree or disagree with the statements below. If you disagree with them, change them so they are true for you.

1 Communication with other passengers is a waste of time. I don't know them and I might never see them again.
2 How far you choose to live from work is a very important decision. There is a connection between everyday happiness and the length of your commute.

PRONUNCIATION

Word stress in nouns ending in *-ion*

3.3 A Listen to the pronunciation of the nouns ending in *-ion* and underline the stressed syllables. Some words may have two stressed syllables.

1 action 2 connection 3 communication

3.3 B Listen again and repeat the words. How is the stress pattern similar?

3.4 C Underline the stressed syllables of the nouns ending in *-ion*. Then listen and check your answers. Repeat the words.

1 decision
2 expectation
3 expression
4 inspiration
5 reaction
6 situation

D SPEAK Work in pairs. Practice saying the words. Listen and check your partner's pronunciation.

SPEAKING HUB

A Go to the Communication Hub on page XXII.

B SPEAK Work in groups. Compare your lists and explain your reasons to each other.

C DISCUSS Decide on the top three most annoying things. Discuss ways of stopping that behavior. Compare your ideas with another group.

- Talk about a difficult trip or travel experience
- Talk about behavior on public transportation

- Evaluate suggestions and justify a choice
- Talk about why a plan didn't work

G articles and quantifiers   P sentence stress: quantifiers   V gradable and ungradable adjectives
S listening for signposting

READING

A SPEAK Work in pairs and discuss the question. Do you think there are too many cars on the road where you live or study?

B READ FOR MAIN IDEA Read *Whatever happened to Helsinki's Kutsuplus transportation service?* Match the headings (a–e) with the paragraphs (1–5).

a The advantages of Kutsuplus
b The disadvantages of Kutsuplus
c How Kutsuplus worked
d Was Kutsuplus a success?
e What was Kutsuplus?

Whatever happened to Helsinki's *Kutsuplus* transportation service?

1 ___
A few years ago, Helsinki, Finland, decided it had a problem: there were **too many** cars. So the Helsinki Regional Transportation Authority decided to hold a three-year trial of an on-demand minibus service designed to reduce the number of cars on the road. It was called *Kutsuplus* and it allowed passengers to choose where they wanted to go.

2 ___
Passengers went online and selected a start and end point for their trip. They then paid online and went to their nearest bus stop. **A minibus** arrived and took them to the chosen end point. If other **people** wanted to go to the same area at the same time, no problem: there was **plenty of** space and they could share **the minibus**! Even if people wanted to go to different places in the same area, **the online service** was able to choose the best route available, so everybody was happy!

3 ___
For passengers, the key benefits of *Kutsuplus* were convenience and cost. They could choose where they wanted to go and they didn't have to wait long for the bus to arrive. During the time of the trial, the average *Kutsuplus* trip cost $5. In comparison, the average cost of a taxi ride started at $6, but could be much more expensive for longer trips. Surely this would make *Kutsuplus* a great success! Well, not really …

4 ___
Although it was more convenient than a normal bus or the subway, unlike a taxi, the minibus wasn't able to take people exactly where they wanted to go. Passengers had to use the nearest bus stops as the start and end points of their trip. Another major problem was that there were very **few** buses in operation. By the end of the trial, *Kutsuplus* had 21,000 registered users, but only 15 buses. This would have a big effect on the result of the trial.

5 ___
In general, Helsinki residents had positive feelings about the service. **A lot of** them felt that it was convenient, especially for people who lived in areas where there wasn't **enough** public transportation. However, with **not enough** buses in operation, it wasn't convenient for everybody. In the end, city officials decided not to continue the service.

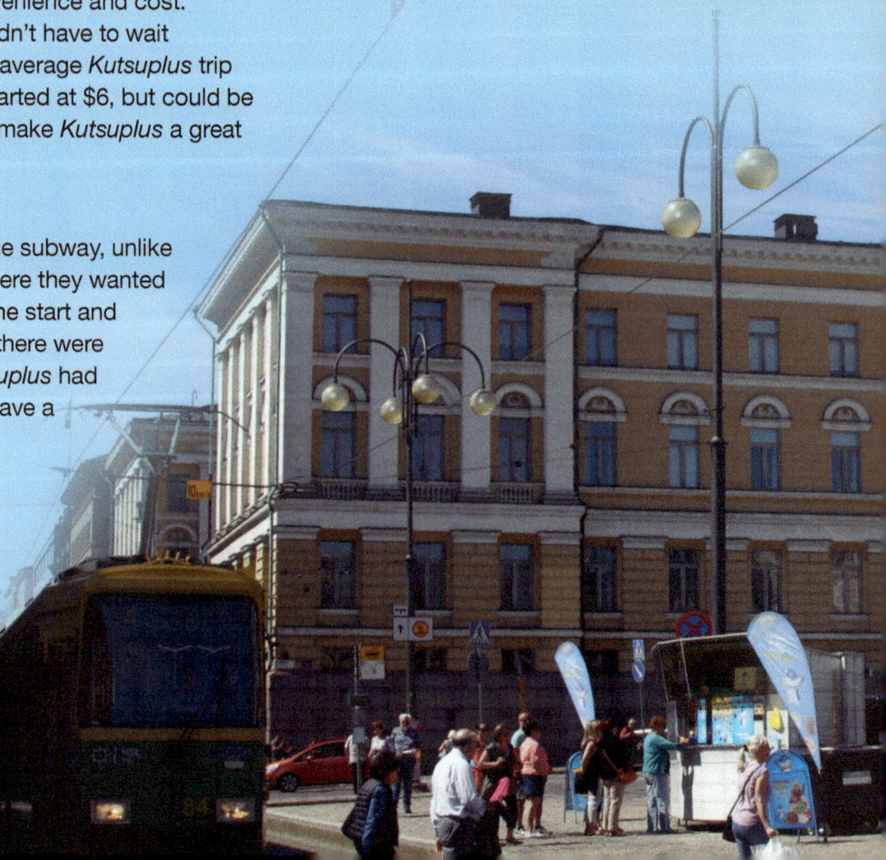

C READ FOR DETAIL Read again. Complete the sentences by choosing a, b or c.

1 The long-term goal of *Kutsuplus* was to encourage people to stop …
- **a** driving cars.
- **b** using the subway.
- **c** hiring minibuses.

2 Passengers could choose the start and end point of their trips by …
- **a** asking at the bus stop.
- **b** calling the driver.
- **c** using the internet.

3 There were … registered users by the end of the trial.
- **a** a small number of
- **b** not enough
- **c** a lot of

4 Overall, people who lived in Helsinki thought the service was …
- **a** useful.
- **b** expensive.
- **c** unfair.

5 The local … stopped the service.
- **a** businesses
- **b** government
- **c** residents

D SPEAK Work in pairs. Do you think the *Kutsuplus* service was a good idea? Why/Why not?

GRAMMAR
Articles and quantifiers

A WORK IT OUT Look at the words in bold in paragraph 2 of *Whatever happened to Helsinki's Kutsuplus transportation service?* Then complete the rules with *a/an*, *the* or – (no article).

Articles

1 We use _____ the first time we mention a person or thing.
2 We use _____ the second time we mention the person or thing.
3 We use _____ when it is clear who or what we are talking about.
4 We use _____ when we talk generally about people or things.

B Find and underline other uses of *a/an*, *the* or – (no article) in the same paragraph and match them with the rules (1–4) in Exercise A.

C Go to the **Grammar Hub** on **page X**.

D PRACTICE Choose *a*, *the* or – (no article) to complete the questions.

1 How long does ***a* / *the* /** – trip from where you live (or are staying) to where you study usually take?
2 Would you like to go by ***a* / *the* /** – different type of ***a* / *the* /** – transportation? If so, which one?

E SPEAK Work in pairs. Ask and answer the questions in Exercise D.

F WORK IT OUT Look at the quantifiers in **red** in the text. Then choose the correct words to complete the rules.

Quantifiers

1 We use quantifiers to talk about ***amounts* / *qualities***.
2 Quantifiers go ***before* / *after*** nouns.

G Go to the **Grammar Hub** on **page X**.

H SPEAK Work in pairs. What is the public transportation system like in your town? Does your town need more or fewer buses, trains or taxis? Why? Tell your partner.

PRONUNCIATION
Sentence stress: quantifiers

3.5 **A** Listen to the sentences from the article. Check (✓) the sentences you hear. Which words are stressed?

1 **a** A lot of them felt that it was convenient. ☐
b A lot of them felt that it was convenient. ☐
2 **a** There were very few buses in operation. ☐
b There were very few buses in operation. ☐

3.5 **B WORK IT OUT** Listen again and repeat the sentences. Do we usually stress the main noun or the quantifier?

C SPEAK Work in pairs. Practice saying the sentences. Listen and check your partner's pronunciation.

SPEAKING

3.6 **A** Listen to an expert explaining why the *Kutsuplus* service was canceled. What reasons does the expert give?

B Work in pairs and discuss the reasons. Do you think the local officials were right to stop the service? Why/Why not?

C Work in groups. Summarize your discussion. Explain your opinions and listen to the opinions of others.

D Work in groups. Plan how you could continue the service or do it differently.

LISTENING

A SPEAK Work in pairs. Look at the poster and discuss the questions.

1 What event is the poster advertising?
2 What happens during that event?
3 Why do cities and towns hold these kinds of event?
4 Does your city or town hold similar events?

3.7 **B LISTEN FOR GIST** Listen to a city council meeting about Car-Free Day and answer the questions.

1 What is Alfred Shaw's view of the Car-Free Day?
2 Do the others at the meeting agree with him?
3 What is Alfred's opinion of cars generally?
4 What two events does Alfred suggest holding instead?
5 What reason does Alfred give for being at the city council meeting?

Glossary

ban (v) to say officially that someone is not allowed to do something
campaign (n) a series of actions intended to produce social change
pedestrian (n) someone who is walking, especially in a town or city, instead of driving or riding

3.7 **C LISTEN FOR DETAIL** Listen again and choose the correct answers.

1 Why don't annual car-free days reduce the amount of traffic?
  a The city has little public transportation.
  b Cars are the most effective type of transportation.
  c You need more than ten car-free days a year.
2 How do car-free days affect pollution levels?
  a They decrease the amount of pollution.
  b They increase the amount of pollution.
  c They do not change the amount of pollution.
3 What might increase the number of people buying electric cars?
  a Providing free electricity-charging stations.
  b Providing opportunities for people to test drive them.
  c Providing online videos showing their advantages.
4 Why do people prefer traveling by car rather than by bus?
  a There are not enough buses.
  b The buses are too slow.
  c The buses are dirty.
5 Why doesn't this city provide bicycles that people can rent?
  a The roads are not very safe.
  b The council has not discussed the idea.
  c It would be too expensive to do.

3.7 **D** Read the information in the box. Now listen again. For 1–7, put the signposting language you hear in the correct position.

Listening for signposting language

When giving a short talk, speakers use signposting language to show the order of points and make their argument easy for people to follow.

- First, I want to talk about the problems.
- [1] First of ________________ …
- To start, …
- Finally, …

They can use it to introduce a new topic:

- Now, let's turn to the solutions.
- Moving on, I'll now discuss my ideas in more detail.
- [2] ________________ look at …
- [3] I'll now ________________ on to …

They can use it to introduce an extra point:

- In addition, …
- [4] Here's another ________________ why …
- [5] And ________________ thing, …
- Also, …

They can also use it to finish a section of a talk or to finish the talk:

- That's all I want to say on that. Any questions?
- In conclusion, …
- [6] In ________________, …
- [7] OK, to sum ________________ …

E SPEAK Work in pairs. Discuss Alfred's arguments and claims. Do you agree or disagree with Alfred?

VOCABULARY

Gradable and ungradable adjectives

A **Underline the adjectives in the sentences from the council meeting about the Car-Free Day.**

1. Some things about cars are fairly bad.
2. That's very funny.
3. That's a really good idea.
4. This may be extremely difficult.
5. Car-free days have a really tiny effect on driving habits.
6. There was an absolutely enormous traffic jam.
7. People were furious about that.
8. Some of our old buses are really filthy.

B **Look at the adjectives in Exercise A. Which are gradable? Which are ungradable? Use the information in the box to help you.**

> **Gradable and ungradable adjectives**
>
> Gradable adjectives can be made stronger and weaker. We can use a range of adverbs to change their strength (*fairly, very, extremely, a little, really*). They have a comparative form.
>
> Ungradable adjectives cannot be made weaker. They already mean *very* + adjective. We can use some adverbs to emphasise the adjective (*extremely, absolutely, completely, really*). They do not have a comparative form.

C **Write the adjectives from Exercise A in the correct place.**

1. very ________ → excellent
2. very small → ________
3. very ________ → terrible
4. very angry → ________
5. very ________ → impossible
6. very dirty → ________
7. very ________ → hilarious
8. very big → ________

D **Match the ungradable adjectives (a–g) with some of the adjectives (1–8) in Exercise C.**

a wonderful ________
b huge ________
c fabulous ________
d great ________
e awful ________
f superb ________
g massive ________

E **Go to the Vocabulary Hub on page XVII.**

F **SPEAK Work in pairs. Describe something you have bought, seen, eaten or done recently using ungradable adjectives.**

I saw an awful play last weekend. The lead actor was absolutely terrible. He kept forgetting his words!

SPEAKING HUB

A **Go to the Communication Hub on page XXIII.**

B **DISCUSS** Work in groups. Discuss the proposals and write notes on their advantages and disadvantages. Think of other ideas you can add to each proposal.

C **PLAN** Decide which proposal would be the best for the city and its people as well as being the best value for money.

D **REFLECT** Share your ideas with the class. Was your thinking similar or different?

- **Evaluate suggestions and justify a choice**
- **Talk about why a plan didn't work**

Café Hub

3.3 Getting there

F – tell a story   P – intonation in responses

COMPREHENSION

A Complete the personal information with *Milly* or *Zac*.

Name:	1 ______	2 ______
Nationality:	American	American
Home town:	Seattle	Seattle
Address:	London	London
Job:	makes video games	owns a clothing store
Hobbies:	playing video games	cycling

B Look at the picture. Where do you think Milly and Zac are going today?

C Watch the video and check your ideas. Then answer the questions.

1 Which famous people does the cabbie say have been in the back of his cab?

2 Why are Milly and Zac amazed at the cabbie's story about his American girlfriend?

3 How does the cabbie react when Milly asks, 'Are you sure this is the right way?'

D Work in pairs. Discuss the last time you took a taxi.

- Where did you go from and to?
- How much did it cost?
- What did you talk about?

FUNCTIONAL LANGUAGE

Telling a story in five stages

A Work in pairs. Complete sentences (1–8) in the grey box with the endings (a–h). Then watch the video again and check.

a … went out with an American girl.
b … what happened the other day.
c … I was putting on a shirt and tie.
d … got my cab licence.
e … I miss you, Molly.
f … who I had in the back of my cab the other week.
g … she loved cycling.
h … she stopped answering my calls.

Telling a story in five stages

Introduction
1 You'll never guess … b
2 You won't believe … ___
3 I once … ___

Background
4 It was a few years ago now, when I … ___
The funny thing was she hated driving.
5 It turned out … ___
This is the best part: she used to run this fantastic little vintage clothes shop.

Problem
Well, a couple of months later, everything was going great, then one day, while I was watching the football, she said to me …
6 Before I knew it ___
All of a sudden things started to change.

Resolution
7 In the end … ___

Comment
8 I still love that girl … ___

Glossary

cycling **(v) (British)** = bike riding **(v) (American)**
cabbie **(n) (British)** = taxicab driver **(n) (American)**
football **(n) (British)** = soccer **(n) (American)**

MILLY SAM NEENA ZAC GABY

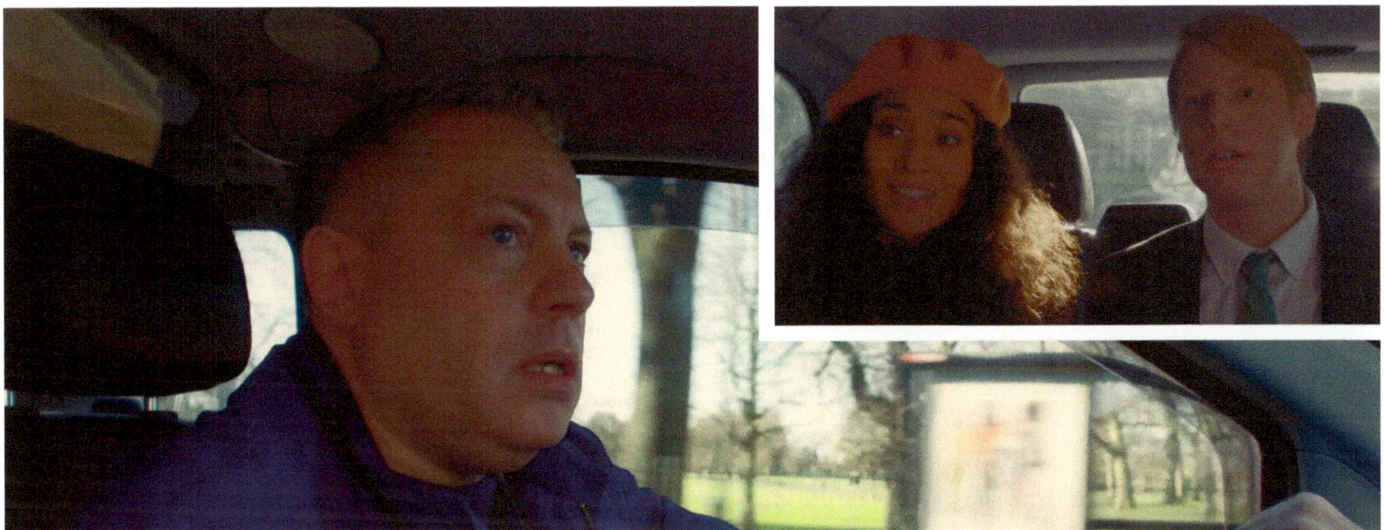

B Work in pairs. Look at Milly and Zac's responses in the box. Student A – retell the cabbie's story. Student B – use the responses at an appropriate moment.

> No way! Really? That's awesome! Really? You're kidding! So what happened? That's tough.

USEFUL PHRASES

A Complete the useful phrases with the correct form of the verbs in the box. There are two verbs you do not need.

> be do joke jump let make take(x2)

1 Whatever, ________________ in the back, Jack.
2 Go on, ________________ a guess.
3 Only ________________!
4 I'll ________________ a short cut.
5 ________________ you two an item?
6 ________________ me tell you something.

B How do you say these useful phrases in your language?

PRONUNCIATION
Intonation in responses

3.8 **A** Listen and write the responses in the table below. Then listen and repeat the responses. Copy the stress and intonation.

B Which two types of responses have similar intonation?

Something is very good	Something is difficult	Something is surprising
		I don't believe it!

C Work in pairs. Student A – use a prompt from the box or your own ideas to begin a conversation. Student B – respond appropriately.

> I found $50 in the street. I earned a perfect score in English. I got tickets to see my favorite band. I won a prize. My dog died. My father lost his job.

SPEAKING

A You are going to tell your partner about somebody you used to spend a lot of time with, but now you do not. Answer the questions.

- Who is this person – a childhood friend, a neighbor, a relative?
- When and how did you meet him/her?
- How often did you use to see him/her?
- What sort of things did you use to do / talk about?
- Why did you stop seeing him/her so much?
- When was the last time you saw him/her?
- What is he/she doing now?

B **DISCUSS** Work in pairs. Take turns talking about the person. Use the functional language to structure your story, and if you are listening, respond in an appropriate way.

Tell a story

➤ Turn to page XXVII to learn how to write an email of complaint.

Unit 3 Review

GRAMMAR

A Complete the story with the correct form of the verbs in parentheses.

We left home early in the morning because it [1] ____________________ (*snow*) heavily. After we had found a parking space at the airport, we [2] ____________________ (*go*) straight to the check-in desk. That was when Kenny realized he [3] ____________________ (*forgot*) his passport. He thought he [4] ____________________ (*leave*) it on the kitchen table!

I [5] ____________________ (*decide*) to travel without him, but this made me nervous because I [6] ____________________ (*not fly*) on my own before. Luckily, when I [7] ____________________ (*wait*) in the line at the security checkpoint, Kenny [8] ____________________ (*call*) me with some excellent news.

He [9] ____________________ (*find*) his passport in the car and [10] ____________________ (*walk*) back to the check-in desk.

B Correct the mistakes in the following passage by using *a*, *an*, *the* or – (no article).

Japan has the famous network of bullet trains. A network is the world's busiest and connects the major cities of the country. Like many the major train networks, it gets very busy at peak times. It is mainly transportation system for long distances.

C Choose the correct quantifiers to complete the sentences.

1. The town center is full of traffic jams during the day. There are just ***too much / too many*** cars on the road.
2. Our city has a bicycle-sharing system. But at peak times it is difficult to get a bike because there are ***not enough / too little***.
3. Overall, our town does not invest enough in transportation systems. This is because the council has ***few / little*** money for this.
4. How ***many / much*** of what the council says about the system is actually true?

VOCABULARY

A Choose the best words to complete the traffic reports.

Storm Anna is over, but there are still problems affecting roads and public transportation. You should only travel if it is essential. The central train station is closed, and they have [1]***canceled / delayed*** all trains. Better news below the roads for the [2]***bus service / subway lines***. There [3]***is good service / are overcrowded trains*** on all lines except for line 3. On that line, there are [4]***severe / slight*** delays of about ten minutes.

Traffic is building up on Bank Street due to the [5]***roadwork / rush hour*** at the corner of Bank and Church Street. You can expect [6]***heavy delays / heavy traffic*** all day there, and probably a [7]***slight delay / traffic jam*** during [8]***heavy rain / rush hour***. That's certainly what happened yesterday.

B Complete the sentences with the nouns in the box.

communication connection decision expectation inspiration situation

1. I don't like to make a ____________ too quickly as I may regret it later.
2. It is important to see the ____________ between the job you want and your own experience and knowledge.
3. Many jobs need strong ____________ skills because talking and writing to people is essential.
4. When your ____________ is realistic, you are less likely to be disappointed.
5. When you cannot change a ____________ you are in, you can learn to accept it.
6. You can waste time waiting for ____________ to produce something. Sometimes it's best to take action.

C Find and correct the mistakes in four of the sentences.

1. Tell Stan that joke about the self-driving car. It's very hilarious.
   ____
2. I'm very angry. The train is late again!
   ____
3. This road is very bad. They need to repair it.
   ____
4. Sometimes, the old buses are very filthy.
   ____
5. These timetables are very impossible to understand.
   ____
6. The New York City bus tour was very excellent.
   ____

FUNCTIONAL LANGUAGE

Complete the dialogue with the words in the box.

awesome best couple dear guess kidding sudden turned way

A: You'll never [1] ____________ what happened on my last trip with Kate. We got lost on a mountain without a map.

B: Really? You're [2] ____________!

A: No, I'm not! It was a [3] ____________ of months ago in Patagonia. I left the map in our hotel.

B: Oh [4] ____________!

A: And even worse, it was dark when we got to the top. Then all of a [5] ____________ Katie remembers she left the flashlight at the hotel, too.

B: No [6] ____________! I can't believe she did that.

A: Yeah, we were a little stupid. But we were lucky. We met two locals and they helped us get back. And you know the [7] ____________ part?

B: What? Tell me!

A: They invited us for dinner. And it [8] ____________ out they owned the most expensive restaurant in town!

A: That's [9] ____________ .

4 CHANGE

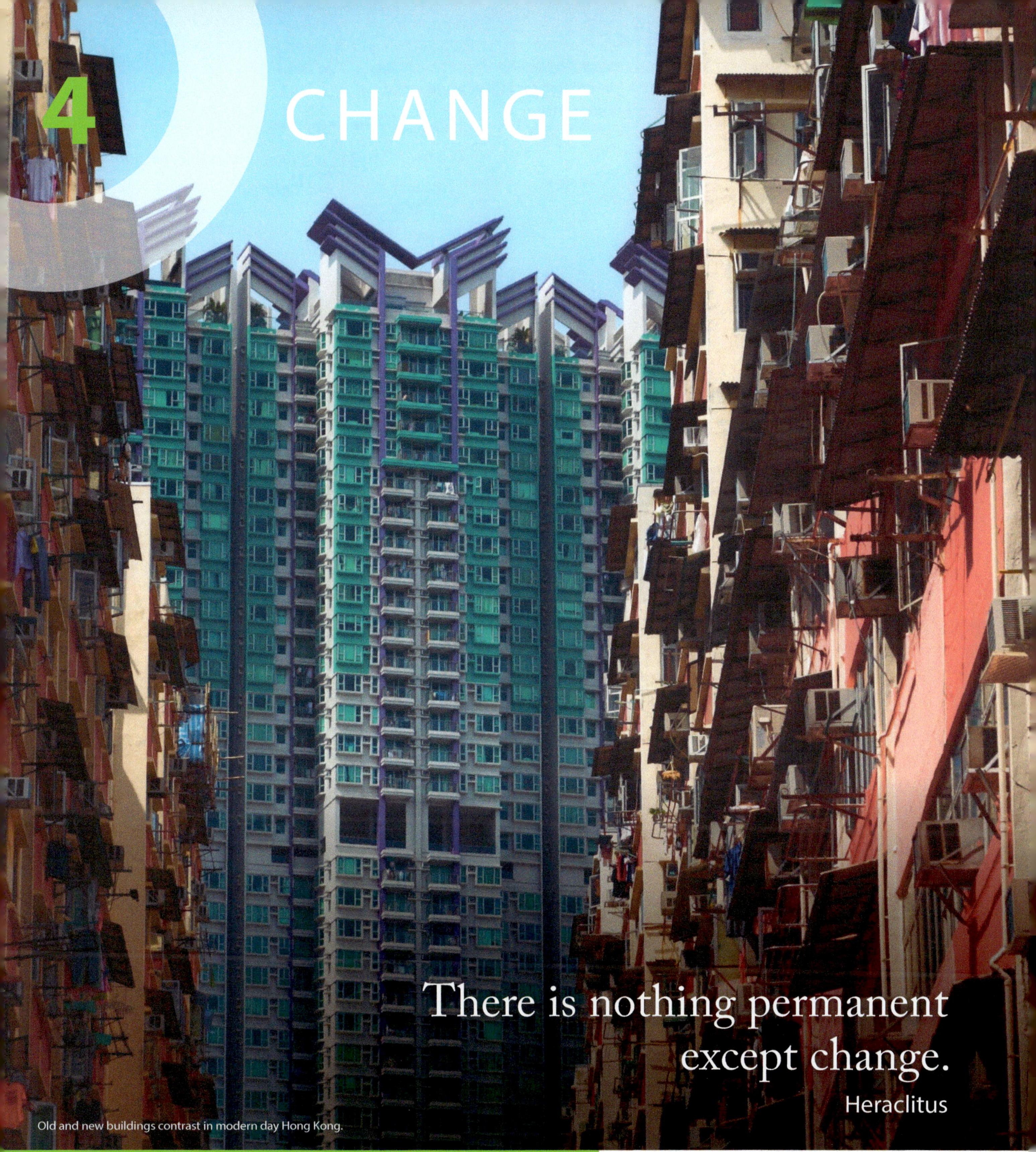

Old and new buildings contrast in modern day Hong Kong.

> There is nothing permanent except change.
>
> Heraclitus

OBJECTIVES

- talk about resolutions and plans
- talk about a life-changing book or movie
- make and discuss predictions
- discuss problems, reasons and consequences
- clarify and ask for clarification
- make and deal with complaints
- write a short essay

Work with a partner. Discuss the questions.

1. Look at the picture. What change does it show? Is it positive or negative?
2. Read the quote. Do you agree with it?
3. What have been the most important changes in your life?

4.1 Personal change

- Talk about resolutions and plans
- Talk about a life-changing book or movie

G future forms
V collocations: goals and resolutions
P intonation for attitude and mood
S summarizing

LISTENING

A SPEAK Work in pairs and discuss the questions.

1 Is New Year's Eve an important celebration:
- for you?
- in your country?

2 How do people celebrate the New Year in different parts of the world?

3 Why do people celebrate the New Year?

4.1 **B LISTEN FOR GIST** Listen to a video call between Julia and Shireen. Then answer the questions.

1 What is their relationship and where are they?

____

2 Check (✓) which of these topics they talk about.
- a their New Year's Eve activities ☐
- b moving ☐
- c buying new clothes ☐
- d making new friends ☐
- e changing jobs ☐
- f learning a language ☐

3 What do you think a New Year's resolution is?

____

4.1 **C LISTEN FOR DETAIL** Listen again. Are the sentences true (T) or false (F)? Correct the false sentences.

1 The weather was cold on New Year's Eve at Times Square in New York City. ___
2 Julia's boyfriend has always been very romantic. ___
3 Julia wants to do more physical exercise. ___
4 Julia can't speak Spanish. ___
5 Julia is looking for a new teacher. ___
6 Shireen thinks Julia reads too many advice books. ___
7 Shireen agrees to stop eating chocolate. ___

D SPEAK Work in pairs and discuss the questions.

1 Look at the list of the ten most common New Year's resolutions. Which do you think are the top three? Go to the **Communication Hub** on **page XX** to check your answers.
- get in shape and get healthy
- get organized
- enjoy life to the fullest
- change the foods you eat
- quit unhealthy habits
- help others achieve their dreams
- fall in love
- spend less, save more
- learn something exciting
- spend more time with family

2 What could people do to achieve these resolutions?

3 Which do you think are the hardest to achieve?

GRAMMAR

Future forms

A WORK IT OUT Look at the sentences (1–7) from the conversation between Julia and Shireen. Check (✓) the sentences in which the speaker made a decision or plan before this conversation.

1 Oh! Oops! I'll do it now. Hold on. ☐
2 I've decided to get in better shape this year, so I'm going to join a gym. ☐
3 I did get pretty cold. I'm going to look for a new hat tomorrow. ☐
4 Sophie's coming here to have lunch. ☐
5 I'm meeting a new teacher on Thursday. ☐
6 Make your mind up now! ☐
7 OK, OK. I'll stop eating it every day. ☐

B Complete the rules with the phrases in the box.

already at a certain time in the future at the time of speaking

Future forms

1 When we talk about future actions and events, we use ***be going to*** when we have ______________ decided to do something.

2 We use ***will*** when we make the decision ______________.

3 We use the present progressive when we have a planned arrangement ______________, usually with another person.

C Go to the Grammar Hub on page XII.

D SPEAK Work in pairs and discuss the questions.

1 What are you doing tonight?
2 Do you have any plans or arrangements for the weekend?
3 What do you intend to do over the next few months?
4 Imagine you have just realized you left your wallet at home. What will you do?

PRONUNCIATION

Intonation for attitude and mood

Intonation for attitude and mood

We change the tone of our voice to communicate our feelings about or attitude toward something. For example, interested/uninterested, surprised/unsurprised, positive/negative.

Our tone of voice can be in a high, mid or low position.

As we speak, our tone may rise and fall to show mood and attitude.

4.2 **A** Listen and write down the five words and phrases that you hear. They are in a neutral tone.

4.3 **B** Listen to the same five words and phrases. Each phrase is said in two different tones. Match each tone (*a* or *b*) with the moods and feelings below.

1 very positive ___
not very positive ___
2 excited ___
unexcited ___
3 interested and surprised ___
not interested ___
4 serious/determined ___
unsure ___
5 pretty surprised ___
not surprised at all (sarcastic) ___

4.3 **C** Listen again and repeat the sentences.

D SPEAK Work in pairs. Student A – go to the Communication Hub on page XIX. Student B – go to the Communication Hub on page XXI.

VOCABULARY

Collocations: goals and resolutions

A Match the phrases (1–6) with phrases with a similar meaning (a–f).

1 make a resolution
2 keep a resolution
3 break a resolution
4 quit a bad habit
5 reach a target
6 cut down on something

a do less of something
b achieve something
c set (yourself) a goal
d not do what you promised
e stick to a plan
f stop doing something that is not good for you

B Choose the best words to complete the sentences.

1 I've made a resolution ***to learn / of learning*** ten English words a day.
2 He managed to keep his resolution ***by / in*** using a fitness app.
3 He quit ***smoking / smoke*** last year.
4 She wants to cut down on ***drink / drinking*** coffee.
5 His goals are not very ***realistic / real***. They're too hard to achieve.
6 Stick to your plan ***until / when*** you reach your target.

C Go to the Vocabulary Hub on page XVIII.

D SPEAK Work in pairs. Discuss your experiences of making resolutions and achieving goals. Find out:

- about resolutions your partner has made, kept and broken.
- how your partner managed to achieve his/her goals and stick to his/her plans.
- if your partner has ever quit, or cut down on, doing something.

SPEAKING

A Work in pairs. It is New Year's Eve, and you have agreed with your friend to each make eight resolutions. Student A – go to the Communication Hub on page XXIV. Student B – go to the Communication Hub on page XXII.

B Talk to your partner about your resolutions, and ask them to make a resolution for each of your topics.

C Compare your resolutions with another pair. Do you think the resolutions will be easy or hard to keep?

READING

A Choose the correct sentence endings.

1 Self-help books …
 a contain instructions for doing something, especially operating a machine.
 b are designed to help you solve your own problems or improve your life.

2 Self-help books are usually written in …
 a a formal style that is for experts only.
 b an informal style for anyone.

B SCAN Read *Life Cycle* quickly. Match the phrases (1–5) with the topics (a–e).

1 Helena Schneiderlin	a a journey
2 *Life Cycle*	b the author's next book
3 Paris to Moscow	c the author's passion
4 cycling	d the author
5 *Inner Pedal Power*	e the author's first book

Life Cycle: How to find what you love and love what you find

About this book

Ten years ago, Helena Schneiderlin was a hard-working mom with no time for herself. Like many people, she didn't know what she really wanted to do with her life. Today, Schneiderlin is a cyclist who is well known for going on long and difficult journeys. She has ridden from Paris to Moscow by herself. She has also ridden across Australia, and last year she rode from the bottom of South America to the top.

Thanks to her cycling experiences, and the effect they have had on her life, Schneiderlin has also become a leading lifestyle expert. Her talks have been watched millions of times online, and she is regularly asked to speak at international lifestyle events and conferences.

In *Life Cycle*, which is her first book, she describes how finding her true passion changed her life, and explains how you can find yours.

'This isn't a book about cycling,' says Schneiderlin. 'It's a book about finding the thing that you enjoy doing most, and helping to make that thing benefit all other areas of your life.'

In *Life Cycle*, Schneiderlin uses her own story as an example for others to follow. She describes how she found her passion for cycling while on vacation with her family, and what it has taught her about commitment, sacrifice and success.

She provides valuable advice and life lessons that apply to all of us, including chapters on getting rid of the things in life that aren't helping, and how to identify the things that make you feel better about yourself.

Schneiderlin says:

> ***"I believe that everyone has a passion, but they may not know what it is. I also believe that when you find that passion, you should use it to improve every area of your life. In my case, it was cycling – but it could have been anything. What's important is finding the thing that you love, and then using it in the right way."***

C SUMMARIZE Read the two summaries of the book *Life Cycle*. Which is the best summary? Why? Use the strategies in the box to help you.

Summarizing

A summary gives a brief explanation of the most important parts of the text.

To write a summary, first identify the details in the original text that don't need to be included in a summary. Then find the main points in the original text. Finally, put these together to make a summary, but try not to copy word for word.

1 Helena Schneiderlin has gone on a lot of long bicycle journeys. Once she rode from Paris to Moscow. Another time she rode across Australia. She has also ridden all the way up South America. She is a mom. She is a lifestyle expert and lots of people watch her talks on the internet. This is her first book. This book is about lifestyle changes. This book is about finding the thing you enjoy doing most. It is not about cycling, but she does talk about how she found her passion for cycling while she was on vacation with her family. This book is also about improving your life.

2 Helena Schneiderlin is a top lifestyle expert and a well-known cyclist who has ridden across continents. In this, her first book, she explains how cycling led to a life change and self-discovery, and gives advice on how to find your true passion. Using her own story as a guide, the author explains what she has learned from cycling, and discusses how these 'life lessons' can apply to all of us, in all aspects of life.

D SPEAK Work in pairs. Would you like to read *Life Cycle*? Why/Why not?

LISTENING

A LISTEN FOR GIST (4.4) Listen to four people talking about books or movies that changed their lives. Write *Maya*, *Lukas*, *Jody* or *Hassan*.

Who talks about …

1 a non-fiction film? ____________

2 a fiction book? ____________

3 doing what the book suggested? ____________

4 the whole of human history? ____________

B LISTEN FOR MAIN IDEA (4.4) Complete the summaries (1–4) with the words in the box. Then listen again and check your answers.

advice characters confident documentary father history impressive journey passion society sport recently

1 Maya read a self-help book about finding your true ____________. She followed the ____________ in the book and now she feels happier and more ____________.

2 Lukas read a book about two ____________ on a ____________ in a strange place. The book made him think about his own relationship with his ____________.

3 Jody learned a lot about the ____________ of the human race in a book she read ____________. She thinks the book is very ____________.

4 Hassan saw a ____________ set in the US. He feels that the story is about more than a ____________; he thinks it also has an important message about ____________.

C SPEAK Work in pairs. Which book or movie from the listening are you most interested in? Why?

SPEAKING HUB

A PLAN You are going to talk about a life-changing book or movie.

1 Choose a book or movie that had a big effect on you.

2 Think about how you can summarize the book/movie:
- What kind of book/movie is it?
- Who wrote/made it?
- What is it about?

3 Think about how it affected you:
- When did you read/see it?
- Why did you read/see it?
- How did it change the way you think/feel?
- Who else do you think should read/see it?

B SPEAK Work in pairs. Tell your partner about the book or movie that changed your life. Listen to his/her description. Ask and answer questions.

Talk about resolutions and plans

Talk about a life-changing book or movie

4.2 Social change

- Make and discuss predictions
- Discuss problems, reasons and consequences

G – making predictions
V – prefixes: *dis-*, *mis-*, *over-*, *re-*, *under-*
P – contraction of *will*; linking final consonant and first vowel sounds
S – paraphrasing

READING

A SPEAK Work in groups. Have you ever predicted something that later came true?

B Look at the headline of the article. Which word means:

a a person who has detailed knowledge about a subject?

b a person who talks about future events and situations?

C READ FOR GIST Read *How super-forecasters could replace professional experts.* Then choose the best summary.

1 Philip Tetlock carried out a study on why experts are good media guests, but make predictions that are generally less accurate than those made by most ordinary people.

2 Philip Tetlock carried out a research project to show that ordinary people who have particular thinking skills usually make better future predictions than experts.

How super-forecasters could replace professional experts

Katy Macnab

'Five minutes left, and Brazil is leading by three goals. They're going to win the World Cup again.' Apart from situations like this, the only certain thing about the future is that our predictions will probably be wrong.

In his early research, Philip Tetlock, of the University of Pennsylvania, showed that professional experts are only slightly better at predicting the future than monkeys. However, his most recent study is more hopeful.

This project involved thousands of ordinary people making predictions about social change. They used the internet, but they did not have detailed knowledge of a topic or access to secret data. Despite this, Tetlock found that 2 percent of them were rather good at it – better than both monkeys and professional experts. These 'super-forecasters' are smart, but not geniuses. However, they do have good thinking skills that anyone can develop.

Super-forecasters are analytical thinkers who update their opinion when they get new information, and they don't let their personal hopes affect their thinking. More importantly, they listen carefully to different views that they then use in their forecast. This perhaps explains why they make their most accurate predictions when working in teams of super-forecasters.

Surprisingly, professional experts usually lack these qualities. They tend to work alone and have strong personal opinions that guide their thinking. They speak with great confidence, stressing they are totally certain: 'I'm sure all cars will be driverless', 'Robots are going to replace office workers', 'We won't have an early election'. This means they are great TV guests and bloggers, but not the best forecasters.

Super-forecasters don't speak in a way that suits TV. They are more cautious: 'There may be an early election', 'People might stop reading newspapers', 'Chinese could become a global language'. They also use percentages to show how likely something is: 'I think this has an 80 percent chance of happening'. In this way, the team can discuss different ideas easily and make a final prediction.

Tetlock also identified three useful techniques, namely looking at current trends, comparing with past events and exploring the possible effects of a prediction: 'If everyone uses electric cars, how will we produce enough electricity?'

In the future, we will definitely develop better computers to make accurate predictions about our society. For now though, teams of super-forecasters are the best crystal balls we have.

Glossary

analytical (adj) using a method of separating things into their parts in order to examine and understand them

genius (n) someone who is much more intelligent or skilful than other people

tend (v) to usually do a particular thing

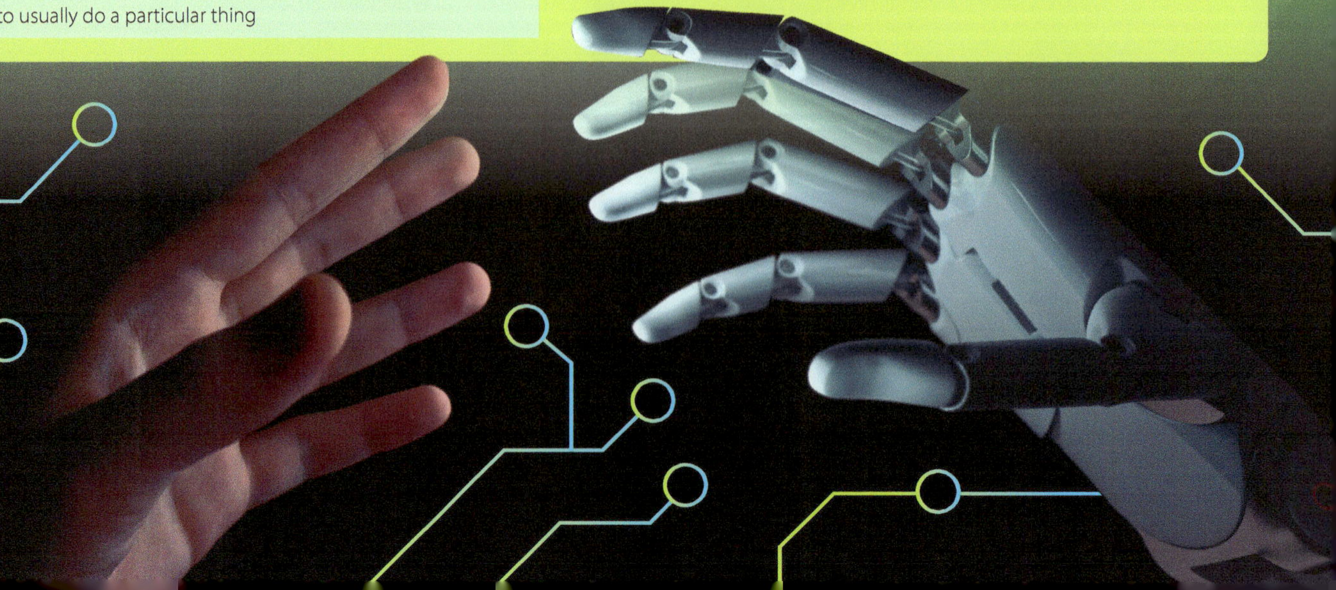

D **READ FOR DETAIL** Read again. Match the sentences (1–6) to the professional experts (PE) or the super-forecasters (SF).

1 They generally work individually. ___
2 They change their ideas when they learn something new. ___
3 They make better predictions when in groups. ___
4 Their personal beliefs influence their thinking. ___
5 They use percentages to show how certain they are. ___
6 The way they speak shows they are really certain. ___

E **SPEAK** Work in pairs. How easy is it to accurately predict these things? Put them in order (1 = easiest, 3 = hardest). Give reasons for your decisions.

a the winner of a soccer competition
b the number of schools we will need in ten years' time
c what life will be like in 100 years' time

GRAMMAR

Making predictions

A **WORK IT OUT** Look at the words in bold in the sentences from *How you could become a super-forecaster.* Which words show that the speaker is less than 100 percent sure of a prediction? Which show that the speaker is 100 percent sure?

1 Brazil is leading by three goals. They**'re going to** win the World Cup again.
2 There **may** be an early election.
3 I'm sure all cars **will** be driverless.
4 Our predictions **will probably** be wrong.
5 Robots **are going to** replace office workers.
6 Chinese **could** become a global language.
7 We **will definitely** develop better computers.
8 People **might** stop reading newspapers.

B Choose the correct words to complete the rules.

Making predictions

1 When we feel certain about a future event or situation, we *use / don't use be going to*, *will* or *won't*.
2 To show stronger certainty, we can add *definitely / probably.*
3 To show we are confident, but not completely certain, we can add *definitely / probably.*
4 There is little difference between *will* and *be going to* for predictions. However, if the present provides strong evidence or reasons for our predictions, we usually use *be going to / will.*
5 When we feel a future event or situation is possible, but are not completely certain, we *use / don't use could*, *may* or *might*.

C Go to the Grammar Hub on page XII.

PRONUNCIATION

contraction of *will*

A Listen to five pairs of sentences. In each pair, which sentence (a or b) uses *'ll*?
4.5

1 ___ 2 ___ 3 ___ 4 ___ 5 ___

B Listen and repeat the subject pronouns + *'ll*.
4.6

C **SPEAK** Work in pairs. Go to the Communication Hub on page XX. Student A – say a sentence. Student B – point to the sentence. Take turns.

SPEAKING

A Follow the instructions.

1 Make two predictions for three of the topics in the box – one prediction for life in ten years' time, the other for life in 50 years.

education housing and domestic life
free time national culture
technology the environment
transportation work and employment

2 Give each of your predictions a percentage mark to show how likely you think it is.
3 What are the reasons for your predictions and percentages? Write notes.

B Work in pairs. Imagine you are a team of 'super-forecasters'. Explain and discuss your predictions. Practice using super-forecasting language from *How super-forecasters could replace professional experts.*

C Decide on your pair's strongest four predictions. Compare your predictions with another pair.

LISTENING

A SPEAK Work in pairs. Student A – describe picture a. Student B – describe picture b. Ask and answer the questions.

1 What are the positive things about living in this place?
2 What are the negative things about living in this place?

4.7 **B LISTEN FOR GIST** Listen to a current affairs radio show. Which is the best description of the show's main topic?

1 They are revealing why a negative prediction, about life in the countryside disappearing, is not very accurate.
2 They are describing the advantages and disadvantages of living in the countryside, in order to understand why the rural population is decreasing.
3 They are reporting on how we can increase the number of people living and working in the countryside in order to stop villages from dying out.

Glossary

expense (n) an amount of money that you spend in order to buy or do something
resident (n) someone who lives in a particular place

4.7 **C LISTEN FOR DETAIL** Listen again. Complete the summaries with the missing word(s) and/or number(s).

Kamiyama, which is [1]_______________ from the city, offers a [2]_______________ to attract new businesses. Toshi Asaka thinks working in Kamiyama doesn't have any [3]_______________ and life is less expensive. Kamiyama is replacing old-style business with [4]_______________ companies.

Nakanoshima fishing village provides opportunities for [5]_______________ to live and work there for [6]_______________ and to discover a more traditional lifestyle. They get inexpensive accommodations and [7]_______________ jobs with farmers and fishermen. Because of this program, residents start new businesses, and that helps keep [8]_______________ in the area.

Mishima Island gives money to [9]_______________ people to pay for romantic dates in the hope that they will stay on the island if they get married and start a family. All [10]_______________ receive a young cow. The meat is valuable (it costs [11]_______________ per kilo), and these cows are [12]_______________ disappearing completely.

D Match the phrases (1–4) with phrases with the same meaning (a–d). Use the strategies in the box to help you.

Paraphrasing

When explaining and describing things, we sometimes paraphrase, which means that we repeat a point, but use different words. We paraphrase for various purposes:

- As the speaker, to make a point clear or to give it extra emphasis.
- As the listener, to check, or show that you understand the speaker's point.
- Both the speaker and the listener may paraphrase to sum up a few points or longer argument.

1 young people are relocating to urban areas
2 offering financial incentives
3 blue-sky thinking
4 these cows are in danger of extinction

a ideas that are different, fresh and unexpected
b they're going to the cities
c offering things like free or cheap housing
d of disappearing completely forever

E SPEAK Work in pairs. Can you think of any other ways to encourage people to move to the countryside?

PRONUNCIATION

Linking final consonant and first vowel sounds

4.8 **A** Complete the sentences from the radio show. Then listen and check your answers.

1 Oh yes, such _______________?
2 Tell _______________ more.
3 What's the next _______________?
4 That sounds like _______________ fun thing to do.
5 But, is _______________ such a good idea?
6 What _______________ did you discover?
7 That isn't _______________ lot of money, is it?
8 That's _______________ lot of money!

4.8 **B** We usually link the final consonant sound of a word to the first vowel sound of the next word. Listen and repeat sentences 1 and 2 from Exercise A.

4.8 **C** Mark the links between the final consonant and first vowel sounds in Exercise A. Then listen again and check your answers. Repeat the sentences.

D SPEAK Work in pairs. Practice saying the sentences. Listen and check your partner's pronunciation.

a

VOCABULARY

Prefixes: *dis-*, *mis-*, *over-*, *re-*, *under-*

Using prefixes

We can add a prefix to a verb, noun or adjective to change its meaning. We use prefixes to show the opposite, to indicate a size or to show repetition. For example:

- *do – **un**do* *circle – **semi**circle* *organize – **re**organize*

A **Underline the prefixes in the sentences from the radio show.**

a Hi, I'm Rita Costa and this is *Rethinking the Future*.

b Many villages and small towns are going to disappear.

c We've talked before about overpopulation in urban areas …

d You've misunderstood the goal of this plan.

e My employees don't feel underpaid now!

B **Match the prefixes in the box with their meanings (a–e).**

dis- mis- over- re- under-

a bad or wrong

b opposite

c too little or too small

d again, but perhaps in a different way

e too much

C **Complete the words in bold with the correct prefixes.**

1 There are many things I ________**like** about where I live. I'd like to move.

2 I know someone who usually ________**works**. They should relax more.

3 I regularly ________**place** things and waste time trying to find them.

4 There are some terrible buildings in my town that they should knock down and ________**build**.

5 I usually ________**agree** with my parents, which sometimes leads to arguments.

6 I think that soccer players are ________**paid**. Some get millions of dollars a year. In contrast, I think nurses are ________**paid**.

D Go to the **Vocabulary Hub** on **page XVIII**.

E **SPEAK** Work in pairs. Rewrite the sentences in Exercise C so they are true for you. Then compare your ideas with your partner.

SPEAKING HUB

A **Look at the predicted problems. Think of solutions to these problems. How can we stop this from happening? What could we do? How can we create a better future?**

1 The use of robots and artificial intelligence will create massive unemployment because many jobs will disappear.

2 Across the world, air pollution will continue to increase and damage human health.

3 Using social media and digital services will lead to a near total loss of privacy, as companies and governments store and use all the data.

B **DISCUSS** **Work in groups. Discuss your ideas. Choose the best two solutions for each problem.**

C **REFLECT** **Compare your group's solutions with another group. Are they the same or different? Which ideas are good examples of blue-sky thinking?**

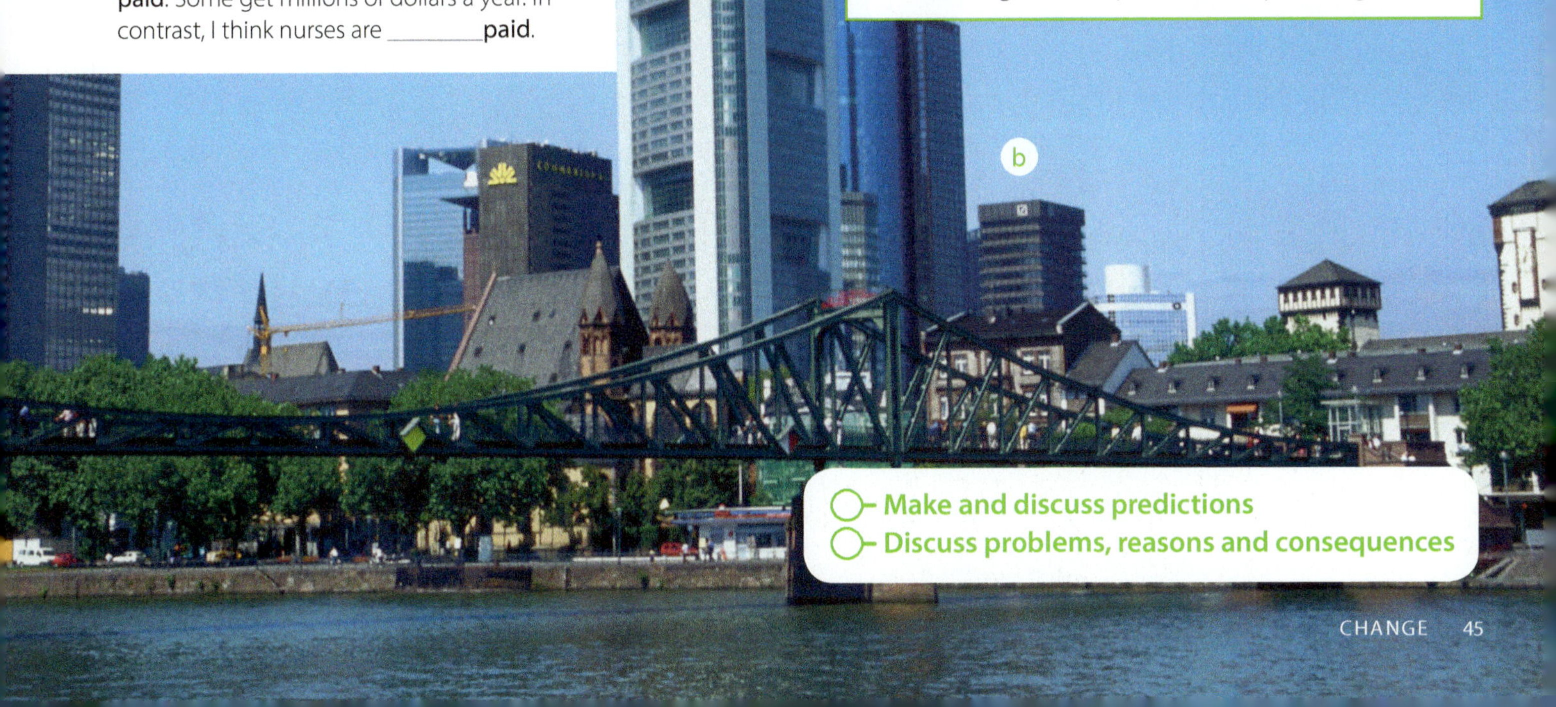

- **Make and discuss predictions**
- **Discuss problems, reasons and consequences**

Café Hub

4.3 Part-time

F– clarify and ask for clarification; make and deal with complaints
P– intonation and stress

COMPREHENSION

A 00:00–02:30 **Work in pairs. Watch the first part of the video without sound and guess the answers to the questions.**

1 How is Gaby feeling?
2 What does Sam suggest?
3 How does Gaby respond?
4 What do they decide?
5 What misunderstanding do they have?

B 00:00–02:30 **Watch the first part of the video with sound and check your ideas in Exercise A. What is the main reason Sam gives for taking Gaby on?**

C 02:30–04:49 **Watch the second part of the video and answer the questions.**

1 What does the customer complain about?
2 What does the customer want Gaby to do?
3 How does Gaby react to the situation?
4 Why does the customer ask to speak to Sam?
5 How does Sam deal with the situation?

FUNCTIONAL LANGUAGE

Clarifying and asking for clarification

A 01:48–04:49 **Complete what Gaby says with the correct form of *get*, *say*, *lose* or *catch*. Then watch the clip and check your answers.**

Clarifying and asking for clarification
1 What did you ______________?
2 Sorry, I didn't ______________ that.
3 I don't ______________ what you're saying.
4 So you're ______________ you want me to …
5 You've ______________ me.
6 Why didn't you just ______________ that?

B **You are going to role-play a similar situation. Invent a conversation.**

Student A: You are Sam. Begin with '… And remember to put the plates under here.'

Student B: You are Gaby. Ask for clarification and use phrases from Exercise A.

MILLY

SAM

NEENA

ZAC

GABY

Making and dealing with complaints

C 02:30-04:49 **Put the words or phrases in parentheses in the correct position to complete the sentences. Then watch the second part of the video to check.**

Making a complaint	Finding out about a complaint	Apologizing
[1]I'm sorry to bother you, but *I'm afraid* there's a problem with … (*I'm afraid*) I want my money back, please. [2]I'm not happy with the service. (*really*)	[3]What is the problem? (*exactly*) What seems to be the problem?	I'm sorry to hear that. [4]That's no problem. I'm sorry about that. (*so*) [5]I'm sorry for the inconvenience, madam; it won't happen again. (*terribly*)

USEFUL PHRASES

A Match the useful phrases in the box with the phrases before or after them from the video (1–6).

How dare you! How's your first day going?
Leave it to me. Something good will come along.
The customer is always right. What's up?

1 ________________ / I don't know, Sam.
2 ________________ / It always does.
3 ________________ / Great so far.
4 Excuse me! Hello? Excuse me! / ________________
5 ________________ / Unless the customer is wrong.
6 ________________ / I want to speak to the manager.

B How do you say these useful phrases in your language?

Glossary
madam **(n) (British)** = ma'am **(n) (American)**

PRONUNCIATION

Intonation and stress

4.9 **A Listen and write down three versions of the question 'What's the problem?'**

1 exactly ________________
2 seems ________________
3 appears ________________

B Practice the questions in Exercise A. Copy the stress and intonation.

SPEAKING

A Work in groups of three: the customer, the waiter, the manager. The customer makes one of the following complaints. Write a funny conversation.

- The soup is cold. (The customer has eaten the soup.)
- The steak is tough. (The customer has eaten the steak.)
- The pasta is too salty. (The customer has eaten the pasta.)

B PRESENT Perform your conversation in front of the class.

Clarify and ask for clarification
Make and deal with complaints

➤ Turn to page XXVIII to learn how to write a short essay.

Unit 4 Review

GRAMMAR

A Choose the best verb form to complete the sentences.

1. I can't tonight, I'm busy. I can't call you tomorrow either. I ***'m visiting* / *will visit*** my parents all day. I ***'m calling* / *'ll call*** you when I'm free.
2. He ***'s going to* / *'ll*** do that this afternoon. It's next on his to-do list.
3. Can I borrow some money? You ***'re getting* / *'ll get*** it back tomorrow, if that's OK?
4. Well, let me check. Yes, I ***'m going to* / *'ll*** lend you $20. Here you are.
5. We're going now. We ***'re meeting* / *'ll meet*** Asif for dinner at seven. Bye!
6. Oh, look – it's raining. Change of plans! I ***'m not bike riding* / *won't bike*** today; I think I ***'m going to* / *'ll*** take the subway instead.
7. My sister's decided to go to Italy for her vacation this year. She ***'s going to* / *'ll*** visit Rome, Florence and Venice.

B Choose the correct words to complete the dialogues.

1 **A:** This game is terrible. Come on – let's leave early.
B: No, let's wait until the end.
A: But there's no point staying. We're losing 5–0. We [1] ***aren't going to* / *probably won't*** win.
B: But we [2] ***might* / *will*** score one at least. You never know!
A: There's no way that [3] ***may* / *will*** happen. Come on. Time to give up.

2 **A:** Flying cars? Of course, I can't say it will [4] ***definitely* / *probably*** happen, but it [5] ***definitely* / *probably*** will.
B: No, it [6] ***might not* / *won't*** happen. I'm sure. Think about it, what would happen if every car were a flying car? It would be too dangerous.
A: But people are definitely [7] ***going to* / *might*** want them in the future. The technology can't be far away. I'm sure we [8] ***'re going to* / *could*** have flying cars in the future!

VOCABULARY

A Which is the odd-one-out in each set of verb phrases? Why?

1. a achieve a target
   b make a resolution
   c set a goal
2. a keep a resolution
   b stick to a plan
   c cut down on something
3. a do less of something
   b quit a bad habit
   c stop doing something
4. a reach a goal
   b break resolutions
   c not do what you promised

B Look at the words in bold. Are the prefixes correct or incorrect? If they are incorrect, write the correct prefix.

1. The fire destroyed a lot of the building. We'll need to **misbuild** it.
2. I'm definitely **overpaid**. Unless I get a pay raise, it'll be time to find a new job!
3. Some money has **reappeared**. It's missing. No one is leaving until we find it.
4. Wait, let me help! It's heavy. Don't **overdo** it. I'll lift it with you.
5. And, don't **disbehave**! We want to impress our school visitors.
6. No, I didn't pass my exam, unfortunately. I have my **overtake** next week.
7. The answer is wrong. You made a **miscalculation**. Do the math again.
8. Urban **underpopulation** isn't a problem now, but it soon will be. The city's population is increasing rapidly.

FUNCTIONAL LANGUAGE

Choose the correct words to complete the dialogue.

A: Hi. I'm sorry to [1] ***excuse* / *bother*** you.
B: Not at all, sir. Please sit down. How can I help?
A: I took one of your courses, 'How to change your life in seven days'. I'm [2] ***afraid* / *not happy*** there is a problem with the course.
B: Oh, I'm sorry. Could I have your name first?
A: Jim Stevens.
B: Sorry, I didn't [3] ***take* / *catch*** the last part.
A: Stevens.
B: Great. What was the problem with the course?
A: I took the course ten days ago. But my life hasn't changed!
B: OK, I'm not sure I [4] ***have* / *get*** what you are saying. Do you mean the course was unhelpful?
A: Yes. I expect results for the price. And the teacher was always late.
B: I'm sorry to [5] ***hear* / *catch*** that. We will talk to the teacher. That won't [6] ***happen* / *bother*** again.
A: And the money?
B: So you're [7] ***saying* / *hearing*** you want your money back?
A: Exactly!
B: Ok, just let me check with my manager …

5 WORK AND BUSINESS

A business that makes nothing but money is a poor business.

Henry Ford

Designers making tough decisions at a studio in Berlin.

OBJECTIVES

- discuss and give advice about employment skills and career interests
- discuss and suggest workplace benefits and changes
- describe and evaluate a small business
- talk about environmental business ideas
- structure a presentation
- write a cover letter for a job application

Work with a partner. Discuss the questions.

1 Look at the picture. What do you think they are doing?

2 Read the quote. Do you agree that a business which makes money can still be poor?

3 What kind of business would you like to work for?

5.1 At work

- Discuss and give advice about employment skills and career interests
- Discuss and suggest workplace benefits and changes

V – employment skills and qualities; verbs of influence
G – past habits and states
P – intonation and rhythm: holding your turn
S – following reference links in a text

a

b

c

d

VOCABULARY

Employment skills and qualities

A SPEAK Work in pairs. Look at the pictures (a–d). What are the people's jobs? What skills do they need to do these jobs?

B SPEAK Work in pairs. Student A – go to the Communication Hub on page XXIII. Student B – go to the Communication Hub on page XXII.

C Read the report about a business survey. Complete the phrases with *be* or *have*.

Many jobs require very specific skills and experience. However, there are also many skills and personal qualities that all employers are looking for. We surveyed **100 Human Resource Managers** to find out which are the most important general employment skills and qualities.

People should:

1 ________ reliable.
2 ________ good communication skills.
3 ________ good digital technology skills.
4 ________ good at time management.
5 ________ good at team work.
6 ________ able to work well under pressure.
7 ________ creative thinking skills.
8 ________ good people skills.

D SPEAK Work in pairs. Match the quiz questions in Exercise B with the employment skills in Exercise C.

E SPEAK For each employment skill in Exercise C, give yourself a percentage score to show your strength. For example, 100 percent = a great strength, no room for improvement. Then work in pairs and explain your answers.

LISTENING

5.1 **A LISTEN FOR KEY WORDS** Listen to the first part of a conversation between Fiona and Michael about work. Choose the correct answer for each question.

1 What is Fiona's job?
  a Human Resources Manager in a company
  b a career advisor
  c a psychologist
2 What is Michael's role in the bank?
  a head of the accounting team
  b a junior member of the property investment team
  c a member of the general management team
3 Why is Michael unhappy in his job?
  a He doesn't work closely with other people.
  b His work doesn't offer enough challenges.
  c He has to meet too many deadlines.
4 In which of these areas hasn't he worked?
  a fashion
  b sports
  c food and drink
5 Which of these things seem most important to Michael?
  a team work
  b digital technology skills
  c time management

5.1 **B LISTEN FOR DETAIL** Listen again. Are the sentences true (T) or false (F)? Correct the false sentences.

1 Michael has worked in five different banks. ___
2 Michael currently uses the skills that the test showed as strengths. ___
3 Michael sometimes bought the clothes that he modeled. ___
4 Michael enjoyed working as a waiter, but not when it was very busy. ___
5 Michael feels positively about training and coaching. ___
6 Michael is interested in setting up his own company. ___

C SPEAK Work in pairs. Look at the pictures (a–d) again. Which job do you think Fiona will recommend for Michael? Why?

5.2 **D LISTEN FOR DETAIL** Listen to the second part of the conversation. Which job does Fiona suggest? Why?

PRONUNCIATION

Intonation and rhythm: holding your turn

5.3 **A** Listen to Michael and Fiona saying *Nice to meet you.* Then answer the questions.

1 Who sounds like they have finished speaking?

2 Who sounds like they are going to continue speaking?

3 What is the difference in how they say *you*?

Holding your turn

We can show that we are going to continue speaking by making a word longer, and sometimes, by using a rising intonation.

We show that we have finished speaking by using a falling intonation on our final word.

5.4 **B** Read the box. Now listen to more examples from Michael and Fiona's conversation. Underline the words the speaker makes longer to show they want to keep speaking.

1 I see you've been there for five years.

2 Well, it's been a good job, but um, I just feel there's something missing.

3 I see, and what is it that's missing exactly?

4 I've recently been made assistant manager, so those skills are important.

5 I mean, you look very neat and well-dressed.

C SPEAK Work in pairs. Practice saying the sentences in Exercise B. Listen and check your partner's pronunciation.

GRAMMAR

Past habits and states

A WORK IT OUT Look at the sentences from the conversation between Fiona and Michael. Which underlined verbs are state verbs and which are action verbs? Which words are used to show repeated actions and events in the past?

1 I used to be a fashion model.

2 They'd usually give us some of the clothes after the shoot.

3 I used to help new members.

4 At busy times, you would always be under a lot of pressure.

5 I used to be tired but happy at the end of each day.

B WORK IT OUT Choose the correct words to complete the rules. Then match the rules (2–5) with the sentences in Exercise A.

Past habits and states

1 We use ***used to*** and ***would*** to describe actions and states in the ***present / past***. These are likely to be actions and states that are finished.

2 To talk about repeated actions in the past, we can use *used to* **and / but not** *would*.

3 To talk about temporary repeated states in the past, we can use *used to* **and / but not** *would*.

4 To talk about permanent states in the past, we use *used to* **and / but not** *would*.

5 We usually use adverbs of frequency with ***used to / would***.

C Go to the Grammar Hub on page XIV.

D SPEAK Work in groups. Discuss some of these topics.

- your childhood vacations
- your grandparents' younger lives
- how you have changed over the years

SPEAKING HUB

A You are going to give and receive some career advice. Think about your employment skills, interests and experience. Then write down three jobs you would like to do.

- What strengths do you have?
- What skills have you used in work, college or your hobbies?
- What is important for you in a job or career?
- What types of work do you like doing?

B PLAN Write some interview questions that will help you find out about your partner's employment skills, interests and experience. Use the audio script on page XXXVI to help you.

C SPEAK Work in pairs. Interview your partner. Listen carefully and make a note of his/her answers. Take turns.

D DISCUSS Choose three jobs that you think match your partner's skills and experience. Are they the same jobs that your partner wrote down before?

READING

A SPEAK Work in pairs. Look at the pictures (a–c) and discuss the questions.

1 Which offices would you like to work in? Why?

2 Which wouldn't you like to work in? Why?

B READ FOR MAIN IDEA Read *Are we in the middle of a workplace revolution?* Which is the best subtitle? Why?

1 Why digital technology companies are so successful

2 Why office life is changing and how to manage it

3 Why modern offices and unusual benefits are bad for business

a

b

c

Are we in the middle of a WORKPLACE REVOLUTION?

Pool tables, nap-pods and free food. **They** sound like things at an all-inclusive vacation resort rather than in an office. However, digital tech companies have redesigned the office and provided unusual benefits to make the workplace a more pleasant and productive place to be. Need a massage to help reduce stress? Want to bring your pet to work? No problem. For these companies, the days of individual cubicles where people would work on their own for eight hours a day are no more.

This trend is now spreading outside Silicon Valley. Bob Randell, director of MiCareer, says, 'Everyone's realizing that tech companies don't provide fancy perks or game areas in order to seem cool and trendy. They want their staff to feel good about themselves and their jobs. Happy employees are less likely to leave to work for a competitor and, most importantly, they are more productive.'

This new kind of workplace also encourages people to collaborate and to be creative. Playing table tennis with a colleague you rarely work with can lead to new ways of working and fresh thinking. Thinking over a problem while lying in a hammock might be the best way to find **its** solution.

However, this doesn't mean employers should immediately offer free ice cream, replace desks with couches or let staff bring pets to work. 'Firms have to make sure their perks are of real interest to their employees, and that **they** can afford them for the long term. If a company stops offering a perk, staff happiness goes down and people are less satisfied,' says Anna Tang, head of HR at DigitalForest.

'We advise our managers to monitor the effects of the perks carefully. We now offer free breakfasts instead of free lunches. **This** persuades people to arrive early and to start work with good energy levels, which makes **them** more productive. Large free lunches just made them feel sleepy.'

This revolution in the workplace is unlikely to slow down. As Randell says, 'All businesses can improve by increasing creativity, collaboration and happiness at work. The most successful ones do exactly **that**, and which companies don't want to be successful?'

C Read again. What do the words in bold refer to? Use the strategies in the box to help you.

Following reference links in a text

We use pronouns (for example *it*, *them*, *this*) instead of repeating the same word many times. They usually refer to a person or thing, but they can also refer to ideas.

In order to improve your understanding of a text, it is important to understand which idea or thing the pronouns refer to.

1 Line 1: They ___pool tables, nap-pods and free food.___
2 Line 21: Its ______
3 Line 25: they ______
4 Line 31: This ______
5 Line 32: them ______
6 Line 37: that ______

D READ FOR DETAIL Read again. Answer the questions.

1 According to the article, which of the following are advantages of modern office design and attractive perks?
   a increasing the quality of work that people do
   b attracting high quality people to the company
   c encouraging sharing ideas with different people
   d stopping people from leaving their jobs
2 What should companies who want to update their benefits and office design do?
   a provide benefits that employees really want
   b consider the future costs of extra benefits
   c avoid canceling benefits
   d offer different perks to other companies

E SPEAK Work in groups. Find and underline the innovations and perks in the article. What is your opinion of them?

VOCABULARY
Verbs of influence

A Look at what Sophia, the boss, said to her employees Simon and James. Match the pairs of sentences with the correct meanings (a or b).

1 Yes, of course, you can do that.
2 Do it now!
   a She allowed him to do it.
   b She told him to do it.
3 Of course, no problem. Feel free to do it.
4 I'll explain why it's a good idea, and then you might change your mind.
   a She persuaded him to do it.
   b She let him do it.
5 You must do it. If you don't, I will fire you!
6 I think you should do it this way.
   a She made him do something.
   b She advised him to do something.
7 Don't worry, I'm sure you are good enough. Try to do it.
8 I would like you to do it, not her.
   a She encouraged him to do it.
   b She wanted him to do it.

B Go to the Vocabulary Hub on page XVIII.

C SPEAK Work in pairs. Talk to your partner about when you were younger. Use the ideas below to help you.

When I was younger, …		
my parents	didn't let	me …
a friend	used to make	us …
my teacher	encouraged	my parents …
I	advised	a friend …

SPEAKING HUB

A Look at picture b on page 52. Imagine that you work in an office similar to this. You are going to a meeting about improving the workplace and employee motivation. Make a list of ideas to take to the meeting.

B DISCUSS Work in groups. Compare your ideas, giving explanations for each one.

C ORGANIZE Choose the best ideas and make a simple plan to show your office redesign and list your chosen perks.

D PRESENT Show your plan to the class. Then take a class vote to decide which plan is the most popular.

— Discuss and give advice about employment skills and career interests

— Discuss and suggest workplace benefits and changes

5.2 In business

- Describe and evaluate a small business
- Talk about environmental business ideas

G – the passive voice V – business collocations P – silent consonants S – listening for examples

READING

A SPEAK How much extra do you think you pay when you buy these products? Match the products (1–3) with the percentages in the box. There are two extra percentages. Then work in pairs and compare your answers.

40 percent 300 percent 600 percent
1,200 percent 4,000 percent

1 bottled water rather than tap water
2 pre-cut vegetables and fruits rather than uncut
3 takeout espresso coffee rather than making it at home

B SPEAK Work in pairs and discuss the questions.

1 How often do you buy the items in Exercise A?
2 What's your opinion of these products and the prices charged for them?

C PREDICT You are going to read an article about a new company, Aethaer. Before you read, answer the questions below. Then work in pairs and compare your answers.

1 Look at the picture and the title of the article. What product does Aethaer sell?
2 Which four of the following topics do you think will be in the article?
  a personal information about the owner of Aethaer
  b the production method
  c Aethaer's business model – product, price and target customers
  d full details of how to order, including delivery costs
  e information about other similar businesses
  f why people buy the product

D READ FOR GIST Read *The new bottled water?* Check your answers to Exercise C.

Business Business

News and views on the business of doing business

The new bottled water?

AETHAER (MoreChaos Ltd)

At ***Business Business***, we are always looking for the next bottled water, and we think we have found it – bottled air.

Businessman Leo de Watts is selling jars of fresh air from the British countryside to the residents of polluted cities around the world. He claims Britain has 'designer quality' fresh air, and he sells Aethaer as a luxury product. Each jar costs a breathtaking £95.

The business was launched two months ago. Orders can be made online only, and already 200 jars have been delivered to China. Not many small businesses achieve sales of £16,000 in their first months, and none have a product that is so cheap to produce. With plans to start marketing Aethaer in India, Watts could be made a millionaire by selling almost nothing, nothing but air.

'Air-farming' is incredibly easy. The air is collected from different places in the countryside, from the seaside to the mountains, from the green hills to the forests. The glass jars are held high in the air, and are closed after a few minutes. That's it – the simplest production process ever. Next, a label saying where the air comes from is put on the jars. Then, after they have been packed for delivery, they are sent overseas. Job done.

There are currently 15 different 'airs' in the product range. Watts claims that each one has different qualities, depending on where they were collected. While some customers do buy the air to inhale, many people buy the jars as gifts that will be kept and won't be opened.

Aethaer air is sold as a luxury item for wealthy people, but other new businesses have started selling cans of compressed air for everyday or sports use. Each can contains 200 breaths of air, and they come with a face mask for efficient and easy use.

People laughed when bottled water was first sold in convenience stores, but now everyone buys it. With urban air pollution increasing, it may not be long until you buy a can of clean air as well as a bottle of water every day.

E READ FOR DETAIL Read again. Complete each sentence with a word or phrase from the article.

1 Aethaer's customers usually live in ______________________.
2 Aethaer air costs £95 per jar because it is a ______________________.
3 Leo de Watts started the business ______________________.
4 If you want some Aethaer air, you must buy it ______________________.
5 There aren't any other businesses with such ______________________ production costs.
6 He may become ______________________ in the future.
7 Collecting the air is ______________________ to do.
8 Before he puts the jars in boxes, Leo adds ______________________ to each jar.
9 ______________________ want to breathe the air, but ______________________ never open the jars.
10 Aethaer's competitors want people to buy air for their ______________________ lives or when they are playing ______________________.

F SPEAK Work in pairs and discuss the questions.

1 Why does the article say bottled air is the new bottled water?
2 What do you think of the idea of buying a jar of air for £95?

GRAMMAR

The passive voice

A WORK IT OUT Look at the sentences from *The new bottled water?* and underline the main verb. Which sentences tell us who did the action?

1 Leo de Watts sells Aethaer as a luxury product.
2 The business was launched two months ago.
3 Orders can be made online only.
4 The air is collected from different places in the countryside.
5 Other businesses have started selling cans of compressed air.

B Choose the correct words to complete the rules.

The passive voice

We form the passive voice with *be* + the past participle of the main verb.

We use the passive voice when:

a we *know* / *don't know* or it is *important* / *not important* who or what did the action.
b it is *obvious* / *not obvious* who or what did the action.
c we *want* / *don't want* to focus on the person or thing affected by the action.

C Go to the **Grammar Hub** on **page XIV**.

SPEAKING HUB

A You are going to choose a business idea as the winner of the *Business Business* Low-cost Business of the Year Award. Read the information about *Fall Memories* below, then go to the **Communication Hub** on **page XX** and compare it to the *Arctic Diamond*.

B PLAN Write notes to help you present the information in the company profile.

C PRESENT Work in pairs. Present the company to your partner. Then listen to your partner's presentation and write down the key information.

D REFLECT Take a class vote to decide which company (including Aethaer) should win the Low-cost Business of the Year Award.

Basic information

Country:	Canada
Business name:	Fall Memories
Slogan:	'Bring nature's beauty into your home'
Founded by:	Jessica Malone
Products:	Fall leaves in a gift box (Three leaves: 1 red, 1 yellow, 1 mixed)
Price:	$30

Production process

picked by hand / dried and pressed for ten days / wrapped in tissue paper / packed in a gift box

Sales

Online business:	130 orders in first three days / $12,000 in first year of business
Current customers:	People from hot, dry states in the US, e.g. Nevada, Texas
Future markets:	India / Saudi Arabia / Dubai

REPAIR, REUSE OR RECYCLE

LISTENING

A SPEAK Work in pairs and discuss the questions.

1 How often do you buy new clothes?
2 Have you ever bought second-hand clothes?
3 Why do you think some people prefer to buy second-hand clothes?

5.5 **B LISTEN FOR GIST** **Complete the sentences (1–3) with the words in the box. Then listen to the *Business Business* podcast and check your answers.**

marketing outdoor second-hand

1 Patagonia is an ______________ clothing company.
2 They launched a ______________ campaign called 'Worn Wear'.
3 It encouraged people to return old clothes and buy ______________ clothes.

5.5 **C LISTEN FOR MAIN IDEA** **Listen again. Are the sentences true (T) or false (F)? Correct the false sentences.**

1 Patagonia makes things that people only wear when they are at work or at home. ___
2 Patagonia is one of many companies in this sector. ___
3 'Worn Wear' is a campaign that persuades people to make their own clothes. ___
4 Customers are encouraged to give their old clothes to be sold second-hand. ___
5 'Worn Wear' is the only time Patagonia has launched an environmental campaign. ___
6 As a company, Patagonia is concerned about its effect on the environment. ___

5.5 **D LISTEN FOR EXAMPLES** **Listen again. Complete the sentences (1–5) with the missing words and phrases. Use the strategies in the box to help you.**

Listening for examples

In longer talks and discussions, speakers give examples to support their claims.

Here are some words and phrases that we usually use to introduce an example:

- *For example, …* • *… like …* • *… such as …*
- *As the survey(s) / results / sales figures show …*
- *Another instance …*

Paying close attention to the examples that follow these words will give you a fuller understanding of the speaker's main ideas.

1 There are lots of others, ______________ North Face, Berghaus and Columbia.
2 'Worn Wear' encourages customers to buy second-hand Patagonia clothes, ______________ old jackets and T-shirts.
3 ______________, their sales have increased because of campaigns like 'Worn Wear'.
4 ______________, they made record profits on Black Friday.
5 ______________ of this is when Patagonia took out a full-page ad in *The New York Times*.

E SPEAK Work in pairs and discuss the questions.

1 Why do you think the 'Worn Wear' and 'Don't Buy This Jacket' campaigns were a success for Patagonia?
2 Would campaigns like these encourage you to buy a company's products? Why/Why not?
3 Can you think of any other environmental business ideas like these campaigns? Give examples.

VOCABULARY
Business collocations

A **Choose the correct verbs to complete the business collocations in the sentences from the podcast.**

1 The company *landed* / *launched* a new marketing **campaign** called 'Worn Wear'.
2 That is an unusual way to *run* / *do* a **business**.
3 It's difficult for a clothing company to *have* / *make* a **profit** selling new clothes.
4 They've *run* / *built* a **brand** based on respecting nature.
5 Patagonia is doing a good job of *attracting* / *adapting* new **customers**.

B **Match the beginnings of sentences (1–5) with the endings (a–e).**

1 Over the last few years, the company has **built**
2 When we **attract**
3 The company tries to **launch**
4 Like any business, we **make**
5 The best way to **run**

a new **investors**, we'll have more money.
b **money** by selling our products for a profit.
c its **reputation** successfully.
d a **company** is to hire good people.
e at least one new **product** every year.

C **Go to the Vocabulary Hub on** **page XVIII.**

D **SPEAK** **Work in pairs and discuss the questions.**

1 What can a retailer do to attract new customers?
2 What campaigns have companies that you know launched recently?

PRONUNCIATION
Silent consonants

5.6 **A** **Listen to the sentences from the podcast. Complete the missing words. Which consonant is silent?**

1 Patagonia strongly believes in taking care of the e________________.
2 Is 'Worn Wear' the first time Patagonia has used such an unusual marketing c________________?

5.7 **B** **Underline the silent consonants in each word. Then listen and check your answers.**

1 climbing
2 design
3 high
4 honest
5 knowledge
6 write

C **Find and correct the mistakes in the sentences.**

1 There's no dout the company sold a lot more clothes as a result of the magazine ad.
2 It's rong to say that all businesses are only interested in profits.
3 To understand advertising, you need to understand people's sychology.
4 You can buy second-hand Patagonia clothes at any of their stores with a 'Worn Wear' sain.

SPEAKING HUB

A You are going to talk about an environmental business idea in a podcast. Student A – read the box below about the company *REI stores*. Student B – go to the Communication Hub on page XXI.

B **PLAN** Plan your talk:

- explain the idea.
- include examples and business collocations.
- be prepared to answer questions.

C **SPEAK** Work in pairs. Role-play presenting a business podcast. Listen to your partner and ask questions about his/her idea. Take turns.

D **REFLECT** Work in pairs. Which idea do you think is the best? Why?

Student A

Company:	REI stores, US
Retail sector:	Outdoor clothing and equipment
Environmental idea:	Close all stores on Black Friday (the busiest shopping day of the year in the US). Employees are paid to take the day off.
Reason:	To encourage people to spend more time outdoors.
Result:	700 organizations, and 8 million people supported the campaign via social media in its first few years.

Describe and evaluate a small business
Talk about environmental business ideas

Café Hub

5.3 Major presentation

F – structure a presentation   P – ordering adverbs

COMPREHENSION

A Work in pairs. Which of the following factors are most important for a successful business presentation?

- be nicely dressed
- have neat, organized handouts
- show interesting slides
- have a clear, confident voice
- be relaxed and in good shape
- be punctual

B ▶ 00:00–02:48 Watch the first part of the video. What problems does Matthew Williams have with his presentation?

C Predict what happens next. Do *Jobs, Jobs, Jobs and Jobs* get the contract?

D ▶ 02:48–04:53 Watch the second part of the video and check your ideas. Why does Neena smile at the end?

FUNCTIONAL LANGUAGE

Structuring a presentation

A Put the phrases in the box into a logical order in the table.

> Do you have any questions? So first of all, I'd like to talk about So, the next question is That brings us to Today's presentation is all about

Structuring a presentation
Welcome
Good morning and thank you for coming.
Introduction
1 ______________ how we can work together in Brazil.
Main points
2 ______________ the benefits.
Let's take a look at the first slide.
We have a great deal of experience in the jobs marketplace.
3 ______________ how to market ourselves in Brazil.
4 ______________ the end of the presentation.
Questions
5 ______________
Summary
Great. So to sum up, we see an exciting future …

B ▶ 00:00–02:48 Watch the first part again and check your answers.

C At what stage of a presentation would you expect to hear sentence beginnings 1–5? Use the headings in the box.

1 Let's move on now to look at … ______
2 In conclusion, … ______
3 The purpose of today's presentation is … ______
4 I'd like to finish with … ______
5 The next point I would like to explore is … ______

Glossary

pay rise **(n) (British)** = pay raise **(n) (American)**

MILLY

SAM

NEENA

ZAC

GABY

USEFUL PHRASES

A Rewrite the useful phrases from the presentation less formally. Use the words and phrases in the box.

agree | lots | write / right away

1 We have a great deal of experience …

____

2 If we can come to an agreement …

____

3 We can put the contract together immediately.

____

B How do you say these useful phrases in your language?

PRONUNCIATION

Ordering adverbs

5.8 **A** Listen and write the ordering adverbs in the correct space.

1 ________ 4 ________

2 ________ 5 ________

3 ________ 6 ________

B Work in pairs. Practice the adverbs in Exercise A. Student A – say a number. Student B – say the adverb.

SPEAKING

A You are going to give a presentation about a personal possession and explain why it is a good one to have. Choose from the personal possessions in the box or your own ideas.

my bag | my bicycle | my car | my coat | my laptop/computer | my cell phone

B Prepare your presentation. Make presentation slides if possible and think about the following:

- Give a 'history' of your personal possession – when, why, how did you get it?
- Talk about the advantages (and any disadvantages) of owning it.
- Say why it has been a good personal possession to have.
- Use at least six examples of functional language.

C **PRESENT** Give your presentation to the rest of the class.

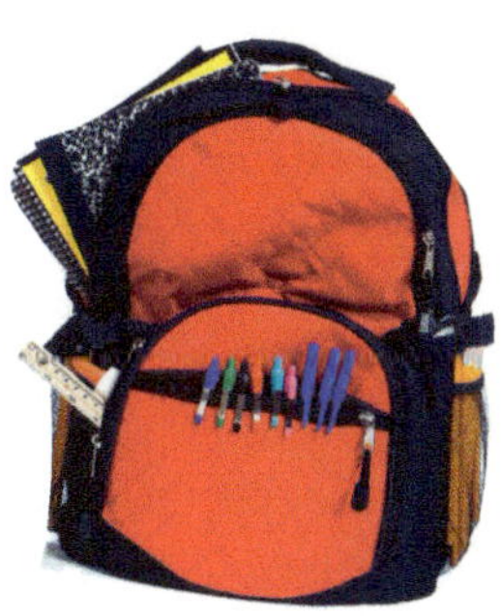

Give a presentation

➤ Turn to page XXIX to learn how to write a cover letter for a job application.

Unit 5 Review

VOCABULARY

A Complete the interviewer's comments with the phrases in the box.

communication skills creative thinking skills people skills reliable teamwork time management

1 Well, he arrived late, so he isn't very good at ______________________.

2 I'd say she has poor ______________________ – she didn't offer any fresh ideas.

3 Her presentation showed she doesn't have good ______________________ – it wasn't engaging, and her voice was rather flat.

4 I wasn't impressed by his ______________________; sometimes he looked annoyed by the questions, and he was a little rude once.

5 But will he be good at ______________________? He's only been self-employed before, as a gardener. Not much group work there.

6 I don't think she is ______________________. She's left her last few jobs after only two months.

B Choose the best verbs to complete sentences. Use the correct tense.

At first, I didn't [1]______________ (*tell / want*) him to go on the rollercoaster, but he kept asking, and finally he [2]______________ (*persuade / advise*) me to buy his ticket. I certainly didn't [3]______________ (*encourage / make*) him to do it, and I [4]______________ (*tell / let*) him to be careful. In the end, it was fine and he enjoyed it, so I [5]______________ (*let / persuade*) him go again.

My boss [6]______________ (*let / make*) my colleague work over the weekend. I couldn't believe it, but the boss is the boss. I [7]______________ (*advise / let*) him to do it this time, but to say no the next time. My boss has [8]______________ (*allow / let*) him to have two days off later in the week, so it isn't so bad. Personally, I think that if they [9]______________ (*want / make*) us to work overtime, they could [10]______________ (*advise / persuade*) us by offering extra money!

C Complete the sentences with the nouns in the box.

customers business profit campaign

1 The company made a big ______________ last year so employees received a bonus.

2 The key to running a successful ______________ is to find the right employees.

3 The gyms have attracted ______________ because they offer excellent amenities.

4 The health stores launched a ______________ about healthy eating.

GRAMMAR

A Find and correct the mistakes in the sentences.

1 A few years ago, I would be an accountant. I loved that job.

____

2 I'd to arrive early most days. I liked it when the office was quiet.

____

3 So I use to have long lunch breaks.

____

4 He didn't used to be such a relaxed boss.

____

5 They would being very quiet when I returned to the office.

____

B Complete the text with the correct form of the verbs in parentheses.

Parmesan cheese, *Parmigiano-Reggiano*, [1] ~~was created~~ (*create*) over 1,500 years ago. It [2]______________ (*have*) a strong and complex savory taste, and its name [3]______________ (*protect*) by EU law since 1955.

Parmesan cheese [4]______________ (*make*) from cow's milk. The cows [5]______________ (*milk*) in the morning, and the milk [6]______________ (*put*) into a large metal container. Key ingredients, such as whey, [7]______________ (*add*), and then the mixture [8]______________ (*heat*) to 35°C. After 15 minutes, the temperature [9]______________ (*raise*) to 55°C for an hour.

FUNCTIONAL LANGUAGE

Complete the conversation with the missing words.

Ian: So, moving on to the next item on the agenda: the new office design. [1]______________ of all, does anyone [2]______________ any questions about the design? No? OK, so …

Kim: Um, just a [3]______________. I just want to say that we should think again. Do we really need a Ping-Pong table?

Ian: I think we've heard enough, Kim. So moving [4]______________ to the next agenda item …

Kim: One minute – I have more to say!

Ian: Sorry, it's time to decide. Before we vote, let's [5]______________ up what we decided. We're saying keep the table, but forget the fish tank, for health reasons and cost reasons. Who agrees?

Kim: No, Ian, you can't make decisions like this. And that [6]______________ me to the next topic we need to discuss: how to make these meetings better.

Endmatter Contents

Grammar Hub

1.1 Simple present and present progressive

	Positive	Negative	Question
Simple present	**He gets up** early.	**It doesn't look** good.	**Do you take** the bus?
Present progressive	**I'm taking** a selfie.	**She isn't watching** TV. **She's not watching** TV.	**Are they smiling**?

- We use the simple present to talk about actions that always/usually/never happen.

  I don't always get up early.
- We use the present progressive to talk about actions that are in progress at the moment of speaking or writing.

  They aren't working this week.
- We also use the present progressive to describe actions in a photo or video.

  What is he doing in this photo?
- We also use the present progressive to describe trends.

  More and more people are getting worried about money.
- We use the simple present, not the present progressive, to talk about our everyday routines.

  Do you write many emails at work?
  NOT ~~Are you writing many emails at work?~~
- We usually use these adverbs of frequency with the simple present: *always, never, rarely, sometimes, usually*.

  *Do you **usually** post photos of yourself on social media?*
- We use stative verbs to describe feelings and ideas. We use the simple present (not the present progressive) with stative verbs.

  *I **love** taking selfies!*
- Some verbs (e.g. *have, look, speak, think*) can be used as both dynamic and stative verbs, depending on the situation.

  *have: She **has** a perfect life. / **Are** you **having** fun?*
  *look: Your new kitchen **looks** really good! / **I'm looking** for a new job.*

1.2 Subject and object questions

Subject questions		
Question word/ Subject	Main verb	Rest of question
What	is	your first language?

Object questions				
Question word	Auxiliary verb	Subject	Main verb	Rest of question
What	do	you	want	to study?

- We use these question words to ask for information: *who* and *whose* (for people), *where* (for places), *when* (for times), *why* (for reasons), *what* (for things), *which* (for two or more different choices), *how* (for the way something is done) and *how long/many/much*/etc (for time, quantity, etc).

  ***Whose** blog is this?*
- We frequently use an auxiliary verb (*be, can, do* or *have*) to form questions. We put the auxiliary verb before the main verb.

  ***Are** they practicing their English?*
  ***Can** I ask you a question?*
  *Why **do** you want to learn English?*
  *How long **have** you known Liam?*
- In subject questions, the question word is the subject of the sentence. We use subject questions when we don't know what/who/which/whose something/someone is. We don't use an auxiliary verb in subject questions and we don't change the word order in the answer.

  Who interviewed him? Mona interviewed him.
- In object questions, the question word is the object of the sentence. We use object questions when we want to know more information about something/someone. We always use an auxiliary verb in object questions. In the answer, we use the normal word order for a sentence.

  Where did he learn to speak English?
  NOT ~~Where he learned to speak English?~~
  What do you want to study? I want to study modern languages.
- With subject questions, the answer is the subject.

  Who told you? Someone told you.
- With object questions, the answer is the object.

  Who did you tell? You told someone.
- With questions using *do, does* or *did*, we don't change the form of the main verb.

  Does she speak English? NOT ~~Does she speaks English?~~
- When a question word is the object of a preposition, the preposition usually comes at the end of the sentence.

  What did you have problems with?

1.1 Simple present and present progressive

A Choose the correct option.

1 Sarah *is showing* / *shows* me her vacation photos. They're amazing!
2 *Are they working* / *Do they work* today?
3 *Are you always getting up* / *Do you always get up* early on weekdays?
4 They *are relaxing* / *relax* on the beach in this picture.
5 We *are not usually* / *don't usually* watch TV but this show is really good!
6 I *am becoming* / *become* more worried about my social media posts.

B Complete the email with the correct form of the verb in parentheses. Use contractions where possible.

Hi Sarah!

We [1] ______________ (*have*) a great time here in Spain! The sun [2] ______________ (*shine*) and the country is beautiful. We [3] ______________ (*have*) a nice room in a little hotel with a view of the beach. I [4] ______________ (*sit*) on the balcony to write this email and I can see Paul down on the beach. He [5] ______________ (*play*) soccer with the boys on the sand. The children [6] ______________ (*like*) it here – they say they [7] ______________ (*not want*) to go home! Hope you [8] ______________ (*not work*) too hard!

See you next week!

Love, Mary

➤ Go back to page 3.

1.2 Subject and object questions

A Read the answers and write questions. Use the question words in the box.

how what where which who why

1 *Why are you taking an umbrella?* — Because it's raining!
2 ______________ — My house is close to the school.
3 ______________ — I'm watching the news.
4 ______________ — I get to work by bus.
5 ______________ — I want to visit Poland.
6 ______________ — David is helping me.

B Put the words in order to make questions.

1 you / want / about / to talk / do / what / ?
What do you want to talk about?
2 I / am / pronouncing / right / this word / ?
____
3 please / say / you / that again, / can / ?
____
4 usually / do / at work / use English / you / ?
____
5 this / phone / whose / is / ?
____
6 the graph / what / does / show / ?
____
7 you / me / help / this / article / with / can / ?
____
8 hours / how / you / English / study / week / do / many / each / ?
____

C Correct the mistakes in each question.

1 How long you have your phone?
How long have you had your phone?
2 Where you are working right now?
____
3 You understand these words?
____
4 Who laptop is this?
____
5 Where you keep your English books?
____
6 How many people do they speak English in the world?
____
7 How long it takes you to get to work?
____
8 Who you met yesterday?
____
9 Where they are learning English?
____
10 Does he uses the app to practice his pronunciation?
____

➤ Go back to page 7.

Grammar Hub

2.1 Present perfect and simple past

	Positive	Negative	Question
Present perfect	**Wilhelm has climbed** Mt. Everest before. **We've visited** the Pyramids already.	**I haven't been** sailing before. **Paula hasn't made** a bucket list yet.	**Have you** ever **met** a movie star? **Have they bought** the tickets already?
Simple past	**Wilhelm climbed** Mt. Everest last month. **We visited** Yosemite National Park a year ago.	**I didn't go** sailing last weekend. **Paula didn't move** out of her parents' house a week ago.	**Did you meet** a movie star yesterday? **Did they buy** the tickets?

- We use the present perfect for actions completed during a period of time that continues to now.

  *Juan **has been** in Asia for three months so far.*
  = He's still there.
- We also use the present perfect for actions completed before now when we don't say exactly when.

  ***She has** already **written** out a bucket list.*
  NOT ~~She already wrote out her bucket list.~~
- We frequently use time expressions such as *before*, *already*, *just* and *yet* with the present perfect.

  Have you finished your exams yet?

- We use the simple past for actions completed during a finished period of time or at a specific time in the past.

  ***Did you stop** using your social media account last week?*
- We frequently use time expressions such as *yesterday*, *two days / a week / a month ago*, or *last week/month/year* with the simple past.
- If we use a specific time reference, we usually use the simple past.

  *She's just **won** a free vacation. / She **won** a free vacation **a moment ago**.*
  *Henri **has already booked** a flight to India. / Henri **booked** a flight to India **yesterday**.*

2.2 Present and past ability

can

	Positive	Negative
I/you/he/ she/it/we/they	**Rosa can ride** a horse.	**They cannot drive.** **They can't drive.**

Question	Positive short answer	Negative short answer
Can you fish in the lake?	Yes, **I can**.	No, **I can't**.

be able to **(simple present)**

	Positive	Negative
I/you/he/ she/it/we/they	**I am able to book** a taxi online.	**Sven isn't able to fly** a plane.

Question	Positive short answer	Negative short answer
Are Tomas and Jaime able to work as volunteers?	Yes, **they are**.	No, **they aren't**.

manage to **(simple present)**

	Positive	Negative
I/you/he/ she/it/ we/they	**He manages to remember** new words every day.	**We don't manage to meet** our friends very regularly.

Question	Positive short answer	Negative short answer
Does Laura manage to stay calm when she presents?	Yes, **she does**.	No, **she doesn't**.

- We use *can*, *can't*, *(not) be able to* and *(not) manage* to talk about our ability or skills in general in the present.

could

Subject	Positive	Negative
I/you/he/ she/it/ we/they	**I could cook** when I was young.	**Paolo couldn't take on** more work.

Question	Positive short answer	Negative short answer
Could your cousin swim as a baby?	Yes, **he could**.	No, **he couldn't**.

- We use *could*, *couldn't* or *(not) be able to* when we talk about our ability or skills in general in the past.
- We use *couldn't*, *(not) be able to* and *(not) manage to* when we talk about our ability to do a specific task on a particular occasion in the past. We usually do NOT use *could*.

  We couldn't solve the problem at that time.
  BUT NOT ~~We could solve the problem at that time.~~
  We were/weren't able to solve the problem at that time.
  We managed / didn't manage to solve the problem at that time.
- When a verb is followed by *-ing* or the infinitive, we can't use *can*. We use *be able to* instead.

  Sebastian enjoys being able to cook.
  NOT ~~Sebastian enjoys can cook.~~

2.1 Present perfect and simple past

A Choose the correct option.

1 I *have swum* / *swam* with dolphins before.
2 Martin *dreamed* / *has dreamed* about the pyramids last night.
3 We *haven't climbed* / *didn't climb* Mt. Everest yet.
4 *Did you hear* / *Have you heard* Leon's good news already?
5 *Did Zac learn* / *Has Zac learned* how to make a fire at camp last summer?
6 *Have you ever taken* / *Did you ever take* a trip to another country?

B Correct the mistakes in each sentence. Use contractions where possible.

1 She ~~has seen~~ saw a beautiful sunset last week.
2 They made a sci-fi movie already.
3 Molly didn't prepare a list yet.
4 Mohammed traveled never around Asia before.
5 Did you deal with a serious problem before?
6 He has come up with a smart plan yesterday.

C Complete each sentence with the correct form of the verb in parentheses.

1 Giralt <u>has never been</u> (*never / be*) to America.
2 Dan ________________ (*just / finish*) a charity walk.
3 Katerina worked hard but she ________________ (*not / achieve*) her goal.
4 When the time was right, the chess champion ________________ (*put*) his plan into action.
5 ________________ (*you / read*) other people's bucket lists before?
6 I ________________ (*already / do*) two parachute jumps this year.

➤ Go back to page 15.

2.2 Present and past ability

A Complete the sentences with the words in the box.

can	could	couldn't	manage	managed	wasn't

1 She didn't <u>manage</u> to make it to the interview on time.
2 Amazingly, Diego ________________ read when he was two and a half years old.
3 They ________________ to find a solution to the complicated problem.
4 We were discussing something important, so I ________________ able to answer my phone.
5 Francisco ________________ stop his hands from shaking because he was so nervous.
6 Michela is amazing because she ________________ work three jobs and not be tired.

B Put the words in order to make sentences.

1 can't / Helena / egg / an / boil
<u>Helena can't boil an egg.</u>
2 a / manage / I / cook / meal / didn't / tasty / to
____
3 our / we / goals / long-term / were / to / able / achieve
____
4 system / very / can / quickly / analyze / the / data
____
5 manage / speech / to / give / Aisha / her / did / ?
____
6 couldn't / easier / suggest / an / plan / they
____

C Choose the correct option.

1 Marina ________________ raise enough money for her trip.
a wasn't able b didn't manage ⓒ couldn't
2 Olaf ________________ paint great pictures of animals.
a can b manages c is able
3 I ________________ watch TV all day as a kid.
a was able b can c could
4 They ________________ to deal with any more problems.
a couldn't b weren't able c can't
5 Hana ________________ to find a good cooking video.
a can't b didn't manage c couldn't
6 She forgot her lines, but she ________________ stay calm.
a could b managed to c was able
7 She ________________ to find the theater with the help of her app.
a was able b manages c can't
8 Fred ________________ sing to other people – he gets too nervous.
a couldn't b manages c can't
9 Poppy ________________ work and study, but she's usually tired.
a manages to b able to c can't
10 I ________________ take my English exam because I was on vacation.
a couldn't b didn't manage c wasn't able

➤ Go back to page 20.

Grammar Hub

3.1 Narrative tenses

	Positive	Negative	Question
Simple past	They **went** to Spain last year.	The train trip **didn't take** long.	Where **did** you **go** on vacation?
Past progressive	It **was raining** when we left the house.	Anna **wasn't enjoying** the trip.	Where **were you going** when I saw you yesterday?
Past perfect	I **had just arrived** at the hotel. We **had missed** the train.	Ben **hadn't arrived** at the office.	What time **had** they **left** the house? **Had** you ever **been** there before?

- We use the simple past to talk about finished actions or situations, and things that happened one after another.

  *I **waited** at the bus stop until my bus **came**.*
- We use the past progressive to describe the background to a story.

  *It **was snowing** and the traffic **was moving** very slowly.*
- When we are talking about two events in the past, we use the past perfect to show that one event happened before the other.

past ← *I **had left** the train station when I saw a bus.* → present

I left the train station. ... I saw a bus.

- We use the past progressive for actions or situations that were unfinished at a past time and which were interrupted by shorter events (described using the simple past).

  *While we **were going** through town, the bus **started** making a strange noise.*

3.2 Articles and quantifiers

Articles

***a*/*an*, *the*, no article**

a/an	We use *a/an* the first time we talk about a singular noun.	I have **a ticket** for the train. There was **an accident** on the main road.
the	We use *the* when we have already mentioned the person or thing.	There was an accident. **The accident** wasn't serious.
	We use *the* with singular nouns when it is clear what we are talking about or when there is only one.	I usually take **the bus** that leaves at 6:15.
	We use *the* with plural nouns when it is clear what we are talking about.	**The trains** that leave in the mornings are overcrowded.
no article	We use no article with the names of people, companies, cities and countries (except *the UK*, *the US*, *the Netherlands*).	My cousin's name is **Sam**. He recently flew to **Colorado**, which is in **the US**.
	We use no article when we talk about things in general.	Do you like **traveling**? **Buses** are sometimes faster than **trains**.

- We use *an* before a vowel sound. We use *a* before a consonant sound, even if the word begins with *a*, *e*, *i*, *o* or *u*.

  an hour, an expensive trip, a university town
- We sometimes use *the* before a type of transportation.

  *We always take **the** bus / **the** train / **the** plane.*
- We use *the* before the names of oceans and rivers and countries whose names are plural.

  ***the** Atlantic Ocean / **the** Nile River / **the** United States / **the** Philippines*

Quantifiers

	Countable nouns	Uncountable nouns
Question	**How many people** use the subway?	**How much traffic** was there on the road?
Positive number	There are **a few people** on the train.	There is **a little ice** on the roads so drive carefully.
	There are **a lot of** / **lots of people** waiting for the bus.	There is **a lot of** / **lots of information** in this booklet.
	There are **enough seats**.	There is **enough space**.
	There are **plenty of buses**.	There is **plenty of time**.
Negative number	There are **few people** on the train.	There is **little chance** of us getting there on time.
	There aren't **many people** here.	There isn't **much traffic** today.
	There aren't **enough seats**.	There isn't **enough space**.
	There are **too many people** on this train. It's **too small**.	There's **too much noise** on the train. It's **too noisy**.

3.1 Narrative tenses

A Complete each sentence with the correct form of the verb in parentheses.

1 We got to the station but we *had already missed* (already / miss) the train.

2 When I arrived at the station, my cousin ________ (wait) for me.

3 The car left the road and ________ (hit) a tree.

4 ________ (you / go) to Berlin before or was it your first time?

5 What ________ (your friend / say) when you finally arrived?

6 We ________ (just / arrive) at the station when we saw our train coming in.

B Choose the correct option.

1 We were excited because we ***didn't visit*** / ***had never visited*** South America before.

2 ***Did anyone wait*** / ***Was anyone waiting*** for you when you got there?

3 Tom arrived at the hotel and ***had gone*** / ***went*** straight to his room for a nap.

4 The reason we were lost was that we ***were taking*** / ***had taken*** the wrong subway line.

5 What ***did you do*** / ***had you done*** when you realized you'd lost your ticket?

6 Didn't you know the train ***was being*** / ***had been*** canceled?

C Correct the mistakes in each sentence.

1 The accident happened because the driver had ~~fell~~ *fallen* asleep at the wheel.

2 I was late, but luckily for me the meeting wasn't starting.

3 We missed the beginning because we were getting stuck in a traffic jam.

4 They had already went to Paris so they decided to go somewhere else.

5 I was worried because I wasn't hearing from my brother for several hours.

6 The traffic didn't move at all so we got out of the taxi and walked.

➤ Go back to page 27.

3.2 Articles and quantifiers

A Find eight more mistakes with articles and correct them.

The trip from my house to my office only takes me about half hour. There is the quicker way – I could take bus – but I prefer to walk. There are many reasons for this. First, the walking is healthy and I find it puts me in good mood. I usually arrive at office awake and ready for work. Going by the bus, on the other hand, leaves me feeling tired and stressed before a day begins!

B Write one word in each blank. Sometimes more than one answer is possible.

1 How *much* time do we have before the train comes?

2 Sometimes we take ________ taxi and share the cost between us.

3 There weren't very ________ passengers on my bus this morning. I wonder why.

4 I find that bike riding is ________ easy way to get through traffic jams.

5 Very ________ people in the town have cars, so the bus service is really important to them.

6 There aren't ________ places to park, and that's why there are traffic problems.

C Check (✓) the sentences that are correct. Write *of* in the right place in the sentences that are incorrect.

1 There are very few buses that go near my house. ✓

2 It will take a little time for the public to get used to the new system.

3 Not enough people used the bus service so they stopped running it.

4 A lot passengers complain of overcrowding on the buses.

5 I don't usually take taxis because they cost too much money.

6 There are plenty people who take their cars to work every day.

7 There are lots taxis where I live.

8 There's plenty money to improve the bus system.

9 There were few free seats on the train today.

10 Is there too much traffic on our streets?

➤ Go back to page 31.

Grammar Hub

4.1 Future forms

- We use *will* when we make a decision at the time of speaking.

  I'll get my coat and we can leave now.
  I won't buy this dress because it's too small.

- We use *be going to* for our intentions (the things we want to do or have already decided to do).

  Salma is going to cut down on the amount of chocolate she eats.
  We aren't going to have a New Year's party this year.
  Are you going to keep your New Year's resolutions?

- We use the present progressive when we have made an arrangement for a certain time in the future, usually with another person.

  Aisa is going shopping with her sister tomorrow.
  He isn't coming out with us tonight.
  What are you doing on New Year's Eve?

Be careful!

- We don't use the present progressive for intentions that haven't been arranged yet. We use *be going to.*

  I'm going to write a book one day.
  NOT ~~I'm writing a book one day.~~

4.2 Making predictions

- When we are certain about a future event or situation, we can use either *be going to* or *will.*

  Panit is going to keep his New Year's resolutions.
  The company won't reach its sales target this month.
  Will the forecaster's predictions be accurate?

- Although there is little difference between the use of *be going to* and *will* for predictions, if there is strong evidence or a good reason for our prediction, we usually use *be going to* rather than *will.*

  Caitlyn is going to have a baby.
  NOT ~~Caitlyn will have a baby.~~

- To add even greater certainty to our prediction, we can use the adverb *definitely.*

  The other team has a lot of points – they're definitely going to win.

- We can use the adverb *probably* to show that we are not completely certain.

  I'll probably stay at home on New Year's Eve.

- We usually use these phrases with *will* when we're making a prediction: *I (don't) think …, I expect …, I'm sure …*

  I don't think the media experts will predict the election results accurately.

- When we feel that a future event is possible, but we are not completely certain, we use *could, may* or *might.*

  You could make some new friends by joining the gym.

Be careful!

- We put the adverbs *definitely* and *probably* after the auxiliary verb in sentences with *be going to* or *will.*

  They're definitely going to win the World Cup.
  NOT ~~They're going to definitely win the World Cup.~~
  I'll probably take part in the project.
  NOT ~~I'll take part probably in the project.~~

4.1 Future forms

A Match the sentences (1–6) to the answers (a–f) to make short dialogues.

1 The phone's ringing! ___
2 Are you staying at home tonight? ___
3 Would you like anything else? ___
4 Josh is having a fireworks party tomorrow. ___
5 I've lost my wallet! ___
6 What time are you meeting the others? ___

a Oh no! What are you going to do?
b Sometime tomorrow morning.
c Sounds amazing. Can I come?
d OK. I'll get it!
e Yes, I'll have a coffee, please.
f No, I'm having dinner with Kate.

B Choose the correct option.

1 **A:** 'I've just heard it's Dan's birthday today.'
B: 'Oh! ***I'll get*** / ***I'm getting*** him a present at lunchtime, then.'
2 Next year, I'm ***going to try*** / ***trying*** to keep my New Year's resolutions.
3 It's all arranged. ***We'll move*** / ***We're moving*** next Tuesday.
4 I made a big decision last week. ***I'll*** / ***I'm going to*** look for a new job.
5 **A:** 'I don't think I'll ever fall in love.'
B: 'Don't be silly. It's ***happening*** / ***going to happen*** soon, I'm sure.'

C Complete the dialogue with the correct form of the words in parentheses. Sometimes more than one answer is possible.

Ashanti: What are you doing on the weekend, Camilla?
Camilla: I [1] ______________ (*not / do*) anything special. Why?
Ashanti: Well, I'm going to a two-day self-help course. Come with me!
Camilla: Self-help?
Ashanti: Yes. I've decided I [2] ______________ (*change*) my life.
Camilla: It doesn't sound like my kind of thing. What time [3] ______________ (*leave*) tomorrow?
Ashanti: Early – at about eight o'clock.
Camilla: In that case, I definitely don't want to come! Tomorrow's Saturday and I [4] ______________ (*not / work*). I [5] ______________ (*sleep*) until eleven o'clock and then have breakfast in bed!
Ashanti: All right. If you're sure. In that case, I [6] ______________ (*call*) you on Sunday evening and tell you all about it.
Camilla: OK. Have a good time!

➤ Go back to page 39.

4.2 Making predictions

A Reorder the words to make sentences.

1 the future / for our children / is / going to / what / be like / ?
What is the future going to be like for our children?
2 probably / in college / study / Modern Languages / Gareth / will
____
3 going / she / buy / definitely / to / a new cell phone / is
____
4 soon / will / he / sure / be here / I'm
____
5 will / don't / to the party / Dimitris / I / come / think
____
6 Jamie / going / is / a new suit / to buy / for the interview / ?
____

B Write a word from the box in each blank to complete the sentences. Sometimes more than one answer is possible.

could	definitely	is	might	think	won't

1 The score is 4-0 – they're ______________ going to lose.
2 She ______________ make a lot of money one day – anything's possible!
3 Don't worry – you ______________ have any problems.
4 She ______________ going to compete in a national sports competition.
5 I ______________ she will need some help moving.
6 The weather's bad today; some people ______________ arrive late.

C Choose the correct option.

1 I'm sure people ______________ fewer hours in the future.
a are working b will work
2 Hundreds of people ______________ their jobs when the factory closes.
a are losing b are going to lose
3 Look out! That driverless car ______________ crash!
a will b is going to
4 People ______________ reading newspapers in the future, maybe, but I don't think they'll stop reading books.
a are stopping b will stop
5 I think Magda ______________ a good mother when she's older.
a is going to be b is being
6 I don't expect that he ______________ get good grades because he never studies.
a will b won't

➤ Go back to page 43.

Grammar Hub

5.1 Past habits and states

	Positive	Negative
I/you/he/she/it/we/they	**I used to be** a waiter in a restaurant.	**They did not use to work** here. **They didn't use to work** here.

Question	Positive short answer	Negative short answer
Did you use to work from home?	Yes, **I did**.	No, **I didn't**.

- We use *used to* to talk about past situations that do not exist now. These include past habits and past states.

  *Past habit: We **used to meet** at the station on the way to work.*

  *Past state: He **used to be** a manager but he left his job.*
- We use *use to* with the auxiliary verb *did*.

  *I didn't **use** to work here.*
  NOT ~~I didn't used to work here.~~

  *Did you **use** to do voluntary work?*
  NOT ~~Did you used to do voluntary work?~~
- In the negative, we can also say *never used to*.

  *I **didn't use** to work here. OR I **never used** to work here.*
- We can use *would* when we talk about past actions. We do not use it for permanent states in the past.

  When I was younger, I would visit London regularly on business. NOT ~~When I was younger, I would live in London.~~
- We usually use *would* when we are telling a story or talking fondly about the past.

  Every year, the boss would take us all out to eat.
- When talking about the past, we rarely use *would* in the negative or question form.

  I didn't use to like it here. NOT ~~I wouldn't like it here.~~

  Did you use to work part time? NOT ~~Would you work part time?~~

5.2 The passive voice

	Positive	Negative	Question
Simple present	**I am expected** to work on weekends.	**You are not allowed** to take time off. **You aren't allowed** to take time off.	**Is he paid** a lot of money?
Present progressive	**The goods are being delivered** now.	**The workers are not being trained** right now. **The workers aren't being trained** right now.	**Is the product being sold** at full price?
Simple past	**I was told** to wait at the front desk.	**They were not asked** to work on weekends. **They weren't asked** to work on weekends.	**Were you given** instructions?
Past progressive	**The product was being used** all over the world.	**She was not being paid** very much. **She wasn't being paid** very much.	**Was bottled water being sold** here 30 years ago?
Present perfect	**The product has** just **been launched**.	**Your order has not been received**. **Your order hasn't been received**.	**Have the workers been told**?

- We use the passive voice when we don't say who or what causes the action (usually because the person or thing is not known, not important or obvious).

  *The business **was launched** last year.*
- We can sometimes say the same thing in the active or passive voice. The choice frequently depends on the topic we are talking about.

  *Active: The company **sells** the product as a luxury item. (The topic is the company.)*

  *Passive: The product **is sold** as a luxury item. (The topic is the product.)*
- We use *by* when we know who does/did an action and we want to mention it.

  *This product was bought **by** both young and old customers.*
- We can use the passive voice with modal verbs.

  *Orders **can be made** online or at one of our stores.*

  *The product **might be launched** in the New Year.*
- We don't use *by* + the agent unless it is important, useful information.

  The product is sold all over the world. NOT ~~The product is sold by store owners all over the world.~~

5.1 Past habits and states

A Complete the sentences with *used to* or *would* and the verb in parentheses. If both options are possible, write both.

1 When I was younger, I *used to dream / would dream* of running my own business. (*dream*)
2 In my old job, I ________________ events. (*plan*)
3 The office has moved. It ________________ closer to my home. (*be*)
4 I ________________ that management skills were important. (*not think*)
5 Joel ________________ his job but he hates it now. (*love*)
6 Work ________________ at eight and nobody dared to be late! (*start*)

B Make questions with *used to*.

1 you / live / New York City / ?
Did you use to live in New York City?
2 Sally / work / restaurant / ?
____
3 things / be better / in the past / ?
____
4 where / you / spend / your childhood vacations / ?
____
5 what / you / do / in your old job / ?
____
6 when you walked to work / how long / it / take you / ?
____

C Make sentences with *used to*. Put a check (✓) or an (✗) to show whether the same idea can be expressed with *would*.

1 when / I / be / younger / I / have / my own business
When I was younger, I used to have my own business. ✗
2 in the past / our manager / not have / good communication skills
____
3 every afternoon / I / try / finish / all the letters
____
4 years ago / people / laugh / at the idea / computers in the home
____
5 you / enjoy / your job / more / ?
____
6 we / not take / a summer vacation
____

➤ Go back to page 51.

5.2 The passive voice

A Correct the mistakes in each sentence.

1 The office *is* located in the center of Manchester.
2 The business was start by two brothers in Cape Town in 2018.
3 The company is knowing for its luxury goods and excellent website.
4 Is the plan been considered right now or is there a delay?
5 The items you have ordered can delivered within two working days.
6 The managers agreed. A decision was taken by them yesterday.

B Choose the correct option.

1 When will we ________________?
a paid b (be paid) c paying
2 My order ________________ yesterday.
a was made b is make c made
3 We ________________ what to do.
a haven't told b didn't tell c weren't told
4 When you called me, I ________________ for a job.
a was being interviewed b was interviewed c am interviewing
5 The food for tonight ________________.
a has been delivering b has just been delivered c was been delivered
6 Is everything ________________ in the box?
a provide b provided c providing

C Rewrite the sentences in the passive voice. Use *by* only when necessary.

1 They usually give us our tasks in the morning.
We are usually given our tasks in the morning.
2 The manager is studying Rob's business plan.
____
3 They started the business last year.
____
4 They have only delivered three jars.
____
5 Matt presented details of the plan.
____
6 When I started, they were making some big changes.
____

➤ Go back to page 55.

Vocabulary Hub

1.1 Seeing and hearing

Match the beginnings of the sentences (1–5) with the endings (a–e).

1 If you **spot** somebody,
2 If you **recognize** somebody,
3 If you **notice** something,
4 If you **observe** something,
5 If you **stare at** something,

a you look at it for a long time, maybe too long.
b you see him/her by chance.
c you see it for the first time.
d you watch it carefully over a long time.
e you see him/her and know who he/she is.

➤ Go back to page 5.

1.2 Languages

A Put the letters in bold in the correct order to make words about language learning.

1 Which is more important when you're speaking English? Speaking **uelcartyac** or **tnulylfe**? Why?
2 Do you know any **midosi** in English? What's your favorite?
3 Are most people in your country **nanoliomlgu** or **ialinglub**? What about in your family?
4 Can you tell where somebody is from just by listening to their **cectna**? In your language? In English?

B SPEAK Work in pairs. Ask and answer the questions in Exercise A.

➤ Go back to page 9.

2.2 Problems and solutions

Complete the advice with the correct form of the verbs in the box. Sometimes more than one answer is possible.

agree on analyze come up with deal with solve suggest

1 If you really want to ________________ a problem, you'll find a way. If you don't, you'll find an excuse.
2 If you are stuck and can't ________________ a solution, go and do something different until you have some fresh ideas.
3 It is best to ________________ a problem in as much detail as you can. This will make it easier to solve.
4 It is not always difficult to say what the problem is at work. The real challenge is to ________________ a solution to your colleagues.
5 People frequently have different ideas about how to solve problems. In those situations, you should find a solution everyone ________________.

➤ Go back to page 21.

3.1 Collocations: travel information

Complete the sentences with the correct travel collocations.

1 We are sorry to announce there are ________________ on line 1, of approximately 45 minutes.
2 Let's leave really early, before rush hour, to avoid the ________________.
3 Don't go that way. It's closed due to ________________ – they're replacing the pavement.
4 It's always very crowded on the trains during ________________, with lots of people standing for a long time.
5 Following the earlier delays, we now have ________________ on all lines. All lines are running normally.
6 We're stuck in a ________________ on the highway; we'll be at least half an hour late.
7 Look, they've just ________________. We'll have to wait another hour now, for the next one.
8 The first ________________ opened in 1863 and went from Paddington station to Farringdon Street station, in London.

➤ Go back to page 27.

3.1 Nouns ending in *-ion*

Complete the sentences with the nouns in the box.

communication connection decisions expectation expression inspiration reaction situations

1 I think _______________ between the engineer and the passengers is important when a train is delayed.
2 In my country, there has been a negative _______________ to driverless cars.
3 Environmental issues don't change the _______________ that I make about transportation.
4 I think it is important to have a _______________ with the people you see every day.
5 There are some travel _______________ that make me annoyed or angry.
6 I generally have a blank _______________ when out in public. I never smile at others.
7 I find people that can talk to strangers an _______________. I wish I were so confident.
8 When I was on vacation, the transportation system was better than my _______________.

➤ Go back to page 29.

3.2 Gradable and ungradable adjectives

Complete the sentences with the adjectives in the box.

enormous excellent filthy furious good hilarious terrible tiny

1 Your hands are absolutely _______________. Wash them before dinner.
2 _______________ work. You made no mistakes at all.
3 We had a really _______________ time on vacation. We really didn't want to come back home!
4 Don't talk to him now. He's absolutely _______________ because you lost his bike. Let him calm down first.
5 Don't go to that restaurant. The food's really _______________.
6 Charlie thought the show was absolutely _______________. He laughed from the beginning to the end.
7 The Gobi Desert is extremely large, but the Sahara Desert is _______________; it's seven times bigger!
8 Compared to Russia, the UK is absolutely _______________. Russia is 70 times bigger!

➤ Go back to page 33.

Vocabulary Hub

4.1 Collocations: goals and resolutions

Complete the sentences with the correct collocations.

1 He didn't stop drinking soda completely but he ________________ to two cans a week.

2 When I make a plan I stick to it. I've ________________ I made last year.

3 She finally ________________ of running for thirty minutes every day.

4 He ________________ eating sugary food three months ago and he already feels healthier.

5 He ________________ to quit eating chocolate last New Year.

➤ Go back to page 39.

4.2 Prefixes: *dis-*, *mis-*, *over-*, *re-*, *under-*

Choose the correct prefix to complete the word.

1 I ***dis*** / ***mis*** like working late and try to make sure I finish on time each day.

2 I moved out of that city because it is ***re*** / ***over*** populated. There are just too many people.

3 I didn't mean that. You ***mis*** / ***dis*** understood what I was trying to say!

4 Many people at the company feel they don't earn enough. Personally I agree that they are ***under*** / ***mis*** paid.

5 I don't think this is the best strategy. We should ***under*** / ***re*** think this.

➤ Go back to page 45.

5.1 Verbs of influence

A Match the beginnings of the sentences (1–4) with the endings (a–d).

1 My boss persuaded me ___
2 My boss made me ___
3 I told him ___
4 My friend advised me not ___

a to work on the weekend, but he refused.
b to work at home because I might feel lonely.
c to work overtime by offering me some extra money.
d apologize to the customer for being rude.

B Match the beginnings of the sentences (1–4) with the endings (a–d).

1 Our company lets us ___
2 I want my boss ___
3 My colleague encouraged me ___
4 My company allows us ___

a to use our personal social media at work.
b to apply for the job, and now I'm her boss!
c to go on vacation forever. I can't stand him.
d leave early on Fridays.

➤ Go back to page 53.

5.2 Business collocations

Which noun cannot be used to complete each sentence?

1 Over the last few years, the company has built its … very successfully.
a brand b reputation c customers

2 Recently, we have done a lot of … overseas.
a money b deals c business

3 The … was launched at the end of last year.
a reputation b product c campaign

4 The sales team are very good at making …
a business. b money. c a profit.

5 The media attention has helped us to attract new …
a customers. b investors. c expenses.

➤ Go back to page 57.

Communication Hub

4.1 Student A

You can only see your side of the conversation. Read through your lines, and practice your intonation. Role-play the conversation with your partner. You will start the conversation. Listen carefully in order to speak at the right time.

A: Hi, [name].

B: ______________________________

A: Oh! Oops! I'll do it now. Hold on. There we go.

B: ______________________________

A: And happy New Year to you!

B: ______________________________

A: Great. We had a good time on New Year's Eve.

B: ______________________________

A: That sounds amazing!

B: ______________________________

A: Oh! I bet it was freezing, too. I'm glad I was at a party.

B: ______________________________

A: Is that one of your New Year's resolutions?

B: ______________________________

A: You haven't? I've made several.

B: ______________________________

A: Well, I've decided to get in better shape this year, so I'm going to join a gym. Also, I'm going to study English more seriously.

B: ______________________________

A: Well, not good enough. In fact, I'm meeting a new teacher on Thursday, for private lessons.

B: ______________________________

A: Well, there's no point in putting things off. What about your chocolate habit?

B: ______________________________

A: You eat some every day, don't you?

B: ______________________________

➤ Go back to page 39.

2.1 Student A

Has your partner done these things? If he/she has, find out more details.

- go surfing
- climb a tree
- hold a snake
- relax in a natural hot spring
- take a bike riding vacation
- bake some bread
- give blood
- see a lion in the wild
- stay in an ice hotel
- learn to fly a plane

➤ Go back to page 15.

5.1 Students A and B

Score 2 points for every time you chose answer b. Score nothing for all other answers.

6–8: You have a very good set of general skills and qualities for employment. Reflect on which are stronger than others, and look for jobs that use your clear strengths. What other employability skills do you have? Can you improve them?

2–5: You have some key skills that are important to employers, but there is room for improvement. Identify those skills, and find out what employers are looking for in those areas. What improvements could you make?

0–1: Employers want people to use their skills in certain ways in the workplace. Learn more about employability skills, and find opportunities to practice, for example group projects or leadership roles. Which skills could you focus on first?

➤ Go back to page 50.

4.2 Students A and B

1 a I'll make a lot of money.
  b I make a lot of money.
2 a You have many friends at college.
  b You'll have many friends at college.
3 a She'll shut the window because she hates the cold.
  b She shut the window because she hates the cold.
4 a He put solar panels on his roof.
  b He'll put solar panels on his roof.
5 a They use cell phones in English classes.
  b They'll use cell phones in English classes.

➤ Go back to page 43.

4.1 Students A and B

The top ten most common New Year's resolutions (in descending order):

1 change the food you eat
2 get organized
3 spend less, save more
4 enjoy life to the fullest
5 get in shape and get healthy
6 learn something exciting
7 quit unhealthy habits
8 help others achieve their dreams
9 fall in love
10 spend more time with family

➤ Go back to page 38.

5.2 Students

Basic information

Country:	Finland
Business name:	Arctic Diamond
Slogan:	'Luxury chilling'
Founded by:	Mika Hakala
Products:	Ice cubes from the Arctic
Price:	$50 for 100 grams

Production process

collected by hand / packed in freezer boxes / delivered by air and courier

Sales

Online business:	15 orders in first two weeks / $20,000 in first year of business
Current customers:	European restaurants and bars, hotels in Abu Dhabi and Dubai
Future markets:	China, United States

Arctic Diamond

➤ Go back to page 55.

4.1 Student B

You can only see your side of the conversation. Read through your lines, and practice your intonation. Role-play the conversation with your partner. Listen carefully in order to speak at the right time. Your partner will start the conversation.

A: ______________________________

B: Hi, [name]. I can't see you – I don't think you've clicked the video button.

A: ______________________________

B: That's better. Good to see you. Happy New Year!

A: ______________________________

B: How's everything going in Spain?

A: ______________________________

B: Well, lucky you! We went to see the fireworks.

A: ______________________________

B: Yeah, it was great! Mind you, it was a long wait. We got there at nine.

A: ______________________________

B: Yeah! Lucky you. I didn't have a hat or anything. In fact, I'm going to look for one tomorrow.

A: ______________________________

B: Actually, I haven't made any resolutions yet.

A: ______________________________

B: Really? What have you decided?

A: ______________________________

B: That's a surprise! I always thought your English was really good.

A: ______________________________

B: Really? That's quick!

A: ______________________________

B: My chocolate habit? What do you mean?

A: ______________________________

B: Well, just a little.

➤ Go back to page 39.

5.2 Student B

Company:	H&M stores, Sweden and worldwide
Retail sector:	Fashion clothing
Environmental idea:	Customers hand in their old clothes (even ones they didn't buy at H&M). The company either sells them as second-hand clothes from, or turns them into other clothing items.
Reason:	To stop old clothes from going to waste.
Result:	In a four-year period, the company received more than 40,000 metric tons of clothing items (enough material to make 150 million T-shirts).

➤ Go back to page 57.

2.1 Student B

Has your partner done these things? If he/she has, find out more details.

- go sailing
- climb a mountain
- hold a monkey
- relax on a beach all day
- take a camping vacation
- bake a cake
- give someone flowers
- see a tiger in the wild
- stay in an underwater hotel
- learn to drive

➤ Go back to page 15.

Communication Hub

1.2 Student B

A SPEAK Work in pairs. Ask and answer questions to complete the information about the percentage of people with English as a first language in different countries around the world.

Percentage of people with English as a first language	
Ireland	93 percent
UK	______ percent
New Zealand	86 percent
______	79 percent
Canada	57 percent
______	37 percent
Jamaica	17 percent
South Africa	______ percent
Sierra Leone	8.5 percent
Pakistan	______ percent

*How many people in the UK **speak** English as a first language?*
*Where **do** 79 percent of people **speak** English as a first language?*

B SPEAK Work in pairs. Are you surprised by any of the information?

➤ Go back to page 7.

4.1 Student B

A Make a resolution for each of these topics.

- work or study
- family and friends
- physical fitness
- the internet and digital media

B Tell your partner about your resolutions and why you have made them.

C Ask your partner to make resolutions for these topics.

D Make resolutions for your partner's topics.

➤ Go back to page 39.

3.1 Students

A Look at the list of annoying behavior on public transportation. Number them in order of how annoying they are (1 = most annoying, 9 = least annoying). Think about the reasons for your choices.

___ people talking loudly on the phone
___ people playing loud music and not using headphones
___ people walking too slowly
___ people eating takeout food
___ people not lining up or not waiting their turn to board
___ people leaving trash behind
___ people not giving up their seats to people who need them
___ people coughing and sneezing because of a cold
___ people trying to talk to me

➤ Go back to page 29.

5.1 Student B

A Take the quiz. Choose the answer that is most true for you.

1 When you get a new piece of picture editing software or an app, do you
a just use the basic functions?
b teach yourself how to use all of its functions?
c ask a friend to show you how to use it?

2 When your teacher suddenly tells you that you are going to do an important speaking test in the next lesson, do you
a get nervous and make extra mistakes?
b enjoy the challenge and do your best?
c say it is not fair and ask to do the test the next day?

3 When you disagree with someone's suggestion, do you usually
a say nothing?
b explain your opinion clearly, and listen carefully to their views?
c tell them directly that it is a bad idea?

4 If you are brainstorming ideas in a group, do you suggest
a similar ideas to other people?
b many, and usually different, ideas?
c very little?

B Ask your partner the questions and take note of his/her answers. Then answer his/her questions.

C Go to page XIX to find out your score and what it means!

➤ Go back to page 50.

2.2 Personality test scores

In general, the higher your score in this test, the better your attitude toward challenging situations and the better your problem-solving skills. The highest possible score is 30.

A low score for a question shows an area to consider improving in order to become a truly effective problem solver.

Questions 1–3 reveal your attitude toward problems.
Questions 4–6 reveal your problem-solving skills.

➤ Go back to page 21.

5.1 Student A

A Take the quiz. Choose the answer that is most true for you.

1 When two friends are arguing about what to do on the weekend, do you
- **a** ignore them until they finish?
- **b** calm them down and help them decide?
- **c** tell them to stop and make the decision for them?

2 When you have many things to do next week, do you
- **a** start doing them this week and see how many you can finish?
- **b** make a plan before starting?
- **c** do nothing at first and then rush to do them late next week?

3 When you work on a group project, do you
- **a** focus on your personal tasks?
- **b** do your tasks and support others with theirs?
- **c** do little, and let others do a lot?

4 When you borrow a little money from someone and say you will return it the next day, do you
- **a** pay it back a few days later?
- **b** pay it back the next day?
- **c** need reminding to pay it back.

B Ask your partner the questions and take note of his/her answers. Then answer his/her questions.

C Go to page XIX to find out your score and what it means!

➤ Go back to page 50.

3.2 Students

The local mayor has decided to cancel the city's Car-Free Day. She wants a new project and campaign to reduce the traffic problems and pollution. Read the proposals.

TRANSPORTATION PROPOSALS

1 Reduce your car use!
Encourage people to leave their car at home. Run a media publicity campaign to promote:
- shopping locally, not using out-of-town grocery stores.
- walking or biking for short trips.
- working from home.
- setting up a city council app for car-sharing on common trip.
- increasing city center car parking fees.

2 Go electric!
Encourage the purchase and use of electric cars:
- Install car-charging points around the city.
- Provide cheap loans for the purchase of electric cars.
- Allow free parking for electric cars.

3 A wheely good future!
Encourage biking:
- Run a media publicity campaign to promote riding your bike to work.
- Introduce a city bike rental system.
- Hold 'Bike Fun Days' in local park.

➤ Go back to page 33.

3.1 Students A and B

SPEAK Work in pairs. Put the pictures in the correct order and use them to retell the two stories.

Junko's story

Alan's story

➤ Go back to page 27.

1.2 Student A

A SPEAK Work in pairs. Ask and answer questions to complete the information about the percentage of people with English as a first language in different countries around the world.

Percentage of people with English as a first language	
________	93 percent
UK	92 percent
New Zealand	________ percent
US	79 percent
________	57 percent
Singapore	37 percent
Jamaica	________ percent
South Africa	9.3 percent
Sierra Leone	________ percent
Pakistan	8 percent

*Where **do** 93 percent of people **speak** English as a first language?*
*How many people in New Zealand **speak** English as a first language?*

B SPEAK Work in pairs. Are you surprised by any of the information?

➤ Go back to page 7.

4.1 Student A

A Make a resolution for each of these topics:

- studying English
- food and diet
- money
- house and home

B Tell your partner about your resolutions and why you have made them.

C Ask your partner to make resolutions for these topics.

D Make resolutions for your partner's topics.

➤ Go back to page 39.

1 Writing

Write a report about trends

W using formal language in reports

A Work in groups of three. Discuss the questions and complete the *Me*, *Partner 1* and *Partner 2* columns in the table.

1. How much time do you spend doing each activity in the table each week?
2. Are you spending more (↑), less (↓) or the same (↔) time on each activity at the moment, compared to last year?

	Me	Partner 1	Partner 2	Average
	hours	hours	hours	hours
checking social media				
sending instant messages				
studying online				

B Now figure out the average number of hours spent doing each activity. Are people spending more or less time on each activity compared to last year? Complete the *Average* column of the table in Exercise A.

C Read the *Report about online trends* and answer the questions.

1. What trends did the writer find? Did you find the same trends?
2. What was different?
3. What is the writer's main prediction for the future?

Report about online trends

[1]These days, online communication is more and more important in our daily lives. [2]But are we actually spending more time online? [3]<u>This report examines</u> the number of hours that people spend on <u>various</u> online activities and explores some recent trends. [4]I interviewed eight members of my English class about their online habits.

How much time do you spend checking social media?

The average number of hours in my group is just over one hour per day. This is surprising, as I expected the total to be higher. <u>One possible reason is that</u> several popular social media sites are showing more advertisements these days.

How much time do you spend sending instant messages?

The average number of hours here is <u>approximately</u> 1.5 hours per day. Almost everybody said that this number is increasing for them. <u>It seems that</u> many people are using instant messaging services for conversations that they had on social media before.

How much time do you spend studying online?

The average number of hours here was 4.3 per week. Two people in my group never study online, and this trend is not changing. Two people study online a lot: 12 and 15 hours a week. This trend is also not changing, as these people both study on long-term courses. However, the other three people's answers were <u>especially</u> interesting: they all spend two to three hours a week studying, but this is increasing very fast, from zero last year. They all use language learning apps to study for pleasure.

Conclusion

<u>There certainly seems to be</u> a trend away from social media and towards messaging apps. <u>However</u>, the main trend I noticed is the increase in online studying, especially the use of language apps. I expect this trend to continue into the future.

D Look at the introduction to the *Report about online trends*. Match the sentences (1–4) with the descriptions (a–d).

- **a** Explain where you got your information, e.g. *Who did you ask?*
- **b** Ask a rhetorical question to make the reader think about the topic.
- **c** Present your reason for writing the report: what does the report do?
- **d** Start by introducing the general topic of your report.

E Look at the box and complete the tips about using formal language in reports. Then find examples of each tip in the report.

Using formal language in reports

We *use* / *don't use* contractions (e.g. *there's*, *isn't*).

In general, most sentences are fairly *long* / *short*.

Most sentences have ***a human subject, e.g. I, Two people*** / ***a non-human subject, e.g. It, This trend***.

F Match the formal phrases (1–7), which are underlined in the *Report about online trends*, with the less formal phrases (a–g).

1. This report examines …
2. various
3. One possible reason is that …
4. approximately
5. It seems that … / There certainly seems to be …
6. especially
7. However, …

- **a** but
- **b** more or less
- **c** Maybe this is because …
- **d** In this report, I look at …
- **e** I think …
- **f** a few different
- **g** very

WRITING

A PREPARE You are going to write a report about current trends in communication. What trends do you notice? You can use the ideas in Exercise A or your own ideas.

B PLAN Choose two or three points to include in your report. These will be your main paragraphs.

C WRITE Write your report (150–200 words). Remember:

- to start with an introduction.
- when you present numbers, show what they mean and how they're connected together.
- to use formal language.
- to end with a conclusion.

D REVIEW Work in groups. Share your reports. Who found the most interesting information? Were you surprised by any of the trends he/she found?

Write an informal email

W– informal writing

A SPEAK Work in pairs. Read the email from Sophie to Marta. What is their relationship?

- **a** family members
- **b** new friends
- **c** elementary school friends
- **d** business colleagues

To: Marta
Subject: Hello and good news

Hi Marta,

How are you? I hope everything has been OK since you left New York. Did you have a good vacation with your family? I guess you're back at college now. Studying or partying hard? [1]___ 🙂.

Sorry I haven't written sooner – I can't believe it's been two months since our course finished! I really miss New York. My English really improved, and I loved getting to know you, Sato and the others. [2]___

Anyway, I have some good news! I have a new job and I've moved to Paris. I'm working for a web design agency. I'm so happy. It's only a small company, but everyone's really nice and [3]___

So, how about coming to Paris to visit me? Would you like to? I remember that you haven't been to Paris before, so now's your chance. Come for a weekend and stay at my place – it's easy to get here from Rome! What do you think? [4]___

Let me know what you think, and let me know when you finally get on Facebook – [5]___

Hugs and all the best.

Sophie

B Read again. Answer the questions.

1. Where did Sophie and Marta meet each other?
2. When did they last see each other?
3. Where do they live?
4. How has Sophie's life changed recently?
5. What does Sophie want Marta to do?

C Complete Sophie's email with the sentences (a–e).

- **a** I'm enjoying the work.
- **b** Or both?
- **c** Have you heard from anyone else from our class?
- **d** I can't believe you haven't done that yet!
- **e** I'd love to see you.

D Put the sections in the order they appear in Sophie's email.

- telling Marta about what she has done recently ___
- making a suggestion/plan for the future ___
- asking about Marta's life ___
- talking about a shared experience ___

E Look at the box. Find and underline features of informal writing in the sentences (1–4).

Informal writing

In emails and letters to friends and family, we usually use an informal writing style. We use:

- contractions, such as *You'll* …
- incomplete grammar, such as *How you doing?*
- informal words and phrases, such as *buddy* (= *friend*).
- informal punctuation, such as *!*, *–*.
- emojis/emoticons, such as 🙂.
- informal opening and closing expressions, such as *Hi*, *Hugs*.

1. I'm going on vacation soon – can't wait!
2. I've just passed my driving test 🙂.
3. All fine here. It's great to be back at college!
4. Big hug and say hi to your mom.

WRITING

A PREPARE You are going to write an informal email to a friend. Think of a friend you want to write to or imagine you are writing to a new friend.

B PLAN Write notes. Think about:

- What can you ask your friend about?
- What shared experience can you write about?
- What news do you have? What have you done recently?
- What suggestion or request can you make?

C WRITE Write your email (150–200 words). Use Sophie's email and the skills box to help you.

D REVIEW Work in pairs. Read your partner's email. Ask for more information about his/her news.

3 Writing — Write an email of complaint

W — using adverbs to give emphasis

A Work in pairs. Add to the list of common causes of complaint for travelers.

- trash on buses and trains
- poor quality in-flight entertainment
- a lack of space
- delays due to technical problems

B Work in pairs. Have you experienced any of the problems you wrote down in Exercise A? Did you make a complaint? Why/Why not?

C Read Asaf King's email of complaint. Are the sentences true (T) or false (F)? Correct the false sentences.

1 When he made the reservation, Asaf paid more money to guarantee his seat. ___
2 Asaf went quickly to check-in because he didn't have much time left. ___
3 There were no seats available on the flight to London. ___
4 Asaf was not able to travel to Bangkok. ___
5 Asaf did not tell the airline staff about his seat reservation. ___
6 He wants the airline to give his money back and to pay extra for his problems. ___

To: LuxAir Customer Services
Subject: A serious complaint: Reservation Reference No. 589RT

Dear Sir or Madam,

a I am writing to complain about the mistakes your airline made with my reservation that meant I missed two flights and lost important business.

b On April 17, I made a reservation with your airline for flight Y33 from Dublin to London on May 23. I also paid extra to reserve my seat.

c I arrived at Dublin airport two hours before the flight and immediately went to the check-in desks. Since I had arrived early, I certainly wasn't expecting any problems, but sadly this was not the case. At check-in, I was told that the flight had been overbooked and was completely full, which meant I couldn't board the plane.

d This was extremely disappointing and incredibly inconvenient because it meant that I also missed my connecting flight, an international departure from London to Bangkok. The new flight to Bangkok cost me $500, and I missed an important meeting.

e The simple fact is that I had paid in advance to confirm my reservation, but you failed to hold my seat. I found your customer service at the airport completely unsatisfactory as your staff totally ignored my seat reservation.

f Because of the extra flight costs, my lost time and the effect on my business, I would like to ask for a full refund for my flight and for additional compensation.

I hope to hear from you soon regarding this matter.

Kind regards,

Asaf King

D Match the descriptions (1–6) with the paragraphs (a–f) in Asaf's email.

1 a detailed description of the main events ___
2 the reason why you are writing the email ___
3 the result you want from your email ___
4 the key dates and places ___
5 a summary of the main complaint ___
6 the effects of the event and problems it caused ___

E Look at the box. Then match the adverbs (1–3) with those that have a similar meaning (a–c). Use the email to help you.

Using adverbs to give emphasis

In the email, the writer uses adverbs to make a word stronger. An adverb usually goes before the adjective or verb that it describes.

- *The flight … was **completely** full.*
- *This was **extremely** disappointing.*

1 certainly	a incredibly
2 extremely	b totally
3 completely	c definitely

WRITING

A PREPARE Choose one of the situations to write an email about.

- Your recent flight was terrible.
- A member of staff gave you the wrong information.
- You experienced a long travel delay.

B PLAN Write detailed notes about what happened. Think about:

- where and when did it happen?
- what result do you want?

C WRITE Write a semi-formal email of complaint (150–250 words).

- Use Asaf's email and Exercise D to help you.
- Use adverbs to explain your problem.

4 Writing — Write a short essay

W using linking words to introduce reasons and consequences

A Read the advertisement for a competition. What can you win? How can you win it?

Happy New Year with Digital Express and Tinto Phones

Enter our New Year competition and win a TINTO X cell phone.

Digital technology has already changed our lives in many ways, and this is going to continue in the future. We want to know how you think digital technology is going to change our lives over the next 20 years.

Write a short essay describing a change that digital technology will bring to our lives, explaining why this will happen and any consequences it will have.

The five winning entries will be published online.

B Read a competition essay entry. Put the paragraphs (a–d) in the correct order (1–4).

1 introduction (what the writer thinks the change will be) ___
2 reason 1 ___
3 reason 2 ___
4 conclusion ___

a Digital technology supports a sharing economy, and that means people will not need to buy so many things. Owning a car will not be necessary **as** you will simply use an app to book a driverless car when you need one. People will share things like bicycles and gardening equipment within their local community by using an app to find what they need. **As a result**, people will own fewer things, but they will have more contact with other people.

b People are always buying things **because** they want to get the latest products. However, in the future, people will probably buy fewer things **because of** the development of digital technology.

c To sum up, digital technology will definitely continue to change our lives, and one of those changes will be that we won't need to own so much stuff.

d In the past, new inventions brought many products into our houses, but digital technology usually replaces these things with a single device. For example, your cell phone can now be your television, radio, music player and alarm clock. In the future, children may play all their games on a phone or tablet, **and so** traditional board games will disappear. **Consequently**, people will have less stuff in their house, although they will spend a lot on digital services.

C SPEAK Work in pairs. Read again and discuss the questions.

1 What two reasons are given for why people will own fewer things?
2 How many examples illustrate each reason?
3 What other things will happen?
4 What do you think of the predictions?

D Look at the linking words in bold in the essay. Write them in the correct column.

Introduce a reason	Introduce a consequence
because	

E Look again at the linking words in bold in the essay. Write them in the correct place in the box. Use each of them twice.

Using linking words to introduce reasons and consequences

We use linking words and phrases to show the relationship between information and ideas.

1 Some linking words connect ideas inside one sentence. For example, *because*, ________, ________, ________.
2 Some connect ideas across two sentences. For example, ________, ________.
3 Some linking words are followed by a clause (subject + verb). For example, ________, ________, ________, ________, ________.
4 Others are followed by noun phrases (such as the increase in pollution). For example, ________.

F SPEAK Work in pairs. Complete the sentences with your own ideas. Then compare your answers with a partner.

1 All cars should be electric because …
2 Children are using social media. As a result, …
3 Every year, more people are only paying for things electronically. Consequently, …
4 Cities are unhealthy places to live because of …
5 People are watching less TV as …
6 Online shopping continues to increase, and so …

WRITING

A PLAN Make a prediction about how digital technology will change the future. Think of the reasons why this change will happen and any consequences it will have.

B WRITE Write your competition entry (150–200 words).

C REVIEW Work in groups. Read and discuss your essays. Have a vote to decide on the two winning entries.

W– **paragraph structure**

A Read the job advertisement. Is it the type of work you are interested in? Why/Why not?

Events Team Assistant (Ref: 783G)

ICE: International Charity Events

This is an exciting opportunity to join our lively and dynamic Events Team. We organize and promote fundraising events and programs for charities across Europe. Typical events include sports, cultural events and adventure challenges and tours.

Essential requirements:

- excellent organizational, communication and marketing skills
- a great team player
- good digital technology skills
- able to meet deadlines

Desired experience:

- experience of working internationally

To apply, email a cover letter and résumé to Marta Safin: M.Safin@ice.nett

B Read Peter O'Malley's application. In which paragraph (1–4) does he cover each topic (a–d)?

a why he is a good candidate for this job ___
b when he is able to attend an interview ___
c why he wants to work for this company ___
d what job he is applying for and why ___

To: Ms. Safin
Subject: Events Team Assistant (Ref: 783G)

Dear Ms. Safin

1 I am writing to apply for the position of Events Team Assistant, currently advertised on Euro_Recruit.com (Ref: 783G). I have attached my résumé. I recently graduated with a degree in Marketing, and I wish to start a career in events organization.

2 The experience and skills that I gained from college make me the perfect candidate for this role. I was a member of the Student Social Committee and I was responsible for our International Food Festival. This demanded excellent organizational skills and demonstrated my ability to meet deadlines. I also improved the marketing for the event, which led to the largest ever attendance at the festival. In addition, I attended frequent meetings, which required good communication skills and the ability to work on a team.

3 Working for your company would be a great opportunity for me to begin my career. I am interested in the wide range of events that you organize and I would love the opportunity to work for an international company.

4 Thank you for considering my application. I am available for an interview at any time, and I look forward to hearing from you.

Sincerely yours,
Peter O'Malley

C Look at the advice about writing a cover letter. Find and underline examples in Peter O'Malley's cover letter.

Writing a cover letter

Write in a professional, formal style that suits a business letter. Do not use informal language such as contractions. Follow a clear structure:

- If possible, address the letter to a named person. Use Dear Mr./Mrs. Do not use the person's first name.
- State where you saw the job advertisement and give its reference number.
- Show your interest in the position on offer and the company.
- Describe the key skills and experience that you have for the role and give examples to support your claims.
- Use standard closing sentences.

D Look at the box. Then read paragraphs 2 and 3 of the cover letter again. Identify the topic sentence and examples for each paragraph.

Paragraph structure

The paragraphs in the main body of a cover letter should focus on a single topic and be carefully organized and well structured. Always:

- start with a topic sentence that makes a clear, relevant point.
- support that point with examples to show how your skills and experience meet those listed in the job ad, or to show your genuine interest in the role.
- only add extra points if they relate to the topic sentence.

WRITING

A PLAN You are going to write a cover letter for the job advertisement below. Think about:

- what language style you need to use.
- the best way to organize the letter.
- what your topic sentences will be and how you will structure each paragraph.

Catering Management Assistant (Ref: 812C)

SCC: Superior Conference Catering

High quality catering for events and conferences in the southeastern United States.

Essential requirements:

- excellent organization and time management skills
- excellent communication and team-working skills
- strong digital technology skills

Desired experience and interests:

- event organization
- food and drink
- languages

B WRITE Write the letter (150–200 words).

C REVIEW Work in pairs. Read your partner's letter. Has he/she covered the key points in the ad and organized the letter well?

Irregular Verbs

Base form	Simple past	Past participle
be	was/were	been
become	became	become
begin	began	begun
break	broke	broken
bring	brought	brought
build	built	built
buy	bought	bought
can	could	been able to
catch	caught	caught
choose	chose	chosen
come	came	come
cost	cost	cost
cut	cut	cut
drink	drank	drunk
eat	ate	eaten
fall	fell	fallen
feel	felt	felt
find	found	found
forget	forgot	forgotten
get	got	got
give	gave	given
go	went	gone/been
grow	grew	grown
have	had	had
hear	heard	heard
hit	hit	hit
hold	held	held
hurt	hurt	hurt
keep	kept	kept
know	knew	known
leave	left	left
lend	lent	lent
let	let	let

Base form	Simple past	Past participle
lose	lost	lost
make	made	made
mean	meant	meant
meet	met	met
must	had to	had to
pay	paid	paid
put	put	put
read	read	read
ride	rode	ridden
run	ran	run
say	said	said
see	saw	seen
sell	sold	sold
send	sent	sent
set	set	set
shut	shut	shut
sing	sang	sung
sit	sat	sat
sleep	slept	slept
speak	spoke	spoken
spell	spelled	spelled
spend	spent	spent
stand	stood	stood
steal	stole	stolen
take	took	taken
teach	taught	taught
tell	told	told
think	thought	thought
throw	threw	thrown
understand	understood	understood
wear	wore	worn
win	won	won
write	wrote	written

PHONETIC SYMBOLS											
Single vowels			Diphthongs			Consonants					
/ɪ/	fish	/fɪʃ/	/uw/	n**ews**	/nuw/	/p/	**p**en	/pen/	/s/	**s**nake	/sneɪk/
/iː/	b**ea**n	/biːn/	/eɪ/	f**a**ce	/feɪs/	/b/	**b**ag	/bæg/	/z/	**z**oo	/zuː/
/ʊ/	f**oo**t	/fʊt/	/ɔɪ/	b**oy**	/bɔɪ/	/t/	**t**ea	/tiː/	/ʃ/	**sh**op	/ʃɒp/
/uː/	sh**oe**	/ʃuː/	/oʊ/	n**o**se	/noʊz/	/d/	**d**og	/dɒg/	/ʒ/	televi**si**on	/'telɪvɪʒən/
/e/	**e**gg	/eg/	/ju/	**u**se	/juz/	/ʧ/	**ch**ip	/ʧɪp/	/m/	**m**ap	/mæp/
/ə/	moth**er**	/'mʌðər/	/aɪ/	**eye**	/aɪ/	/ʤ/	**j**azz	/ʤæz/	/n/	**n**ame	/neɪm/
/ɜː/	w**o**rd	/wɜːrd/	/aʊ/	m**ou**th	/maʊθ/	/k/	**c**ake	/keɪk/	/ŋ/	ri**ng**	/rɪŋ/
/ɔː/	t**a**lk	/tɔːk/				/g/	**g**irl	/gɜːrl/	/h/	**h**ouse	/haʊs/
/æ/	b**a**ck	/bæk/				/f/	**f**ilm	/fɪlm/	/l/	**l**eg	/leg/
/ʌ/	b**u**s	/bʌs/				/v/	**v**erb	/vɜːrb/	/r/	**r**oad	/roʊd/
/ɑː/	**ar**m	/ɑːrm/				/θ/	**th**ing	/θɪŋ/	/w/	**w**ant	/wɒnt/
/ɒ/	t**o**p	/tɒp/				/ð/	**th**ese	/ðiːz/	/j/	**y**es	/jes/

Audio scripts

UNIT 1

Lesson 1.1, Listening, Exercise C

1.1 **J = Jackson O = Olivia**

J: Hello. Welcome to the Tec-cast. I'm Jackson, and this is my big sister, Olivia.

O: Hello. In this week's podcast, we're looking at phones. Or rather, we're not looking at our phones for a whole week!

J: Yes, that's right. Our experiment runs for seven days. We started on Monday and today's Thursday, so we're halfway through it.

O: Exactly. And instead of our phones, we're both carrying around one of these voice recorders all week, so we can record our experiences. And it's been an interesting week! I arranged to meet Jackson outside the university on Monday afternoon, but it didn't really work, did it, Jackson?

J: Uh, no. Sorry. Let's listen to our recordings from earlier in the week.

Lesson 1.1, Listening, Exercise D

1.2 **J = Jackson O = Olivia S = Sebastian**

O: Hi. Olivia here. It's 4:20 on Monday afternoon and I'm waiting for Jackson. We arranged to meet here, outside the university, at four o'clock, but I can't see him and it's starting to rain. So it looks like he isn't coming and I'm not sure what to do. Hmm, I can't call him because I don't have my phone. OK, I know. I'll go and wait in that bakery over there – at least I'll stay dry, and I'll be able to see Jackson through the window when he arrives.

J: Hi. This is Jackson. It's Monday afternoon and I'm late meeting Olivia. I think. I don't actually know the time because I never wear a watch; I always use the clock on my phone. Anyway, I missed my bus and I couldn't check the time of the next one – the timetables are all online now. So I decided to walk. But then I got lost because I didn't have a map – I usually use the map on my phone! And I couldn't call Olivia to tell her I'd be late. And now it's raining! OK, so I'm just arriving at the university now and I'm looking for Olivia, but I can't see her. Hmm, now I don't know what to do.

S: Excuse me. Are you looking for Olivia?

J: Uh, yes. Why?

S: Hi. I'm Sebastian. I'm a student here at the university. I listen to your podcast every week, and I watch all your videos. I love them!

J: Really? Wow! Thanks. Uh … but how do you know I'm looking for Olivia?

S: I spotted her here a few minutes ago. I recognized her from your videos. She went into that bakery over there.

J: Oh, excellent. Thank you so much. Look, do you want to come and join us? I'll buy you a cupcake to say thank you, and you can tell us what you think of our podcasts.

S: Yeah, that sounds like a great idea. Thanks a lot.

Lesson 1.1, Listening, Exercise E

1.3 **J = Jackson O = Olivia**

O: Hi. Me again. It's eleven fifteen on Tuesday morning, and yes, I'm waiting for Jackson, again. He's 15 minutes late, again, but it's OK because we arranged a plan B: what to do if something goes wrong. So I'm enjoying a nice outdoor concert in the park right now, by a really cool band. Maybe you can hear the music in the background. Our new friend Sebastian told us about the concert yesterday – he plays the guitar in the band, and he sounds really good. It's strange because all the other people in the audience are filming the concert on their cell phones, but I think they're missing half the fun! I'm just listening and enjoying it – and it's much better. In fact, I think I'll stop recording now so I can listen!

J: Hi. It's Tuesday morning, and I'm late for a meeting with Olivia, again, but it's OK because we discussed where she'll be at 11, 11:30, 12:00 and 12:30. And yes, I'm wearing a watch today – an old one from when I was a teenager. It doesn't look great, but it's good for telling the time! Anyway, today I decided to walk the same way I came yesterday – so I checked a map before I left home! I wanted to come back to this part of town because I noticed that the buildings are really beautiful and interesting. I don't normally look at the buildings around me – I usually just stare at my phone. But it's really nice to look around and think about where I am and … how to get to the park from here. So I'm not exactly lost again; I'm just exploring the city a little more than usual.

Lesson 1.1, Listening, Exercise F

1.4 **J = Jackson O = Olivia**

O: Hello again. So, as I said, it's now Thursday, and we're halfway through our experiment. How's it going for you, Jackson?

J: Surprisingly well! I mean, I think I'm seeing a lot more than usual – now I'm looking at the real world, not my phone all the time.

O: Yeah, me too. I really enjoyed observing all the people outside the university on Monday! So what about those amazing buildings? Did you take any pictures?

J: Uh, no. Because I didn't have my phone! But I can tell you about them, if you want.

O: Wow! You usually just show me your pictures. You see! We're talking more than before, too! Our experiment is working! So tell me about those buildings!

Lesson 1.2, Listening, Exercise B

1.8 **M = Mona J = Juan**

M: Hey, Juan. I'm writing a blog post for our website. I thought it might be good to interview you. Can I ask you a few questions?

J: Yes, of course. Go ahead. But why do you want to talk to me? What do you want to talk about?

M: Well, I hear you've just returned from a trip across Europe. It'd be nice to hear about your experiences of using English during your trip.

J: Oh, right. Yes, no problem.

M: Great. I'll just turn on my microphone … OK, so thanks, Juan, for agreeing to talk to me today about your recent trip to Europe. Which countries did you visit?

J: Well, I started in Russia, and then I traveled through Belarus, Poland, Germany, the Netherlands and England. It was a long journey, but I met a lot of great people and I had some amazing conversations. It was a good way to practice my English.

M: Yes, I'm sure it was! It sounds like a great way of practicing. Was it hard to communicate in English?

J: No, actually I found it really easy to communicate all the way from Russia to the Netherlands. But when I got to England … well, it was terrible!

M: Really? What happened in England?

J: Everybody spoke so fast! And they used really strange words and phrases – lots of idioms that I'd never heard before. Plus, the people had very strong accents, so I couldn't understand very much at all!

M: Oh, no! So what did you do?

J: I just asked people to slow down. 'Can you say that again, please?'; 'Could you speak slowly, please?', and so on!

M: And did that help?

J: Yes. I mean, the people were very nice, and they were happy to talk to me. But they speak very strange English! I guess it's because English is changing all the time.

M: Really? How is English changing? Can you give me an example?

J: Yes, of course. When I was in London, I heard many people speaking a new variety of English called MLE – Multicultural London English. It's becoming extremely popular.

M: Really? I've never heard of it. Who uses MLE?

J: Mostly young people in London.

M: So how is MLE different from normal English?

J: Well, it's mostly a question of pronunciation. But there are also grammar differences. For example, in MLE, they don't say 'you were'; they say 'you was'. 'I was', 'you was', 'he was', 'she was', 'we was', 'they was'. And then in negative sentences, it's 'I weren't', 'you weren't', 'he weren't', 'she weren't', and so on.

M: What? That's terrible! But isn't that a mistake?

J: Well, it isn't Standard English, of course. But millions of people speak like that, so how can it be wrong?

M: Hmm … what do you mean by 'Standard English'?

J: Well, Standard English is the form they use in books and newspapers. It's a kind of cleaned-up version of English. But it isn't the only form of English, and most native speakers don't speak Standard English – at least, not all the time. There are hundreds of other forms of English all over the world – like Jamaican English, Nigerian English, Indian English and so on. They're all different, but I think that's really cool!

M: OK, but isn't it just a question of good English and bad English? Surely Standard English is better, isn't it?

J: No. I don't think so. 'Standard' doesn't always mean 'the best'. When I traveled by train across Europe, I went by 'standard class', not 'first class'. And I think Standard English is like 'standard class' in a train: simple and basic, but a little boring. I think non-standard English is much more interesting.

M: So are you saying we need to learn non-standard English?

J: No, not at all. Standard English is perfect for international communication. As I say, Standard English worked well for me all the way from Russia to the Netherlands. I only had a problem when I got to England. So it depends what you need English for. I think for most learners of English around the world, it's better to learn Standard English. We don't need to speak like native speakers. In fact, as I learned on my trip, it's usually better when we don't speak like native speakers.

M: Wow! Yes, I see what you mean, and I certainly agree with you on that last point. OK, so thanks a lot for that interview, Juan. You've given me a lot to think about … and to write about on the blog.

UNIT 2

Lesson 2.1, Listening, Exercise C
2.2 I = Interviewer E = Emma

I: Welcome to *Dreams Come True*, the podcast that finds out about people's life-long dreams and how they've turned them into reality. My guest in the studio today is Emma Sykes from New York.

E: Hello, thanks for having me!

I: Glad you could be here. Now, Emma, you are 35 and you are the owner of a successful advertising agency, is that right?

E: Yes, that's right.

I: So you've already had a lot of success in your life.

E: Yes, you could say that. I've worked very hard and the agency is doing well, but I still have dreams – well, one dream anyway.

I: And I believe that dream involves big plans on water! Tell us a little more about it.

E: That's right, John. Ever since I was young, I've been fascinated by the water. I love swimming and diving, and for the last few years I've been learning how to sail. My ultimate dream, the thing I've wanted to achieve my whole life, is to live on a yacht and sail around the world.

I: Wow, that's a big dream! And it doesn't sound easy. Tell us, just how have you made this dream a reality?

E: Well, that's the thing … I haven't. Not yet. Not completely.

I: So, you haven't sailed around the world?

E: No, I haven't. It's just not practical at this time in my life. Yachts are very expensive. I've saved a fair amount of money, but not enough yet. Plus, I don't have enough skills or knowledge yet to go sailing on my own across the oceans.

I: Well, that does sound very complicated! So how do you keep going with your plan when it seems so far away?

E: For me, the most important thing is to make a decision to put a plan into action. Once you've made the decision, you can set short-term and long-term goals that will help you achieve your dream.

I: I see. Yes, that's a good point. So what are some of your short-term goals? How are you going to work toward that ultimate goal?

E: Well, there's the sailing lessons, obviously. But actually, I've turned one part of the dream into reality already.

I: Really? What's that?

E: A year ago, I sold my house and used some of the money to buy a houseboat. It isn't a yacht, and it won't take me around the world, but it's a home and it's on the water. OK, I'm on freshwater, not saltwater, but I now live on a boat.

I: Wow, that's already a pretty big change! But does living on a houseboat really prepare you for sailing around the world?

E: Yes, I think so. The important thing here is to stay motivated and not lose heart, and this step helps me to do that.

I: And of course, you're getting some experience of what it's like to live on the water.

E: Exactly! I'm learning to live in a small space, and I'm also finding out what it's like to live in a home that can move from place to place. OK, I'm cruising along canals, not crossing oceans, but doing something similar to my dream – it's a start.

I: And now that you've made that start, do you think your plan to sail around the world is more achievable?

E: Absolutely. On the whole, I think the hardest part of any journey is the first step. Now that I've made the break from the land to the water, I'll be able to take the next step of my journey with more confidence.

I: Well, thank you for coming to talk to us, Emma. I hope you can join us again once you've achieved your ultimate dream. Will you do that?

E: Yes, of course. I look forward to it.

I: Thank you, Emma. Now, next up, I'll be speaking to …

Lesson 2.2, Listening, Exercise B

2.4 **M = Matt S = Suzanna N = Nancy R = Roberto**

M: You know, when you move away from home, arrive in a new place, there are lots of different challenges, and for me the biggest one was eating. Well, not eating, but cooking. I mean, I could make a salad or a sandwich, but not cook anything, like, I couldn't boil an egg. I know that sounds silly, but I simply had no idea. Anyway, I looked at some books and also found some excellent 'how to cook' videos online. To be honest, the books didn't help, but I started to teach myself with the videos. I wasn't very good at first – the first time, I didn't manage to make anything at all; I just watched the video and then ordered a takeout! But, I never gave up. I kept practicing. And when my parents came to see me six months later, I managed to cook them a really tasty meal. They were so surprised.

S: I really hate standing up in front of people to give a talk or a presentation. So, when my brother asked me to make a speech at his wedding, I didn't know what to do. I couldn't say no to him. Luckily a friend of mine, an actor, helped me. Basically, we created a character for me to play when giving the speech, so that I didn't think it was actually me standing up to speak. Also, I learned my speech by heart so that I didn't need to use any notes. Just like an actor. On the big day, I wasn't able to stop my hands from shaking, but I remembered everything and I played that character. And, incredibly, I was able to complete the speech. That was a big day for me, as well as for my brother.

N: I worked as a volunteer in a village school in China for about six months, and the language was my biggest problem. I was able to speak very basic Chinese, but I couldn't remember many new words. I studied each day, but didn't achieve much – the words went in one ear and then straight out the other! Then, I had a great idea. I had my guitar with me, so I started to write simple songs with all the new words. They were kind of like children's songs. I asked a Chinese friend to check my grammar was correct, and then tried to learn the songs. And, you know what, it worked. Each day, I was able to remember those new words, and I even started singing the songs to the kids. I was actually pretty nervous the first time I sang to them, but I managed to do it without mistakes, although I think my pronunciation was pretty poor, from the way the kids were laughing at me.

R: When I was a child, I never learned to swim, and, when I started going on beach vacations, I really regretted that. My friends spent all day swimming in the ocean, but I wasn't able to swim. All I could do was sunbathe! So, I asked my sister to teach me. She was very patient, but, after a few months, I gave up because I still couldn't swim. Then, after another vacation just sitting on the beach, I decided to try again. This time, I paid for lessons at the local pool. And yes, after a few more months, I finally managed to swim 50 meters. That felt so good. And then, that next vacation, I was finally able to swim in the ocean with my friends – that felt incredible. A real achievement!

UNIT 3

Lesson 3.1, Listening, Exercise B

3.1 **B = Presenter (Bobby) J = Junko A = Alan**

B: OK, our first caller is Junko. Hello, Junko.

J: Hello, Bobby. Well, my story happened some time ago, when I first came to the US to study English. I was only 18 then.

B: OK. Can I ask, where are you from, Junko?

J: Japan.

B: Japan? OK, but you aren't calling from there, are you?

J: No, no. I've lived here for ten years now.

B: OK. Well, Junko, thank you for calling. Tell us your story. What problem did you have?

J: Well, the problem was a public holiday. New Year's Day to be exact!

B: New Year's Day was a problem? That is pretty unusual. What happened?

J: Well, I'd arranged to go to a classmate's house for dinner. Of course, I knew it was a holiday. But what I didn't know was there was no public transportation. So in the afternoon, I went to the subway station. It was snowing, not very heavily, but it was really cold. Anyway, the station was closed when I got there, so I couldn't get a train. I thought it was because of the snow, but the roads were OK, so I decided to try to get a bus.

B: But there were no buses either?

J: Mmm, exactly. But I didn't know. Anyway, I found a bus stop and sat down to wait.

B: Oh, no! Did you wait for long?

J: Actually, not so long. I was very lucky.

B: You got a taxi?

J: Not exactly. A police car was driving by when it suddenly stopped and one of the officers got out. She asked me if I was OK and explained there were no buses today. I felt so embarrassed and stupid. But then, guess what?

B: What?

J: She told me to get in the car. I was worried. Had I done something wrong? But they were both smiling, so I just asked why.

B: So then what?

J: They took me to my friend's place.

B: What? Like a taxi?

J: Exactly. I couldn't believe it. So kind. You know, we went right across the city. When I arrived, my friends hadn't started dinner. So, I wasn't late at all. Perfect!

B: How nice, Junko. I guess it was a quiet day for everyone, even the police. A great example of the New Year's spirit in action. Thank you. OK, now let's hear from Alan. Hello, Alan. Tell us your story.

A: Sure. Hi, Bobby. Yeah, so, I'd been out of work for a few months when I got this interview for a job in another city. I really needed the job, so I decided to leave really early – you know, I didn't want to be late and all that.

B: Not for an interview, no!

A: Right! Well, it was raining when I left, so I took a taxi to the station. That didn't take long, but when I got there, I found out that they'd canceled my train. I wasn't too worried though – the next one was in half an hour, and I had plenty of time. So I took the next train, but after about 30 minutes, that train broke down and we were just stuck there. Not moving or anything. And, stupidly, I'd left my phone at home. Yes, I'd changed my jacket just before I left, and my phone was in that first jacket, so I couldn't even call the company.

B: How unlucky, Alan. So how long were you stuck there?

A: About an hour! And all that time I was getting more and more stressed. The train started moving again, but really slowly, and we arrived about two hours late, and that meant I had already missed the interview by over an hour. So, I jumped in a taxi, but that only made things worse.

B: In what way?

A: The traffic was awful – you know, it was still raining. We ended up stuck in a traffic jam. After about 20 minutes we were still not moving, so I got out and walked. So, when I finally got to the office, I was really late, stressed and wet from the rain. I looked like a mess.

B: I can imagine. Nightmare! Did they still interview you?

A: Well, that's the funny thing. I was standing at the reception desk, waiting to make my excuses to the receptionist when this guy stepped in front of me. I was about to complain when the receptionist said 'Mr. Hammond, you've arrived. At last'. And, can you guess who he was?

B: Another candidate?

A: Oh, no, not another candidate. He was the manager, the interviewer! It turned out he'd been on the same train as me! I introduced myself immediately, and we had a laugh about the whole trip.

B: Amazing! What a coincidence. And so I have to ask: did you get the job?

A: Well, after all that bad luck, things had to change, and yes, I got the job.

Lesson 3.2, Listening, Exercise B
3.7 **C = Chairperson A = Alfred C1 = Councilor 1 C2 = Councilor 2**

C: OK, everyone, before we make our final decisions on this year's Car-Free Day, I'd like to invite some members of the public to give their views. First, let me introduce Alfred Shaw, a lecturer in business studies.

A: Thank you. OK, well, it's clear what most of you think about a car-free day. An absolutely wonderful idea, right? However, I'm here to disagree. Actually, it's a really terrible idea.

C1: What? You can't be serious!

C2: Nonsense, it's an excellent idea.

A: OK, you say that, but it really isn't. Let's look at the facts. First of all, they don't solve the traffic problem. And, anyway, cars are, very simply, great.

C2: Great? Come off it! We know they cause some awful problems.

A: OK, some things about cars are fairly bad, but they're clearly the best way to get around, and so they're never going to disappear. We've held this Car-Free Day 15 times before, but the rush-hour traffic jams have not gone away. Car-free days have a really tiny effect on driving habits, if any at all.

C1: But it's still better than doing nothing.

A: Is it? Here's another reason why we should think again. Car-free days don't even help the environment. Think about it. Although there may be no cars in the city center for that one day, those cars are still out there on the roads, just on different roads. So, all you're doing is moving the pollution.

And another thing, the car-free day causes massive traffic problems in the city, as drivers have to find other ways to go. Remember what happened last year, when that truck got stuck under the railroad bridge because we'd closed the main road? Because of that, there was an absolutely enormous traffic jam, trains were canceled and thousands of dollars of damage was caused. People were furious about that, and rightly so.

In short, car-free days are absolutely useless because they change nothing, and they create huge problems, not solutions. I'll now move onto what we should do instead.

C1: About time!

C2: Like what? A pedestrian-free day?!

C1: Ha ha. That's very funny.

A: Hmm, hilarious. You're clearly missing my point. We shouldn't ban anything, we should just improve everything.

First, we should start a campaign to encourage people to buy greener cars. Let's get more people using electric and hybrid cars. This may be extremely difficult, but it isn't impossible. We could hold an e-car festival and give people a chance to try the cars out in order to see their benefits. That would be a superb way to change things.

Also, we need to improve public transportation and get people using it. We need more buses, and cleaner buses – some of our old buses are really filthy, so it's no wonder people choose cars first. Let's invest some money, and then, why don't we run a 'Use Public Transportation Week', instead of banning cars for a day?

C1: Actually, that's a really good idea.

A: Thanks – an extremely good idea, I'd say. Finally, we should encourage a healthier and greener lifestyle all year round, rather than just for one day a year. Let's get people back on bikes. Let's teach people of all ages how to bike safely. Other cities have city bike rental systems – why don't we? We haven't even had a meeting to discuss it because you're too busy planning for car-free day.

OK, to sum up, there are alternatives to car-free days that are actually better for the environment and that actually reduce car use. Let's try them out, instead of holding another useless car-free day. OK, any questions?

C2: Um, isn't it true that your brother runs an electric car dealership? Maybe that's ...

A: Hey, what's that got to do with anything? Really! I just want our city to be a great place to live, that's all.

UNIT 4

Lesson 4.1, Listening, Exercises B and C
4.1 **J = Julia S = Shireen**

J: Hi, Shireen.

S: Hi, Julia. I can't see you; I don't think you've clicked the video button.

J: Oh! Oops! I'll do it now. Hold on. There we go.

S: That's better. Good to see you. Happy New Year!

J: And happy New Year to you!

S: How's everything going in Spain?

J: Great. We had a good time on New Year's Eve; there's a real party atmosphere in Madrid. We were at a house party, and then out on the streets at midnight, eating grapes, dancing and drinking hot chocolate – just wonderful!

S: Well, lucky you! Sounds better than mine. We went to see the ball drop at Times Square in New York City.

J: But that sounds amazing!

S: Oh, I'm sure it was – it's just we never actually saw it.

J: Oh no! What happened? You didn't get lost again, did you?

S: Not exactly – we just weren't early enough. There was a massive crowd and we got stuck on a side road. We could hear the countdown, but couldn't see a thing.

J: Oh! I bet it was freezing, too. I'm glad I was at that party and had that hot chocolate at midnight.

S: Yeah, I can imagine. We were outside for hours, and I lost my hat. To be honest, I did get pretty cold. I'm going to look for a new hat tomorrow; Sophie's coming here to have lunch, and then we're going shopping.

J: That's nice. Is that one of your New Year's resolutions? Are you going to finally buy some new clothes? No more going out in your sister's old ones?

S: Haha, very funny. Actually, I haven't made any resolutions yet.

J: You haven't? I've made several.

S: Really? What've you decided?

J: Try and guess.

S: OK, OK! Let me see. So, are you going to get married this year? Time to copy me?

J: Ooh, that's a big question to ask! No, no plans yet, but Alberto's said he's going to buy me flowers every month. He's going to try to be more romantic, for a change.

S: That's great. He sounds sweet. Let's hope he keeps that one. So, what are yours?

J: Well, I've decided to get in better shape this year, so I'm going to join a gym. Also, I'm going to study Spanish more seriously. I find it pretty hard to follow Alberto's friends.

S: That's a surprise! I always thought your Spanish was really good.

J: Well, not good enough. In fact, I'm meeting a new teacher on Thursday, for private lessons.

S: Really? That's quick!

J: Well, there's no point in putting things off. Just get started and then stick to the plan. I was reading a self-help book about this the other day: *How to Reach Your Goals and Change Your Life*.

S: Another self-help book? I think you should make a resolution to stop reading them.

J: Well, I think you should read some. It'd be good for you.

S: Really? I'll leave that to you, I think.

J: Oh, come on – now's the time to make some resolutions. What do you want to achieve this year? Or change? What about your chocolate habit? Resolutions are a great way to quit bad habits.

S: My chocolate habit? What do you mean?

J: You eat some every day, don't you?

S: Well, just a little. At work, you know.

J: Shireen, I really think you should cut it out of your diet. I was reading about how we've all become sugar addicts and …

S: That's a surprise! Another book! But, yeah, I know what you mean. It's just that I get really bored at work. I don't think I can totally quit, but I'll cut down on the amount I eat. Happy now?

J: Cut down by how much? There's no escape – make your mind up now!

S: OK, OK, I'll stop eating it every day. I'll have chocolate on Fridays only, as a treat.

J: Great, and I'll make sure you don't break that resolution.

S: Great, and how are you going to do that? Going to come to work with me each day?

J: Hmm, I'll put a webcam on your office desk.

S: Well, at least you can see how boring my job is then.

4.4 Lesson 4.1, Listening, Exercise A
A = Announcer M = Maya L = Lukas J = Jody H = Hassan

A: Maya

M: I never usually bother with self-help books. I usually prefer fiction, especially things like sci-fi and fantasy. But last year, I read a book that totally changed the way I feel about myself. It's called *Life Cycle* and it's by a famous cyclist and lifestyle expert named Helena Schneiderlin. The book explains how you can find the real you and be a happier person when you find your true passion. It gives you advice on how to find the thing that you love and how to use it to improve the quality of your life. I followed the advice in the book, and since then I've become much happier. It's definitely changed how I feel about myself. It's changed my life really. I'm much more confident now.

A: Lukas

L: I think the one thing that changed my life most of all was a book called *The Road*. It's by Cormac McCarthy and it's about a father and son on a journey through a strange and unwelcoming place. It might be the future after a terrible event – the book doesn't say exactly. Really, I think it's about the relationship between the two characters. Even though their situation is very bad, the love they have keeps them strong. I'll never forget the first time I read this book. It made me think about my own relationship with my father. We don't always get along, but I think *The Road* has helped me to understand him better.

A: Jody

J: There's a book called *Sapiens*. I only read it last year, but honestly, I can't think of another book that has had such a strong effect on me. It's a history book, and it tells the story of the human race – everything, from how we started as hunters, and then became farmers, on to how we developed cities and industry. It's written by Yuval Noah Harari. He talks about religion, money, countries, law – everything. It's a very impressive piece of work, and it really helped me to see things in context. I feel I have a better understanding about who we are now that I've read that book.

A: Hassan

H: Seeing *Hoop Dreams* was a life-changing moment for me. It's a documentary about two teenagers in Chicago who want to be professional basketball players. It follows six years of their lives, as they try and make it to the top. Both boys come from poor backgrounds, and the film is about a lot more than just basketball. It's about society, and it's about how a life can change in an instant. I was really into basketball when I was young, and I went into the movie theater that day wanting to be a basketball player, but by the time I walked out of the movie theater I wanted to be a film-maker instead. And that's what I am now. *Hoop Dreams* inspired me to make documentaries.

4.7 Lesson 4.2, Listening, Exercise B
R = Rita Costa J = John Malone T = Toshi Asaka

R: Hi, I'm Rita Costa, and this is *Rethinking the Future*, when we look at how we can stop pessimistic predictions from coming true.

OK, so, today's prediction is that rural life has no future. Many villages and small towns are going to disappear, or only have older residents because young people are relocating to urban areas – that is, they're going to the cities to find work and a new, modern life. We've talked before about overpopulation in urban areas, but what about the problem of under-population in rural areas? Like many countries, Japan faces that problem, but it is trying to deal with it. Our reporter John has been there to find out more. Hi, John.

J: Hi, Rita. Yes, I visited several places and saw some great ideas for repopulating small villages, for getting people to exchange their life in the city for one in the country.

R: I guess that means offering financial incentives, you know, offering things like free or cheap housing, low business taxes and relocation expenses.

J: Yes, and some local governments are certainly doing that, but I'm talking about examples of blue-sky thinking, and by that I mean ideas that are different, fresh and unexpected.

R: Oh yes, such as?

J: Well, the fresh thinking involves foreigners, the internet, cows and love.

R: That sounds fascinating. Tell us more.

J: Sure. My tour started in the small mountain town of Kamiyama, where the city feels far away. At first, it all seems very traditional and underdeveloped – you know, there are very few signs of modern life. However, to encourage companies to relocate from urban areas the town council provides a super-fast internet service, faster than Tokyo's. And now, if you look inside some of those traditional buildings, you'll see signs of a growing digital start-up economy, teams of young designers and programmers working away on their computers.

R: Do you mean like small digital design and app companies? Like in those urban creative business centers?

J: Exactly. Here's Toshi Asaka, the owner of one.

T: I decided to move here from Tokyo because of the internet service. I can do my work anywhere, and here the quality of life is wonderful. There are no drawbacks, no disadvantages, about living here– my employees don't feel underpaid now!

J: Kamiyama Council has managed to reinvent the local economy, moving from traditional to modern digital business.

R: Right, using modern technology to create opportunities for young people. That makes sense. What's the next idea?

J: Well, other places are using tradition rather than technology to change their future. The small fishing village of Nakanoshima has its eye on young people, too, but not young Japanese. They offer special six-month Working Holiday Visas to foreign visitors who want to experience a truly traditional Japanese lifestyle. You stay in cheap, shared accommodations, in a traditional building and do part-time agricultural work, that is, you have a job in the farming or fishing industries.

R: That sounds like a fun thing to do. But is it such a good idea? I'm not sure it really helps the village to grow. I mean, the visitors only stay six months.

J: But then, new businesses like restaurants, cafés and language schools open up, and that encourages local young people to stay and not go to the city, so the visitors are an opportunity for the locals.

R: OK, so the experience of the foreign visitors is only half the story. What else did you discover?

J: My final stop was Mishima Island. Like the other places, they provide financial help like cheap accommodations and relocation expenses, but if you are single and looking for romance, they will also pay for your dates.

R: Pay for your dates? Cute, but, that isn't a lot of money, is it?

J: Well, perhaps you've misunderstood the goal of this plan… its intention. It isn't about attracting new people; it's about keeping them. What I mean is, they want people to move to their village, and to then stay forever. What better way to do that than to help them to find love and perhaps start a family. Isn't that both sweet and smart?

R: OK, I get it now, but what about married couples? It doesn't help them, does it?

J: Not really, no, but they also give every new resident a young cow.

R: A cow? I'm not sure that will get me moo-ving there.

J: Oh, not just any cow. Mishima cows are extremely rare, and their beef is incredibly expensive, with a kilogram worth $500.

R: That's a lot of money! I can't believe it.

J: Yeah, but it really is that expensive. And the thing is, just like the village life, these cows are in danger of extinction, of disappearing completely forever, so they're another thing the new residents are helping to save.

R: The thing I love about the Mishima Island approach is that it creates emotional bonds to a place. What I mean by that is people soon make a strong connection to their new home, either through finding love or raising a cow. Definitely blue-sky thinking.

UNIT 5

Lesson 5.1, Listening, Exercise A

5.1 **F = Fiona M = Michael**

F: Hello, sorry I'm late. You must be Michael. I'm Fiona.

M: Hi, Fiona. Nice to meet you.

F: Nice to meet you, and thank you for coming, and for waiting. I hope we can help you. So, I've had a quick look at your personality test and, in today's session, I'd like you to tell me why you're thinking about changing careers, and to find out more about the kind of work that you like doing.

M: Sure.

F: OK, so you're currently working in a bank. I see you've been there for five years, since leaving college, so why do you want to leave that behind?

M: Well, it's been a good job, but um, I just feel there's something missing. I studied business and finance in college, and getting a banking job seemed like the right thing to do at that time, but I'm not so sure now.

F: I see, and what is it that's missing exactly? Your personality test showed you have good people skills. Does your work involve using those much? And your organizational skills are strong. I'm sure that's important at the bank.

M: Yeah, absolutely. You definitely need to be well organized, to both meet deadlines and manage the money carefully. Um, I work in a local branch of the bank, so I have to deal with customers face to face, and I've recently been made assistant manager, so those people skills are important, and I do more general planning now, like team planning, you know, to make sure the work gets done – that sort of thing. I think the thing is that basically every day is pretty much the same. I rarely have to think on my feet, or deal with surprises.

F: OK, you want a little more variety in your work. So, this has been your only job since college. Did you have any part-time jobs before?

M: Well, this may surprise you, but I used to be a fashion model.

F: A fashion model? Well, now that you've told me, it isn't so surprising, I mean you look very neat and well-dressed.

M: Thank you. I didn't do it for long, um, but it was really fun. I really enjoyed the photo shoots. It's good doing something creative together; the teamwork was good and important. And, well, they'd usually give us some of the clothes after the shoot, which was great for me as a student!

F: I can imagine, and also very different from working in a bank. Um, anything else?

M: The other thing was working as a waiter. I joined an agency for part-time catering work, so I used to serve food at conferences and events, or I'd work in a café or restaurant for a few days, you know, if their employees were sick or something.

F: Well, that's great experience to have. Did you like doing that?

M: Oh, yeah, for sure. You have to work hard. At busy times, you would always be under a lot of pressure, but in a good way. I liked helping the customers enjoy the event. I used to be tired but happy at the end of a day. But, you know, that was only student work for me. It did get me into food and cooking though; that's one of my hobbies now – home baking and stuff like that.

F: Well, it's certainly interesting to hear that you liked working under pressure. Um, you just mentioned hobbies. Do you have any other interests? Anything that might involve skills that you could use in a job?

M: Well, you obviously don't mean going to the movie theater. I love skiing. Um, before college, I was a member of a ski club at a local ski center. One thing then, I used to help new members, you know, I'd coach them a little, and just help them as they were learning. That was pretty rewarding. There was a nice sense of achievement, you know.

F: Is that feeling missing from your work in the bank?

M: In a way, yes. But I don't want to be a ski instructor, you know, that's just like having your own business. I want a steady job, to have a career in a good company, but, well, just not in a bank.

F: Sure, sure. Well, from what you've said, I do have an early suggestion for you to consider.

M: Already? OK, well, what are you thinking?

5.2 Lesson 5.1, Listening, Exercise D
F = Fiona M = Michael

F: Sure, sure. Well, from what you've said, I do have an early suggestion for you to consider.

M: Already? OK, well, what are you thinking?

F: Well, it's clear you like using your people and communication skills, and your personality test shows you're good at organization and time management.

M: That's all true, I think.

F: Yes, and you're looking for a job that has a lot of variety. And you enjoy working on a team.

M: Uh huh.

F: So, have you thought about a career in catering? Not as a waiter or chef, but as the person who organizes the catering at events. You used to work as a waiter at them, how about running them? A catering manager is a good career, and it requires all those skills.

M: Well, I don't know, um, sounds interesting, but, I mean, I don't have any training in that area.

F: But you do have experience of those events, and actually catering companies do look for people with a business studies degree.

M: Do they?

F: Uh huh. And I think that the work of planning and running an event should suit you and your skills.

M: And food and cooking is a hobby of mine.

F: Exactly.

M: OK, well, I'm interested. Let's find out more.

5.5 Lesson 5.2, Listening, Exercise B
C = Clive E = Ella

C: Welcome to the *Business Business* podcast. Today, we're discussing environmental business ideas, and we're starting with the retail sector. I'm talking to our retail expert Ella Stevens.

E: Hello, Clive.

C: Ella, I understand you're going to tell us about a clothing company with some very unusual marketing ideas.

E: Yes. I'm talking today about Patagonia. It's an outdoor activities clothing company based in the US. It was started by Yvon Chouinard in 1973. He used to be a rock climber, and at first, Patagonia made climbing equipment. Since then, it has changed its focus to outdoor clothing.

C: So they make and sell clothing for activities like hiking and skiing, as well as climbing?

E: That's right. Patagonia is one of the largest brands in the outdoor clothing sector, but there are lots of others, such as North Face, Berghaus and Columbia. These brands are now so popular that you see people wearing their clothes all the time, not just when they are out in the country.

C: So what's different about Patagonia?

E: Well, a few years ago, the company launched a new marketing campaign called 'Worn Wear', which encourages customers to buy second-hand Patagonia clothes like old jackets and T-shirts.

C: That is an unusual way to run a business. It's difficult for a clothing company to make a profit selling new clothes if everyone chooses to buy second-hand instead.

E: That's a good point, Clive, but Patagonia goes even further. They also actively encourage their customers to give them their old Patagonia clothes so that they can then sell them as second-hand items.

C: Really? Why are they doing this? There must be a good reason.

E: Well, Patagonia strongly believes in taking care of the environment. They've built a brand based on respecting nature, and they are trying hard to reduce the negative impact that the company has on the world we live in. They believe that by encouraging people to repair their clothes and return them so they can be bought second-hand, they are helping the environment.

C: And is this strategy working for them?

E: Yes, it is, Clive. Patagonia is doing a good job of attracting new customers. As the results show, their sales have increased because of campaigns like 'Worn Wear'. For example, they made record profits on Black Friday a few years ago, and they donated the whole amount to environmental organizations.

C: That's incredible! And I imagine this helped them to make even more money in the long term.

E: It's certainly made their brand more attractive to customers who are concerned about the environment.

C: Is 'Worn Wear' the first time Patagonia has used such an unusual marketing campaign?

E: No, it isn't. Another instance of this is when Patagonia took out a full-page ad in The New York Times that encouraged people NOT to buy one of their jackets because of the damage it would do to the environment. Consequently, they got a lot of media attention.

C: I can imagine – that seems like a fairly risky strategy. Did they sell more jackets?

E: Probably, but there's no doubt that the company has helped to increase people's knowledge about the effect the clothing industry can have on the environment.

C: And it's a very interesting approach to building a brand. Thank you for coming in to talk to us today, Ella. Next on the podcast we're looking at …

Notes

Macmillan Education Limited
4 Crinan Street
London N1 9XW

Companies and representatives throughout the world

American Language Hub Level 3A Student's Book ISBN 978-1-380-04724-3
American Language Hub Level 3A Student's Book with Student's App
ISBN 978-1-380-04718-2

Written by Jeremy Day and Gareth Rees.

With thanks to Signature Manuscripts for the Grammar Hub pages.

First published 2020

Designed by emc design ltd
Illustrated by Rasmus Juul represented by Lemonade Illustration Agency, Daniel Limon (Beehive Illustration)
Cover design by Restless
Cover photograph by Peathegee Inc/Getty Images
Picture research by Emily Taylor and Victoria Gaunt
Café Hub videos produced by Creative Listening
Café Hub video scripts written by James and Luke Vyner

The authors and publishers would like to thank the following for permission to reproduce their photographs:

www.AETHAER.com p54(jar); **Alamy Stock Photo** Cultura Creative (RF) p17(bl), JTB MEDIA CREATION, Inc. p44, EVREN KALINBACAK p51, Iain Masterton p20(tmr), David L. Moore – JPN p56; **Ages** scyther5 p22(camera); **Flickr RF** Martin Pickard pXXIII(m); **Getty Images** andresr pXVII, Howard Berman p52(tr), Phil Boorman pXXV, Marco Bottigelli pXX(l), Paul Bradbury pp29, 28(tr), Peter Cade p21, Helmut Meyer zur Capellen p11(b), Ian Cumming p14(bl), Robert DalyThomas_EyeDesign p26(tr), Stephen Frink p15(bl), Photo By Gabriel@@ p35, Bert Hardy Advertising Archive p52(cr), p52(tl), Creativ Studio Heinemann p55(red leaf), Hinterhaus Productions p28(cr), Hero Images pp17(tl), 52(cl), Mohammad Hossain/EyeEm pXXVII, iStockphoto/DaniloAndjus pXXIII(l), iStockphoto/laurence123 p47(background), iStockphoto/miflippo p59(br), iStockphoto Thinkstock Images pp59(bl), iStockphoto Thinkstock Images/Vladimir Arndt pXXVIII, iStockphoto Thinkstock Images/XiXinXing pXXIII(r), Johner Images p40, George W Johnson p16(l), jgroup pp22-23(Background), LeoPatrizi p45(t), Joe McBride p13, Mediaphotos p20(tr), Betsie Van der Meer pXXVI, Helmut Meyer zur Capellen pp8(t), 9, Morsa Images pXIX(t), Naga Film pp30-31(b), Dimitri Otis p27(br), oversnap pXXI(l), PeopleImages p39(t), PhotoDisc pp34(background), 58-59(background), Sergey Podvarsky/EyeEm p26(tl), Monty Rakusen p50(tr), Photo - Lyn Randle p14(br), VisitBritain/Ben Selway p16(r), stefaniedesign p55,Tetra Images pXX(r); **Helsinki Region Transport** p30(tl); **Hemera** Thinkstock Images p43; **Hero Images** XXI(r); **Imagesource** pp45(b), 10-11(background); **iStockphoto** alexsl p59(bml), taratata p59(bmr); **REX/Shutterstock** Solent News p52(bcr); **Shutterstock** Matveev Aleksandr p55(yellow leaf), Alfazet Chronicles p19(H/S Avatar), goodluz p3(b), Mila Supinskaya Glashchenko p2(t), maxuser p42, Yulia Mayorova p3(b), Pressmaster p50(tmr), wavebreakmedia p50(tml), Wedding Stock Photo p20(tml); **SWNS.com** pp18(t,b); **Thinkstock Images** pidjoe p52(br), Purestock pXIX(b), Rana Faure/Corbis/VCG p19(br), Volhah pp14(H/S Avatar), Andrew Watson p38, Westend61 pp20(tl), 52(bcl), Dong Wenjie, Wenjie Dong pXVI, Oscar Wong p1; **123RF**/anyka p54(background), delcreations p8(b), Kzenon p4, Vitalii Nesterchuk p17(tr), Cathy Yeulet p50(tl).

Commissioned photographs in the Café Hubs by Creative Listening.

The authors and publishers are grateful for permission to reprint the following copyright material:

p8 Extract from 'Why being bilingual helps keep your brain fit' by Gaia Vince. Originally published in Mosaic Science, August 6, 2016. © The Wellcome Trust Limited 2018. Republished under a Creative Commons licence. https://mosaicscience.com/bilingual-brains/

p18 Extract from 'War veteran, 89, posts ad for job to stop him 'dying of boredom" by Alexandra Topping. Originally published in The Guardian, November 29, 2016. Copyright © Guardian News & Media Ltd 2018. Reprinted with permission of The Guardian.

p18 Extract from 'Eager 89-year-old seeks job: café snaps him up' by Alexandra Topping. Originally published in The Guardian, December 1, 2016. Copyright © Guardian News & Media Ltd 2018. Reprinted with permission of The Guardian.

p28 Epley, N., & Schroeder, J. (2014). Mistakenly seeking solitude. Journal of Experimental Psychology: General, 143(5), 1980–1999.

Printed and bound in Brazil

2025

10

American Language Hub

LEVEL 3A
Workbook

with Key + access to Audio

macmillan education

Macmillan Education
4 Crinan Street
London N1 9XW
A division of Macmillan Education Limited

Companies and representatives throughout the world

American Language Hub Level 3A Workbook with Key ISBN 978-1-380-04727-4
American Language Hub Level 3A Workbook with Key + access to Audio
ISBN 978-1-380-04721-2

Written by Signature Manuscripts

Signature Manuscripts has asserted their right to be identified as the author of this work in accordance with the Copyright, Designs and Patents Act 1988.

First published 2020

Designed by SPi Global based on original design by emc design ltd
Cover design based on original design by Restless
Cover image by Getty Images/Peathegee Inc

The authors and publishers would like to thank the following for permission to reproduce their photographs:

Alamy/Cultura Creative p21, Alamy/Antonio Guillem Fernandez p11, Alamy/Rico Ploeg p22, Alamy/Tetra Images p7; **Getty Images** pp6, 31, Getty Images/Cultura RF p25, Getty Images/Dougal Waters Photography Ltd p23(bl), Getty Images/DrAfter123 p8, Getty Images/Hindustan Times p29, Getty Images/iStockphoto pp9(tl), 30, 37, Getty Images/JGI p9(tr), Getty Images/Johner RF p35, Getty Images/Maskot p20, Getty Images/OJO p5, Getty Images/Onoky p16, Getty Images/Rawpixel Ltd p26, Getty Images/Chris Ryan p23(tl), Getty Images/SSPL/NMeM/Daily Herald Archive p33(tr), Getty Images/The Image Bank p14, Getty Images/VisitBritain p28, Getty Images/Tom Werner p17, Getty Images/Westend61 p12; **PhotoDisc**/Getty Images p15; **Shutterstock** p27, Shutterstock/Dean Drobot p10, Shutterstock/Igor0077 p4, Shutterstock/Aigars Reinholds p24; **Macmillan Education Limited** /Paul Bricknell p33(b); **Thinkstock** pp19.

Printed and bound in Mexico
by Compañía Editorial Ultra, S.A. de C.V.

2021 2020
04 03 02 01

Contents

GRAMMAR

Simple present and present progressive

A Underline the correct options to complete the sentences.

1 How many languages *do you speak* / *are you speaking*?

2 I *take* / *am taking* the Number 36 bus to work every morning.

3 Misha *learns* / *is learning* Spanish right now.

4 Ahmed *seems* / *is seeming* to like living in another country for now.

5 I *look* / *am looking* for my tablet. Have you seen it anywhere?

6 They *become* / *are becoming* increasingly depressed with the wet weather.

7 Don't worry – the movie *doesn't contain* / *isn't containing* anything unsuitable for children.

8 My husband *thinks* / *is thinking* of buying a smartphone.

B Complete the table with the verbs in the box.

believe belong bring complain cost get include know mean need own prefer relax seem show take understand want watch write

Stative	Dynamic

C Complete the blog post with the simple present or present progressive form of the verbs in parentheses.

Blog post

My Travel Adventures

2/23/2018 I 12:26pm I 3 comments

What a week we had! I [1] __________ (*relax*) at home now because I [2] __________ (*need*) a good rest. I [3] __________ (*have*) a very busy life but I [4] __________ (*not think*) it's something to complain about. I [5] __________ (*travel*) all over the world for work and I [6] __________ (*love*) that aspect of my job. Last week, we were in Russia. That's me in the photograph, in St. Petersburg. I [7] __________ (*smile*) because it was a beautiful sunny day. It usually [8] __________ (*snow*) in February!

Like | Comment | Share

VOCABULARY
Seeing and hearing

A **Complete the sentences with the correct form of the verbs in the box. You will need to use some of the verbs more than once.**

hear listen look see sound watch

1 Ava ________ like she's been very sick.
2 Do you want to ________ to the podcast about rock climbing?
3 Can you ________ that strange noise coming from the computer?
4 Ute didn't ________ the step in the hallway and tripped over it.
5 I can't talk now because I ________ my favorite comedy series.
6 In today's lesson, we ________ at the use of technology for language learning.
7 That song ________ a lot like an old folk song my father used to sing.
8 Does this dress ________ good on me?

B **Read each sentence. Circle the correct answer, a, b or c.**

1 With her bright pink hair you can always ___ Sandra in a crowd.
 a observe
 b spot
 c stare
2 Part of his job is to ___ people's behavior in group situations.
 a spot
 b recognize
 c observe
3 He edits his selfies so much that sometimes I don't ___ him!
 a recognize
 b observe
 c spot
4 It's very rude to ___ at other people like that!
 a notice
 b stare
 c observe
5 Luckily, my teacher didn't ___ when I arrived five minutes late for class.
 a recognize
 b spot
 c notice

C **Complete the following sentences so that they are true for you.**

1 I enjoy watching ________ (*type of sports/ movies/TV shows*).
2 I've been told I look just like ________ (*family member or celebrity*).
3 I really hate/love the sound of ________ (*noise*).
4 I've been listening to ________ (*music or podcast*) a lot lately.
5 I'm good at noticing when ________ (*thing or action*).

PRONUNCIATION
Schwa /ə/

A **Underline three schwas in each sentence.**

1 We speak a lot of English at home.
2 The Spanish exam was difficult, but I think I passed.
3 I don't usually listen to podcasts.
4 A photo doesn't always show the real you.
5 I met up with an old friend at the park.
6 That's me in the photograph with my family.

1.1 **B** **Listen. Check your answers to Exercise A.**

1.1 **C** **Listen again and repeat each sentence.**

GRAMMAR
Subject and object questions

A Correct the mistakes in each question.

1 What do you guys go out the other night?

____

2 Which do you want, an ice-cream cone?

____

3 What Jack want to do for his birthday next week?

____

4 How much did she have to wait at the bank?

____

5 Who shoes are these?

____

6 How doesn't Laura come to the party with us?

____

B Rewrite these sentences as questions. The underlined words are the answer to each question.

1 <u>Kyoko</u> speaks English with a strong Japanese accent.

Who speaks English with a strong Japanese accent?

2 Danny learned Spanish <u>at a school in Madrid</u>.

____

3 The language lab is open <u>from 10 am to 9 pm</u>.

____

4 You can improve your English <u>by watching English movies</u>.

____

5 <u>Yes</u>, we should ask the teacher what this word means.

____

6 <u>Shakespeare</u> is considered the greatest writer of modern English.

____

7 I'm studying <u>modern American literature</u> this semester.

____

8 We speak <u>Jamaican English</u> at home.

____

C Complete the conversation with one to four words in each space.

Charley: Simone, [1] *how many languages* are spoken in South Africa?

Simone: Well, officially there are 11 languages.

Charley: Wow, that's a lot. [2] ______________ all of them?

Simone: Yes, I can. Well, … a little bit of all of them, and one or two completely.

Charley: [3] ______________ language is your native language?

Simone: I speak Southern Sesotho, which is also called *Sotho*. This language is also commonly spoken in Lesotho.

Charley: Ah, interesting. [4] ______________ for English speakers to learn?

Simone: Yes, it's difficult to learn, unfortunately. It's very different from English.

Charley: Oh, [5] ______________ different?

Simone: Well, there are 9 vowels and 35 consonants, and 3 of the consonants are clicks, written as *x*, *c* and *q*.

Charley: Oh, I've heard about that. [6] ______________ that sound?

Simone: You make it by clicking your tongue against your mouth. It takes some practice to get used to it, but anyone can learn!

Charley: Cool! I'd like to try that. [7] ______________ me how to do it sometime?

Simone: Of course I'll teach you! But [8] ______________ so interested in languages?

Charley: I suppose because I enjoy communicating in very different ways.

1.2 Communication

Who owns English?

VOCABULARY

Languages

A **Match the words (1–7) with the definitions (a–g).**

1 phrase	**a** the way someone pronounces words
2 bilingual	**b** able to speak only one language
3 fluently	**c** (speaking) correctly, without making mistakes
4 accent	**d** able to speak two languages
5 accurately	**e** any small group of words that form a single meaning
6 monolingual	**f** a group of words which, when used together, have a different meaning from the individual words
7 idiom	**g** (speaking) easily, without difficulty

B **Complete the sentences with the words from Exercise A.**

1 When teachers want you to use a dictionary to find out the meaning of a word, they usually use the ________________ *Look it up!*

2 His tongue wasn't literally tied; to 'have your tongue tied' is a(n) ________________ meaning that you have nothing to say.

3 I can't speak Russian ________________, but I can understand it when I hear it.

4 Many English speakers are ________________ because they don't have a major need to learn another language.

5 I can tell by her ________________ that she's from Argentina.

6 If you don't spell the words ________________, you will lose points.

7 Canadians living in Quebec are usually ________________; they can speak both French and English.

PRONUNCIATION

Pronouncing questions

1.2 **A** **Listen to the speakers and underline which question you hear.**

1 **a** What do you learn in class?
b What did you learn in class?

2 **a** What do you want for lunch?
b What did you want for lunch?

3 **a** How do you like your class?
b How did you like your class?

4 **a** How do you know Marcus?
b How did you know Marcus?

5 **a** Do you want to use my phone?
b Did you want to use my phone?

B **Practice saying the questions in Exercise A.**

1.2 **C** **Listen again and check your pronunciation.**

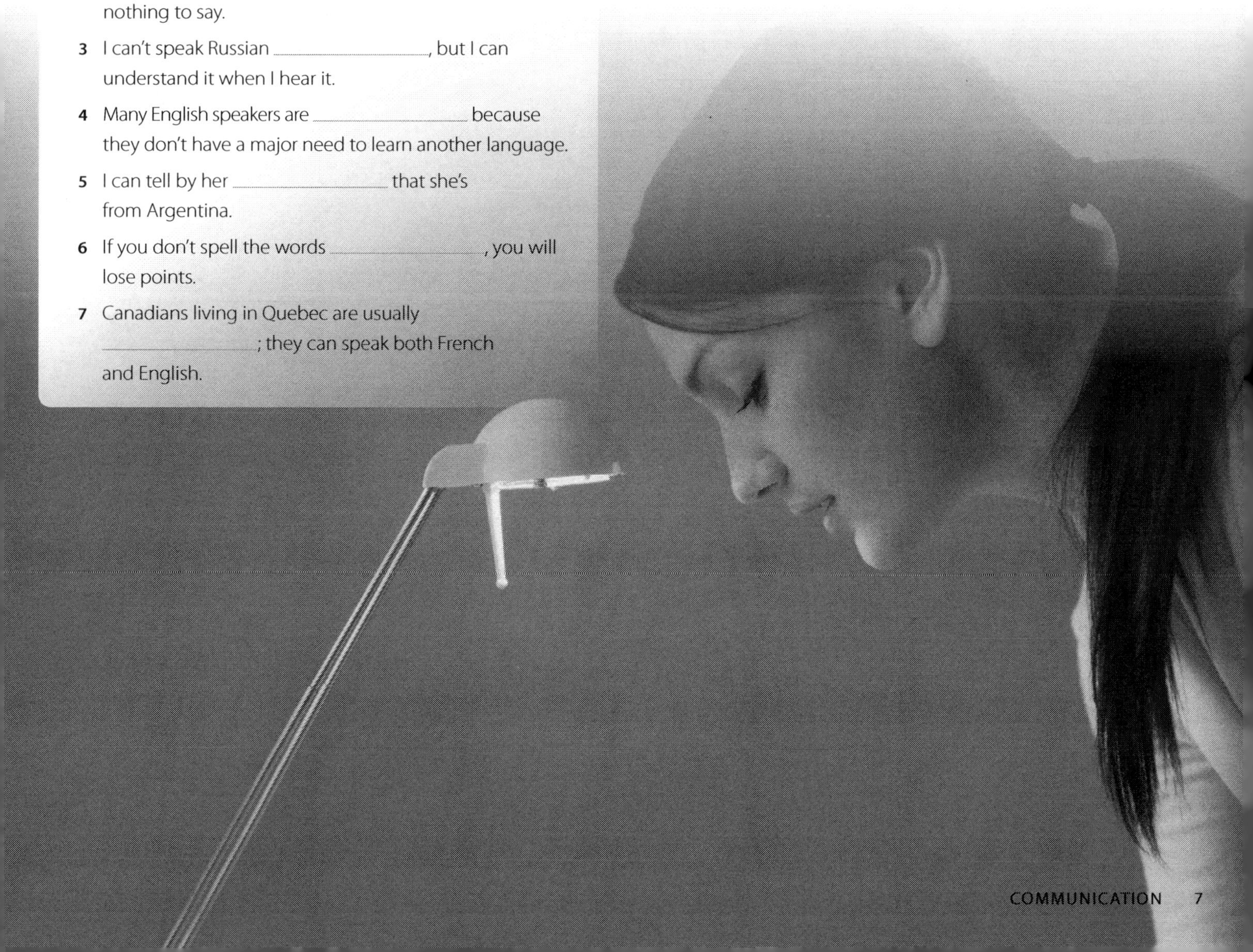

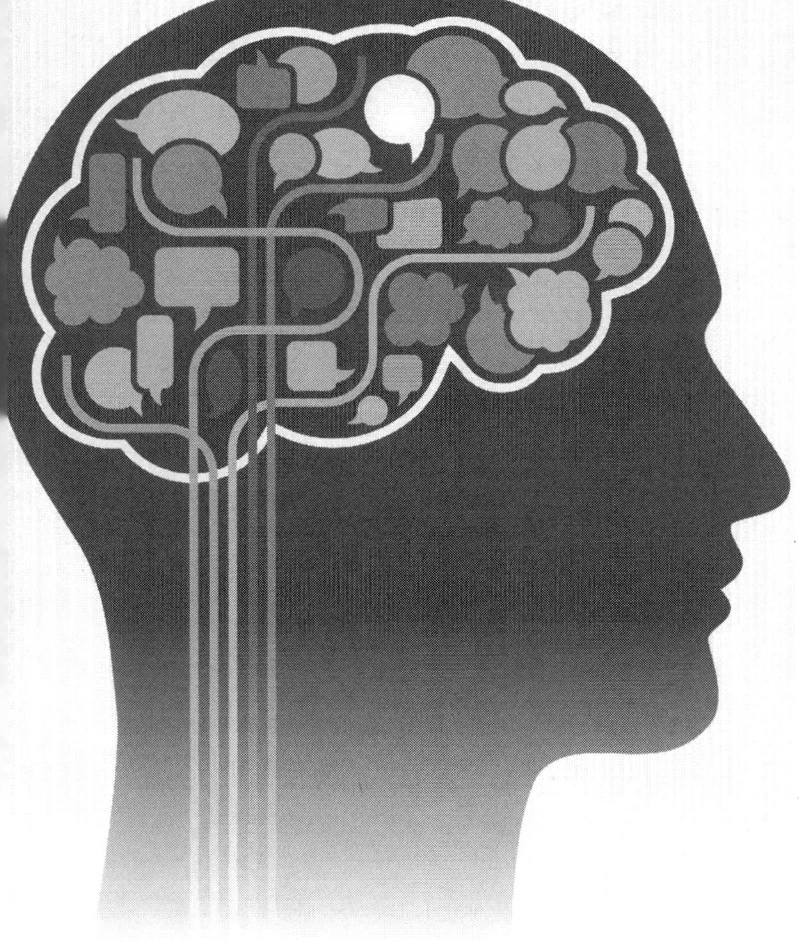

READING

A PREDICT What are some possible answers to these questions?

1. Are there countries where more than ten languages are spoken?
2. How many languages do you think it's possible for one person to learn?
3. Does learning a new language make us more intelligent?

B READ FOR GIST Read *Secrets of the super language learners* quickly to check your predictions.

C READ FOR DETAIL Match the rhetorical questions with paragraphs 1–3 of the article. There are two rhetorical questions you do not need to use.

a. What are the benefits of speaking other languages?
b. Do monolinguals have better memories?
c. How many languages is it possible for one person to learn?
d. Are hyperglots smarter than the rest of us?
e. What's the record number of languages spoken?

Secrets of the super language learners

1 ___ Some European citizens may use two or three languages regularly, but the number of languages spoken in some African countries is incredible. Cameroon in Central Africa has an amazing 250! People who have learned several languages through hearing them on a daily basis are known as *multilinguals*. A different type of learner altogether is the *hyperglot* – a person who has spent their entire life learning and perfecting dozens of different languages.

2 ___ This question is difficult to answer as some of the world's most famous hyperglots lived many years ago. Emil Krebs, who was born in 1867, spoke and wrote 68 languages fluently and also studied another 120 languages. In more recent times, Kenneth Hale, an American college professor, probably holds the modern-day record with 50 languages spoken. What's more, he could pick up a new language with incredible speed and was able to have a basic conversation after just 15 minutes of listening to a native speaker.

3 ___ Studies have shown that the brain activity of both multilinguals and hyperglots is very different from that of people who speak only one language. The act of learning a new language, like any cognitive process, builds new neural pathways and actually increases the size of the brain. Other benefits include improved ability to focus and better memory.

Glossary

cognitive (adj) related to mental processes such as memory, reasoning, etc
neural pathway (n) nerve cells that receive messages from your brain
pick up (phr v) to learn a new language without effort or study

D REFLECT Think about the answers to these questions.

1. Do you think learning many languages is a good idea?
2. Which new language(s) would you like to learn? Why?

1.4 Communication

Listening; Functional Language

5:15 pm: In today's *TechHub*,
presenter John Grimes examines the selfie phenomenon.

LISTENING

1.3 **A PREDICT** Look at the pictures and the magazine listing and circle the best answer. Listen to the introduction and check your answers.

1. I'm going to hear *an advertisement for a selfie camera / part of a radio show.*
2. The recording will be about *selfie addiction / a new selfie app*.

1.4 **B LISTEN FOR GIST** Listen to the full interview and answer the questions.

1. The purpose of *Meitu* is to
   - **a** share your personal information.
   - **b** create the perfect selfie.
2. *Meitu* is
   - **a** the same as other similar apps.
   - **b** better and more advanced than other similar apps.

Glossary

facial recognition technology (n) computer technology used to scan and recognize human faces
launch (v) to start selling a new product or service
retouch (v) to make small changes to a photo or picture

1.4 **C LISTEN FOR DETAIL** Are the sentences true (T) or false (F)? Correct the false sentences. Then listen again and check your answers.

1. *Meitu* is a new app.
2. It is only available in Asia.
3. *Meitu* is for people who want to look perfect.
4. The user ends up looking like a different person.
5. The app is now being used by airport security companies.
6. *Meitu* is different because it has access to all your personal information.

D REFLECT Think about the answers to these questions.

1. How important is it to look good in selfies?
2. Are you worried about phone apps accessing your personal information? Why/Why not?

FUNCTIONAL LANGUAGE

Asking for, offering and responding to help

A Complete the conversation with one or two words in each space.

Jess: Would you [1] ________ me a hand with something?
Matt: I'd be happy [2] ________. What's the problem?
Jess: I'm trying to download *Meitu* onto my phone. It's a Chinese photo-editing app.
Matt: First go to your settings and click on *clear cache*.
Jess: OK. I've done that.
Matt: Now you need to restart your phone. Do you want me [3] ________ that?
Jess: That [4] ________ great. If [5] ________ mind.
Matt: No problem. There you [6] ________.
Jess: Thank you so much.

B Circle the correct words to complete the conversation.

Milo: Do you want a [1]*hand / help* with your project?
Fiona: Hi, Milo. Yes, I could use your [2]*hand / help*. I have to Photoshop this picture I drew in art class.
Milo: Hmm. That isn't going to be [3]*nice / easy* because your computer is slow. Why don't you use my laptop?
Fiona: Thanks, Milo. You're [4]*a myth / amazing*! I owe you one!
Milo: Actually, I need a [5]*help / favor*, too. My drawing is terrible. Can you help me draw it again?
Fiona: Of course I can.

WRITING

A Look at the results of a college survey and answer the questions.

Where do you get your news?

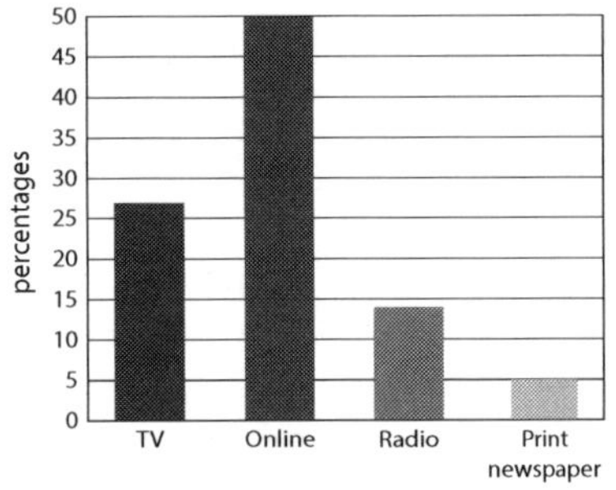

1 Are these results surprising? Why/Why not?
2 Where do you and your friends usually get your news?

B ORGANIZATION Match the sections (a–g) from a report about trends in news media with the paragraphs in which you think they will appear. Then read the report to check your ideas.

a Where they got their information.
b A summary of the situation.
c The purpose of the report.
d Information about TV news.
e Information about radio news.
f Information about print newspapers.
g Information about online news.

Introduction: ___, ___
Paragraph 1: ___
Paragraph 2: ___
Paragraph 3: ___, ___
Conclusion: ___

C Match the headings (a–f) to the paragraphs (1–3) in the report. There are three headings you do not need to use.

a Nobody watches TV these days.
b Digital is more popular than print.
c Where most students get the news.
d Newspapers are boring.
e Why television scores low.
f Online news tops the charts.

Report about trends in news media

Statistics suggest that young people today are not particularly interested in *hard news*. We [1]***conducted / did*** a survey to see how true this is. While our results might seem to confirm the statistics, they do not give the whole picture.

1 ___

Half of those surveyed got their news online. [2]***A lot of them said / Many claimed*** that they did not have time to keep up with all the news and preferred to read brief summaries. If there was a big news story, they followed it in greater detail.

2 ___

The surprisingly low figure for television news is partly explained by the fact that few of them have televisions. This does not suggest [3]***they don't like / a lack of interest in*** the news.

3 ___

The very low percentage of print newspaper readers is [4]***due to the fact that / because*** most newspapers have an online version. Those that got their news from the radio said that it was because they had the radio on most of the time anyway.

Conclusion

While it is true that few young people read print newspapers or watch television news, this is a sign of the times. [5]***I know that / It seems that*** they get the news they want online and are as well-informed as any previous generation.

D USING FORMAL LANGUAGE Circle the more formal phrases to complete the report.

WRITING PRACTICE

A PREPARE You are going to write a report about trends in the use of technology for education.

- Choose two or three points to include in your report. These will be your main paragraphs.

B WRITE Write your report in 150–200 words. Remember:

- to start with an introduction, stating the purpose of your report and where you got your information.
- to provide suitable headings for each paragraph.
- to use formal language.
- to end with a conclusion.

PRONUNCIATION
's and 've

2.1 **A Listen to eight sentences. Complete the sentences with a missing word or contraction.**

1 ________________ planted a tree.
2 ________________ finished my work.
3 ________________ made a list.
4 ________________ started an online course.
5 ________________ saved a lot of money.
6 ________________ climbed a mountain.
7 ________________ started a new job.
8 ________________ made our decision.

B Practice saying the sentences in Exercise A.

GRAMMAR
Present perfect and simple past

A Complete the conversation with the present perfect or simple past form of the verbs in parentheses.

Alex: So, [1] ________________ you ever ________________ (*make*) a bucket list?

Bex: Yes, I have. I [2] ________________ (*write*) one about five years ago. But I [3] ________________ (*not do*) many of the things yet!

Alex: How many [4] ________________ you ________________ (*do*) so far?

Bex: Only one, actually! On my last birthday, I [5] ________________ (*go*) skydiving. That [6] ________________ (*be*) wonderful. So, only 99 more things to do! How about you?

Alex: Oh, I [7] ________________ never ________________ (*make*) a bucket list. My brother [8] ________________ (*write*) one, though. He's always doing the things on his list.

Bex: Such as?

Alex: Well, for example, already this year, he [9] ________________ (*learn*) how to fly. Last December, he [10] ________________ (*go*) swimming with dolphins. He loves doing new and unusual things if he has the money.

B Underline the correct option to complete the sentences.

1 I *still* / *yet* haven't visited Australia, but I will one day.
2 My friend *has gone* / *went* swimming with dolphins last year.
3 Where is the most memorable place you *have ever been* / *ever went*?
4 I've *still* / *just* solved a difficult problem we had at work.
5 Philippe *has been* / *was* here for three months so far.
6 I've *just* / *never* wanted to do anything daring, like climbing a mountain.
7 Marta *went* / *has gone* skydiving on her 30th birthday.
8 I've been so busy that I haven't answered that email *already* / *yet*.

C Complete the blog so that it is true for you.

Have you ever ...? blog

When I was younger two of my dreams were ________________ and ________________.

Unfortunately I haven't ________________ yet, but I have ________________.

I achieved my dream ________________ (*when*) in ________________ (*where*). I was with ________________ (*who*) at time. I felt so ________________ (*emotion*).

VOCABULARY
Collocations: making big decisions

A Complete the collocations with the verbs in the box.

lose make (x2) put set stay take turn work

1 ________ the next step
2 ________ a plan into action
3 ________ a dream into reality
4 ________ short-term and long-term goals
5 ________ heart
6 ________ the break
7 ________ toward a goal
8 ________ motivated
9 ________ a decision

B Complete the sentences with the collocations from Exercise A.

1 Don't ________ – we'll get to the top of the mountain in the end.
2 We have to find a way to stay ________, otherwise we'll never finish this project.
3 Making a list of your plans and ambitions is great in theory, but you won't achieve them unless you put those plans ________.
4 Leaving home is a difficult decision, Anya, but I really think you need to make ________ and learn to be independent.
5 You came first in the local talent contest, but are you ready to take ________ and audition for the national contest?
6 I have to make ________ – do I stay at this job or look for something better?
7 Giles is working toward ________ of becoming a successful businessman.
8 We all have a dream, but some of us manage to turn that dream ________.
9 I know what I want to achieve in the long term, but it's important to set ________ along the way.

VOCABULARY
Dependent prepositions (verb / adjective + *for / of*)

A Match the beginnings of the sentences (1–8) with the endings (a–h).

1 This job would only be suitable
2 Management doesn't seem to be aware
3 It was typical
4 Niaz has asked for
5 Sally is very proud
6 In my first job I worked
7 It can be difficult to prepare
8 Are you looking

a of Joel to try to solve the problem on his own.
b for an animal charity as a volunteer.
c for someone who speaks Japanese.
d for your first job interview.
e of herself for learning how to surf.
f permission to take the day off.
g of how big the problem is.
h for a new job now?

B Complete the sentences with the collocations from Exercise A.

1 Anyone who takes up mountaineering should be ________ the dangers involved.
2 Sandra was going to take her kids to see a new fantasy movie; luckily her sister warned her that it wasn't ________ children before she bought the tickets.
3 The dishes in the restaurant were very ________ the region – all the food was delicious!
4 Thomas spent all morning ________ his keys, but he still couldn't find them.
5 Melissa is ________ a big tech company in California. She absolutely loves it there.
6 Lara's parents were so ________ her when she graduated from college last year.
7 The couple in the café ________ their bill.
8 Claire has been ________ her first marathon for the past six months.

Problems and solutions

C Complete the letter of advice with the correct form of the verbs in the box.

agree analyze cause come deal solve suggest

Dear Carlo,

In your letter you told me that you don't know how to [1] ________ with a difficult situation at work. Well, first you need to think about what's [2] ________ the problem. You say that whenever you [3] ________ solutions for problems at work, your boss is very negative and just rejects them all. Have you tried [4] ________ up with a variety of different solutions? Do you try to look at all the different ways you can [5] ________ a work problem? Maybe your boss thinks that your ideas aren't flexible enough. And finally, get together with your colleagues to [6] ________ each issue as it occurs. Maybe if you work together and [7] ________ on a plan of action, your boss will be less likely to reject it!

PRONUNCIATION
Word stress: verbs with two syllables

A Put the verbs in the box in the correct column.

achieve focus manage regret study suggest

Verbs with stress on first syllable	Verbs with stress on second syllable
________	________
________	________
________	________

2.2 **B Listen to the verbs. Check your answers to Exercise A. Listen again.**

GRAMMAR
Present and past ability

A **Circle the correct option to complete the interview.**

Interviewer: Today, my guest is 52-year-old Lydia Maleknia. Lydia, you have completed two full marathons now, but you told me earlier that two years ago you [1]***couldn't / can't*** even run 200 meters without getting tired!

Lydia: That's right! I started running a couple of years ago to get in shape and now I [2]***am able to / could*** run 26 miles in under four hours.

Interviewer: Amazing. You also said that you found the motivation to train when you read about the difficulties other women marathon runners had faced in the past.

Lydia: Yes, I did. Kathrine Switzer, for example, is an inspirational athlete. She only [3]***could / managed to*** get a place in the 1967 Boston Marathon because the organizers didn't realize she was a woman.

Interviewer: [4]***Could she / Was she able to*** finish the race?

Lydia: Yes, she finished the race – and she proved that both women and men [5]***are able to / manage*** run marathons.

Interviewer: You also [6]***managed to / could*** show your friends and family that it isn't only young people who [7]***can / could*** run marathons.

Lydia: Yes, that's right. My daughter was so happy when I got a medal for the fastest time in my age group that she [8]***didn't manage to / couldn't*** stop crying!

B **Complete the second sentence so that it has a similar meaning to the first sentence, using the word given. Use between two and five words.**

1 How is Kate able to work and take care of her children?
MANAGE
How ______________ work and take care of her children?

2 Joe Bartley likes the fact that he can work part-time at the café.
ABLE
Joe Bartley enjoys ______________ part-time at the café.

3 Callum didn't manage to do much preparation for the interview.
NOT
Callum was ______________ for the interview very well.

4 Helga's low wage means that she can't spend much money on clothes.
SPEND
Helga's low wage means that she is not ______________ much money on clothes.

5 Were you able to speak French before you went to France?
COULD
______________ French before you went to France?

6 We weren't able to solve the problem.
DIDN'T
We ______________ a solution to the problem.

7 Just think what it would be like to swim with dolphins!
IMAGINE
Can you ______________ to swim with dolphins!

Walk on the Wild Side

READING

A READ FOR GIST Read *Walk on the Wild Side* quickly and circle the correct option for each sentence.

1 The article is about people who *don't want smartphones / want a simpler life*.
2 Dan Usher is *a TV announcer / somebody who lives in a remote place*.
3 According to Tessa, her lifestyle is suitable *for everyone / for some people*.

B Read the article again. Match the words and phrases in bold from the article (1–6) with their meanings (a–f). Underline the parts of the text which helped you understand the meanings.

1 off the grid ____	a easy to find or get to
2 the rat race ____	b things you need to live
3 accessible ____	c with no modern technology
4 supplies ____	d fixing
5 maintaining ____	e change ideas or behavior
6 adapt themselves ____	f modern life

C READ FOR DETAIL Read the article again. Are the sentences true (T) or false (F)?

1 The people on the TV show reject modern technology. ____
2 They sometimes have to share their homes with rats. ____
3 You cannot get to the island by helicopter. ____
4 Tessa and Jack had to transport all the things they would need. ____
5 They have to be good at fixing things. ____
6 Dan thinks the couple is good at solving problems. ____

Glossary

isolation (n) the state of being alone
lighthouse (n) a tower built next to the ocean with a flashing light to warn ships of danger
readings (n pl) measurements
remote (adj) far away from other people or places

D REFLECT Think about the answers to these questions.

1 How would you feel about living off the grid?
2 Would you like to live on Maatsuyker Island? Why/Why not?

For some people, the idea of being without their smartphone for an hour is enough to send shivers down their spine. But how about being without an internet connection, without electricity, without a car – completely **off the grid**? Who would willingly put themselves into such a situation? The answer is – a growing number of men and women who want to leave behind the security of a nine-to-five routine to explore the wild places of the Earth.

In the new series of *Walk on the Wild Side*, Dan Usher travels to the remotest corners of the Earth to meet some of the daring people who have left **the rat race** behind to find a way of life that is simpler and more satisfying.

In the first episode, Dan visited Maatsuyker Island, Australia's southernmost lighthouse station. Tasmania Parks and Wildlife Service advertized for a couple to live on the island for a period of six months. **Accessible** only by helicopter, a six-month stay on the island means total isolation and very little communication with the outside world. However, this didn't daunt Tessa and Jack Littleton who made the decision to come and live here.

'Although we have a landline, it's usually out of order and our only other means of communication is the emergency radio,' explains Jack. 'Obviously there's no internet or email. At the beginning of our stay, we had to bring all the **supplies** we would need for six months – food, fuel, clothing and bedding.'

I asked Tessa what everyday life is like. 'Our jobs on the island include cutting the grass, taking weather readings, **maintaining** the buildings and the lighthouse – things are regularly broken or damaged by the wind and rain. It isn't for everyone, but we love the challenge.' Weather conditions on the island are extreme with strong winds and frequent storms which cause a variety of problems.

At the end of his visit to the island, presenter Dan told viewers, 'What was most interesting about these people was that they are able to deal with change on a daily basis. They have an amazing ability to accept new situations and **adapt themselves** to new surroundings.'

LISTENING

A PREDICT Look at the picture and the caption. Check (✓) the things you think a guidance counselor does.

1 analyzes situations ☐
2 teaches students ☐
3 solves problems ☐
4 suggests solutions ☐
5 deals with money ☐

2.3 **B LISTEN FOR THE MAIN IDEA** Listen to an interview with a guidance counselor and check your ideas from Exercise A. Complete the job description with the words in the box.

adults dealing decisions pressure solve support

Children and young [1]________ need guidance and [2]________, especially when it comes to [3]________ with academic, personal, parental and social [4]________. A guidance counselor assists young people by listening to their concerns and uses different techniques to help them to [5]________ problems and make the right [6]________.

2.3 **C LISTEN FOR DETAIL** Listen again and complete the sentences (1–7) with one word in each space. The first letters have been given to help you.

1 The main focus of the interview is how Gareth helps young people to make l________-ch________ d________.
2 Young people have to deal with f________ t________, exams, as well as worrying about their career prospects.
3 Gareth asks young people to write down a l________ of advantages and disadvantages.
4 Sometimes parents d________ a________ with the choices their children are making.
5 Gareth believes that it's important to set l________-t________ g________ and not just to think about the near future.
6 It can be helpful to imagine that you are giving a________ to a friend.
7 It's possible to spend too much t________ and e________ thinking about a difficult situation.

Glossary

fatigue (n) tiredness
imaginary (adj) not real, only existing in the mind

D REFLECT Think about the answers to these questions.

1 Have you ever spoken to a guidance counselor? Would you like to?
2 Do you think that Gareth's suggestions for making decisions were helpful? Why/Why not?

Come and talk to our guidance counselor
– any time between 9 am and 5 pm.

FUNCTIONAL LANGUAGE

Asking for, giving and refusing permission

Complete the conversation with the words and phrases in the box.

can call can we start if I ask I'd like I'm afraid I'm sorry must be would it be

Tania: Hi. Is this the right place for the skydiving club?
Jamal: Yep! Let me see. You [1]________ Tania. I saw your name on the list of new members.
Tania: Yes, that's me! But you [2]________ me 'Tan' – all my friends do.
Jamal: OK, Tan. Well, I'm going to need a few details from you. Is it alright [3]________ you a few questions?
Tania: No problem. What do you need to know?
Jamal: [4]________ with your height? How tall are you, Tan?
Tania: [5]________, but I don't understand why you need to know that.
Jamal: It's for the safety equipment. I need to have your measurements so I can provide you with the right kit.
Tania: Oh, OK. I'm one meter and 70 centimeters.
Jamal: Good – that's fine. And, how old are you?
Tania: I'm 17.
Jamal: Oh dear. You're too young; our rules say that you have to be 18 to join the club.
Tania: [6]________ OK to *say* I'm 18? It doesn't matter, does it? Just write down '18'.
Jamal: [7]________ that isn't possible. We take safety very seriously, Tania. [8]________ to help, but at the end of the day I'm responsible for you and the other club members. You'll just have to come back again next year.
Tania: What a disappointment!
Jamal: Sorry, Tania.

WRITING

A Which of these sentences or phrases are you most likely to see in an email from a friend or family member?

1 I look forward to hearing from you.
2 A friend of mine's just gotten married.
3 Yours truly
4 You'll never guess what happened!
5 Lots of love
6 I'm writing in reply to your email from July 7th .
7 Hi Mike
8 Know what I mean ☺?

B USING INFORMAL LANGUAGE Rewrite these sentences in informal language.

1 I apologize for not having written sooner.
2 I am most grateful for the advice you gave me.
3 I hope this email finds you in good health.
4 I didn't attend due to the fact that I was unwell.
5 I haven't found suitable accommodations yet.

C Read Heike's email to Adriana and circle the best answers.

1 Heike ***rarely*** / ***regularly*** writes to her friend, Adriana.
2 Heike has some ***good*** / ***bad*** news.
3 She is ***sure*** / ***not sure*** about her plans for the future.
4 She thinks Adriana ***will not*** / ***will*** be able to help her.

D USING INFORMAL LANGUAGE Find at least one example of each of these in Heike's email.

1 informal opening and closing expressions
2 sentences with incomplete grammar
3 informal punctuation
4 contractions
5 informal words and phrases
6 an emoji

WRITING PRACTICE

A PREPARE You are going to write an informal email to a friend telling him/her about some good news you've received and asking for advice. Think about the answers to these questions and write notes.

1 Who are you writing to?
2 What's your good news?
3 What advice do you need from your friend?

B WRITE Write your email in 150–200 words.

- Use your notes and ideas from Exercise A.
- Remember to use an informal writing style.

To: Adriana

Subject: Hard choice

Hi Adriana,

What's up? It's been a couple of weeks since I last wrote, but a lot of stuff's been happening. Remember I told you I was applying for jobs at fashion magazines? I thought I'd made a mess of the interviews, but obviously not. Guess what? I've been accepted by two!!! Woo-hoo!

Trouble is, though, I don't know which one to go for! They're both well-paid, but the one that pays best is in London! The other one's here in New York. So what to do? I'll be far away from my friends and family if I go to the UK. Plus, I'll have to find somewhere to live, make new friends … I know it's a great opportunity, but … what do you think?

It would be so cool if we could talk about this in person. How about going out for coffee? It would really help me to talk it all through with you. Great new café has opened near me – it's called *Bean There* (like 'coffee bean' – get it? lol ☺). Let me know if you can make it.

Love to you & Dave & the baby,

Heike

GRAMMAR
Narrative tenses

A Circle the correct answer, a, b or c.

1 I ___ down the street when a bus passed by and splashed water all over me!
   a was walking
   b walked
   c had walked

2 It was a typical Monday morning commute; the trains were running late and everyone ___ about it.
   a complained
   b was complaining
   c had complained

3 Elsa took her seat on the plane, but after ten minutes, the flight attendant ___ a delay.
   a had announced
   b was announcing
   c announced

4 She turned around to pay the taxi driver, but he ___ off and was nowhere to be seen.
   a already drove
   b had already driven
   c was already driving

5 Hamish saw a great travel deal online and ___ it immediately.
   a was reserving
   b had reserved
   c reserved

6 Because Hank ___ a cheap ticket, he couldn't change it without paying a penalty.
   a bought
   b had bought
   c was buying

7 Although the weather was bad, it ___ when the accident occurred.
   a was raining
   b rained
   c wasn't raining

8 She wanted to sit in the back by the window, but someone ___ the seat already.
   a had taken
   b took
   c was taking

B Rewrite the verbs in bold in the story using the correct forms of the simple past, past progressive or past perfect.

Chapter one: An observation

While Louis [1]**drove** ___*was driving*___ to work one day, he noticed a bike lane on his street.

He [2]**didn't see** ______ it before, so he guessed that it was new. He mentioned it to his neighbors, but they said it [3]**was** ______ there for months. 'How did I not notice that?' Louis wondered to himself.

He [4]**had decided** ______ to give the *new* bike lane a try. So, the next day, he got his bicycle out of the garage and [5]**was leaving** ______ home half an hour early, to give himself more time to get to work. As he rode down the street, he [6]**had suddenly found** ______ that he was looking at his neighborhood in a completely new way.

He [7]**had seen** ______ the children walking to school, the trees by the side of the road and his neighbors calling out greetings. He [8]**was never noticing** ______ these things before because he usually took his car to work. Now commuting to work had become the best part of his work day!

VOCABULARY
Collocations: travel information

A Match the beginnings of the sentences (1–8) with the endings (a–h).

1 Be careful driving here; the road	___	a rain, so drive slowly on the way to Revi's house.
2 If I leave during rush	___	b light is red and I have to wait for it to turn green to go!
3 Is there a subway	___	c hour, the highways will be packed.
4 I really hate overcrowded	___	d buses because there's never anywhere to sit!
5 We're in a terrible traffic	___	e work up ahead, so we'll have to go by a different route.
6 Steven, the traffic	___	f sign says there are falling rocks.
7 The forecast is for heavy	___	g line that runs below this building?
8 There is road	___	h jam – we haven't moved for 20 minutes!

Nouns ending in *-ion*

B Rewrite the following verbs as a noun using *-ion*. Other spelling changes may be necessary.

1 connect ____________
2 decide ____________
3 pollute ____________
4 act ____________
5 react ____________
6 situate ____________

C Complete the blog post with the nouns from Exercise B.

Goodbye, car! Hello, clean air!

I've finally made the [1] ____________ to stop using my car and start using public transportation. Well, we all know that there is a direct [2] ____________ between cars and air [3] ____________.

But what was my inspiration for making this choice? The [4] ____________ in my home city is particularly bad; the air quality is just terrible. One day, I noticed an ugly brown cloud hanging over the city and my [5] ____________ was one of disgust. And that was it – I parked my car in the garage and that's where it's going to stay.

Now I use buses and I usually walk short distances. We simply can't have the expectation that our environment will improve if we ourselves do not take [6] ____________.

PRONUNCIATION
Word stress in nouns ending in *-ion*

A 3.1 Listen to two speakers saying the same sentence. Check (✓) the speaker who pronounces the *-ion* word correctly.

1 *information*
Speaker A: ☑ Speaker B: ☐

2 *reaction*
Speaker A: ☐ Speaker B: ☐

3 *decision*
Speaker A: ☐ Speaker B: ☐

4 *destination*
Speaker A: ☐ Speaker B: ☐

5 *expression*
Speaker A: ☐ Speaker B: ☐

6 *situation*
Speaker A: ☐ Speaker B: ☐

B Practice saying the *-ion* words in Exercise A.

GRAMMAR
Articles and quantifiers

A Fill in the blanks with *a/an, the* or – (no article).

Bicycles are better

Everyone wants to live in 1 _______ town or city without pollution. And, naturally, we also want 2 _______ town or city where we live to be people-friendly and easy to get around. But, like all 3 _______ city-dwellers, we know there's 4 _______ issue with transportation. How do we get around without causing pollution? The city of 5 _______ Helsinki is 6 _______ European capital that has always embraced bikes and bike riding, so why not here in 7 _______ US, too? Officials in American cities throughout the country need to do more to encourage people to use 8 _______ bicycles by creating more bike lanes and safe spaces for bike riders.

B Circle the correct option to complete the sentences.

1 How *few / much / many* luggage are we allowed to take on the plane?
2 There aren't *much / enough / plenty* trains during rush hour, so they're usually very crowded.
3 I have very *enough / much / little* money so I can't afford to buy a new car.
4 There's *plenty of / little / too much* time until the train leaves – let's go and get some coffee.
5 Would you like *very few / a lot / a little* sugar in your tea?
6 The Kutsuplus service had *enough / a lot of / too many* advantages.
7 *Few / Little / A few* people use the local bus service, so it's in danger of being canceled.
8 I can't hear you – there's *plenty of / not enough / too much* noise in this train car!

C Complete the sentences with one word in each space.

1 There was _______________ of traffic in the city center today.
2 We'd better buy some gas because we don't have _______________ left.
3 There aren't _______________ seats for everybody to sit down.
4 There's _______________ chance of finding a taxi at this time of the day.
5 _______________ of pollution is created by private cars.
6 Sadly _______________ few people in my town use bicycles as a means of transportation.

PRONUNCIATION
Sentence stress: quantifiers

3.2 **A** Listen and underline the quantifiers the speakers stress in each sentence.

1 A lot of people were angry about the delay.
2 There were a few trains operating on Sunday.
3 Were there many people on the bus?
4 There's too much traffic in the city center.
5 Do you have enough money for the tickets?
6 There's little chance of leaving early today.

B Practice saying the sentences in Exercise A with the correct intonation.

VOCABULARY
Gradable and ungradable adjectives

A Underline the correct answers to complete the letter to a newspaper.

Dear Sir/Madam,

Yesterday's article on reducing traffic in towns and cities was [1]***really / completely*** interesting and I wanted to add my thoughts on the issue.

Many of my friends find it [2]***absolutely / a little*** surprising that I have never learned to drive. I point out to them that since I live in a big city, it is [3]***completely / very*** easy to get around using public transportation.

Some of them are [4]***very furious / furious*** when I point out that driving cars is [5]***extremely / a little*** damaging to the environment and the number one cause of air pollution in our cities. I find it [6]***very funny / very hilarious*** how people react to unpleasant truths.

I look forward to more articles on this topic.

Sincerely,
Femi Oke

B Which adjectives collocate with *very*? Put a check mark (✓) or an ✗ in the box.

1 brilliant ☐
2 enormous ☐
3 smart ☐
4 impossible ☐
5 filthy ☐
6 excellent ☐
7 dirty ☐
8 large ☐

C Complete the sentences using an adjective from Exercise A or Exercise B.

1 The exam was almost __________. No one in the class got more than 30%!
2 Stephen Hawking was considered to be one of the most __________ physicists of his generation.
3 The skyscraper being built in the city center is going to be __________.
4 My boss was __________ with me when I accidently deleted some important files.
5 Simon's van is absolutely __________. He really should get it cleaned.
6 We knew the movie would be funny, but it was __________. I'd definitely recommend seeing it.

READING

A PREDICT Look at the title of the article and the picture and answer the questions.

1 What do you think the article is going to be about?
2 Will the tone of the article be positive or negative?

B SKIM Read the article quickly, paying particular attention to the paragraph headings. Complete each paragraph with the missing topic sentences (a–e).

a Maybe the most important, but also the most expensive, innovation will be the insertion of thousands of tiny sensors into the surface of highways and main roads.
b Smart road technology, including solar-powered road surfaces, wi-fi communication and embedded sensors, will transform road transportation as we know it.
c The term *smart road* covers a range of developing technologies which scientists believe will transform the future of road transportation.
d Modern roads have been in existence for more than a hundred years.
e While the electronic surface-to-vehicle system will help drivers, a different kind of technology is being developed to help the environment.

C READ FOR DETAIL Read the article again. Circle the correct answer, a, b or c.

1 What has changed during the last 100 years?
 a Only cars
 b Only roads
 c Cars and roads
2 The term *smart roads* refers to
 a road safety applications.
 b a range of technologies.
 c the use of solar energy.
3 Using smart road technology, drivers will be able to
 a ignore traffic lights.
 b communicate with each other.
 c make time-saving choices.
4 The vehicles of the future will
 a work better in winter.
 b be powered by the road.
 c be made of glass.

D REFLECT Think about the answers to these questions.

1 What are the advantages of smart road technology?
2 When do you think this technology will exist in your country?

Glossary

congestion (n) when a road is crowded with vehicles, so that it is difficult for them to move
fossil fuel (n) a fuel such as gas, oil or coal
relay (v) to communicate information
sensor (n) an electronic device that reacts to changes such as the amount of heat or movement

Smart roads: the transportation technology of the future?

What is the situation today?

1 ___ The smooth, solid surface allows us to drive cars, trucks and buses over short and long distances, connecting us to other people, cities and faraway places. Modern cars, with their incredibly powerful engines, GPS systems and excellent safety features, would be unrecognizable to the road user of a hundred years ago. However, the roads they drive on remain largely unchanged by time or technology.

What are *smart roads*?

2 ___ Some technological advances include the creation of road surfaces which will generate power using solar energy, and wi-fi communication between vehicles and the road surface. Another advance is the monitoring of road traffic in order to reduce congestion and improve driving times and road safety.

How can they improve traffic congestion?

3 ___ The sensors will register the number of cars passing over them. This information will be relayed to the traffic control system which will change speed limits, traffic lights and recommended routes, depending on the volume of traffic. The information could also be sent directly to drivers who can choose to change their route in order to avoid delays.

How can they help the environment?

4 ___ Solar panels embedded into glass road surfaces will power electric cars as they drive along them. Alternatively, electric cars can recharge their batteries while parked in solar-powered parking lots. In addition, the road surface will contain LED lights and road markings as well as heating elements to melt snow and ice during the winter months. Glass is renewable, environmentally friendly and as strong as traditional road surfaces. This technology will allow road transportation to become independent of fossil fuels as vehicles will no longer be using gas-driven engines.

What will the future bring?

5 ___ These emerging technologies will save time and money for drivers, leading to faster and more economic road transportation. They will improve road safety, especially in poor weather conditions, and most important of all, they will contribute to slowing down climate change by reducing greenhouse gas emissions from today's gas-driven engines. Smart road technology may still be at an experimental stage, but it won't be long before it becomes a part of our everyday lives.

3.4 On the move

LISTENING

A Look at the pictures and answer the questions.

1 Are car accidents a problem in your country?

2 Do young people have more accidents than older drivers?

3 What could be done to improve the situation?

3.3 **B LISTEN FOR SIGNPOSTING LANGUAGE Listen to a talk about road safety. Check (✓) the phrases you hear the speaker use.**

1 First, I want to talk about … ☐

2 Now, let's turn to … ☐

3 Moving on, I'll now discuss … ☐

4 In addition, … ☐

5 That's all I want to say … ☐

6 In conclusion, … ☐

3.3 **C LISTEN FOR DETAIL Listen again. Underline the correct option to complete the sentences.**

1 Drivers who are over 40 are *more / less* likely to die in a car accident.

2 *Older / Younger* drivers are better at seeing possible dangers on the road.

3 Young drivers want to *live dangerously / gain more driving experience*.

4 The speaker thinks that young people shouldn't be so *confident / excited* about their driving skills.

5 *Family members / Different groups of people* must help young people to deal with problems.

6 The speaker believes that young adults should go through *a more difficult test / different stages* before gaining a full license.

7 Young people should be encouraged to *wait until they are older / learn to ride a bicycle* before taking their driving test.

Glossary

fatal (adj) which causes death
hazard (n) danger
trial period (n) period of time during which you test somebody's abilities, skills, etc
vital (adj) very important, necessary or essential

D REFLECT Think about the answers to these questions.

1 Were your ideas about improving road safety similar to the speaker's?

2 Do you agree with the speaker's possible solutions? Why/Why not?

FUNCTIONAL LANGUAGE

Telling a story in five stages

Complete the conversation with one word in each space.

Camila: You'll never [1] ________ what happened to me when I was taking that class last week.

Matias: What?

Camila: Well, after class, we could use the campus athletic facilities. On Wednesday, I [2] ________ just had a really tough class, so I decided to go to the swimming pool.

Matias: And?

Camila: There were some other kids from the program at the pool … mostly boys and just a couple of us girls. The funny [3] ________ was that I had just gone there to relax – I didn't have any other plan in mind. Well, [4] ________ I was just floating in the water, I noticed that the boys were organizing a race among themselves.

Matias: So what did you do?

Camila: I lined up at the end of the pool along with the boys. One of them turned to me and said, 'You're a girl. Do you really want to race against us? You know you're going to lose.' I just looked at him and didn't reply. Then somebody yelled 'Ready, Set, Go!' and we were off.

Matias: So, what [5] ________?

Camila: Well – this is the [6] ________ part – I beat them all!

Matias: No way! You're [7] ________?

Camila: Nope. I've been training as a swimmer since I was little you know. In the [8] ________, the boy apologized for being so rude to me. I'm still laughing about it now!

WRITING

A ORGANIZATION Look at the points (a–d) from an email of complaint. Match the points with the main paragraphs in the email.

a the effects of the event, the problems it has caused Paragraph ___

b the result you want from your email Paragraph ___

c a description of the main complaint Paragraph ___

d the reason for writing Paragraph ___

B Complete the email with the adverbs in the box.

definitely extremely regularly seriously totally unnecessarily

< > X

Subject: Local buses

Dear Sir or Madam,

I am writing to complain about the new bus schedule for the town of Bedford, because I am [1] ___ concerned about how this has affected the lives of residents.

Up until two years ago, the bus came [2] ___ every half an hour. Now there is an hour and a half wait between buses. This is [3] ___ unacceptable. It has made life for those without their own transportation [4] ___ difficult and I know of several people who have missed important appointments – for example, with the doctor – because of it.

If, for example, you have a dentist appointment at 9:45, you must catch the 8:00 am bus because the next one is at 9:30 and you [5] ___ risk missing the appointment. In addition, now there is only one bus during school times and it is usually packed with noisy students, with no room for older people to sit down.

In short, we in the town [6] ___ want to see a return to the old schedule.

I hope to hear from you soon regarding this matter.

Kind regards,

Bernard Wise

WRITING PRACTICE

A PREPARE You are going to write an email of complaint about a problem you had while traveling. Choose one of these topics to write about.

- A travel agency booked you into a terrible hotel.
- Your train/plane was rerouted to a different destination.
- There was no transportation to take you from the airport to your vacation destination.
- The car you rented was badly maintained and broke down.

B PREPARE Think about the answers to these questions and write notes.

1 What happened? What are the key dates, events, etc?
2 What problems did this cause?
3 What result do you expect after writing this email?

C WRITE Write your email in 150–200 words.

- Use your notes and ideas from Exercise B.
- Remember to use adverbs to give emphasis to your writing.

GRAMMAR
Future forms

A Complete the sentences with the correct future form using the prompts.

1 *I / meet / Sarah* ______________ tomorrow at 6 pm.
2 *We / have* ______________ a test on Tuesday.
3 Petra says *she / run* ______________ her own business one day.
4 *I / try* ______________ hard to finish my classes this year.
5 I forgot to call Danny – *I / do* ______________ it now.
6 *What / you / do* ______________ tomorrow morning?
7 Carl will be in town tomorrow because *he / buy* ______________ a new coat.
8 If you don't like the music, *I / turn* ______________ it down.

B Complete the conversations with the correct future form of the verbs in parentheses.

Ben: So, have you made any resolutions for this year?
Tom: Just one. I [1] ______________ (*learn*) to drive.
Ben: Finally! Let me know when your classes are; I [2] ______________ (*make sure*) I keep off the roads then!
Tom: Very funny. What about you? You said you wanted to get in shape. What about riding your bike to work?
Ben: Yeah, but I don't have a bike.
Tom: No problem. I have a spare one. I [3] ______________ (*lend*) it to you.
Ben: Oh wow! Thanks a lot! Can I pick it up next week?
Tom: Yes, but I [4] ______________ (*start*) my first class on Monday, so I won't be at home then.

Anna: Hi Claire! What are you doing with all those Italian books? [5] ______________ (*you / learn*) Italian?
Claire: Yes, I am! We [6] ______________ (*go*) to Rome in the summer.
Anna: But you [7] ______________ (*not be*) able to learn Italian in six months!
Claire: No, I know. I just want to be able to speak a little of the language – that's all.
Anna: Oh, I see. Anyway, a few of us are meeting up later. [8] ______________ (*you / do*) anything tonight?
Claire: No, I'm free.
Anna: Great! I'll call you later and give you details.

C Choose the correct option (a, b or c) to complete the sentences.

1 Ian promised his professor that he ______________ harder in class this semester.
 a 'll try
 b 's trying
 c 's going to

2 ______________ to the party with us or with Liz?
 a Will Sarah come
 b Is Sarah coming
 c Is Sarah going to come

3 We ______________ in the ocean if it's freezing. We'll have to see how cold it is when we get there.
 a won't swim
 b aren't swimming
 c aren't going to swim

4 I think I ______________ the steak and fries please.
 a 'll have
 b 'm having
 c 'm going to have

5 William ______________ a candidate for the job tomorrow afternoon.
 a 'll interview
 b 's interviewing
 c interviews

4.1 Change
Personal change

PRONUNCIATION
Intonation for attitude and mood

4.1 **A** **Listen to eight sentences. Circle the option that best describes each speaker's attitude or mood.**

1 I'll help you if you want.	*happy to help / not interested*
2 Are you going to go to that restaurant again?	*excited / bored*
3 I need to make some changes starting tomorrow.	*determined / unsure*
4 Peter's coming for lunch tomorrow.	*negative / positive*
5 Really? You do surprise me.	*surprised / sarcastic*
6 OK, OK. I understand.	*thoughtful / angry*
7 What are you going to do?	*nervous / curious*
8 Thanks a lot!	*ironic / excited*

B **Practice saying the sentences in Exercise A using the same intonation.**

4.1 **C** **Listen again to check your intonation.**

VOCABULARY
Collocations: goals and resolutions

A **Complete the collocations with the verbs in the box. Use each verb only once.**

break cut keep make quit reach

1 __________ down on something
2 __________ a resolution
3 __________ a target
4 __________ a resolution
5 __________ a bad habit
6 __________ a resolution

B **Match the collocations in Exercise A to the correct definition.**

1 stop doing something that isn't good for you __________
2 not do what you promised __________
3 set (yourself) a goal __________
4 achieve something __________
5 do less of something __________
6 stick to a plan __________

C **Complete the sentences with one word in each space. Use words from Exercise A and B.**

1 You should cut ________ on eating chocolate and candy.
2 Linda has finally managed to ________ drinking coffee.
3 I'm determined to ________ my resolution to pass my English exam by working extra hard.
4 If your target is not realistic, you'll never ________ it.
5 I've made a ________ to stop playing video games until I have finished my work.
6 You will never ________ success if you don't try.
7 I've ________ myself a goal – I want to be ready to run in the next marathon.
8 We decided to ________ to the original plan.

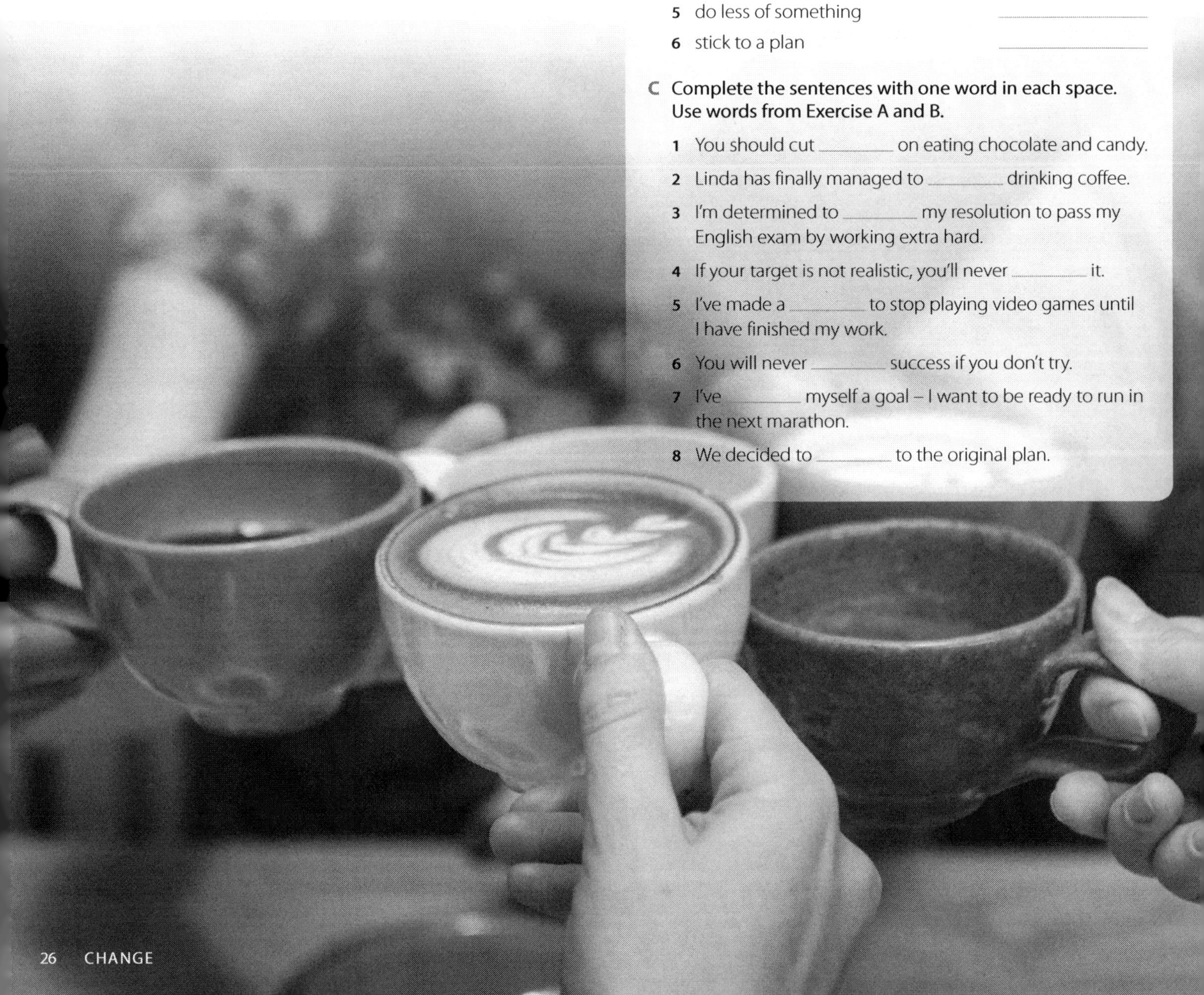

GRAMMAR
Making predictions

A Circle the correct option to complete the sentences.

1 The council ***will*** / ***is going to*** knock down that old building because it's dangerous.

2 She ***may*** / ***will*** take a job with a media company, but she hasn't decided yet.

3 I'm ***definitely*** / ***probably*** going to attend the climate change conference – I'm one of the speakers!

4 We ***will*** / ***might*** use less paper if we receive all our bills electronically – that's much more environmentally friendly.

5 I think we need industry to survive, but companies ***are going to*** / ***could*** try to pollute less.

6 You ***will probably*** / ***are going to*** make a huge difference in the world – I just know it!

7 They ***won't*** / ***might not*** come tonight – it depends on how tired they are after work.

8 Danielle ***probably will*** / ***will probably*** move out of the city if she can find a house she likes.

B Complete the sentences with one word in each space.

1 They ________ definitely support our program; they plan to donate $1 million!

2 She's ________ to work with her neighbors to set up a community garden.

3 I'll ________ see you later tonight, but I'll see how tired I am when I get home.

4 Lionel ________ be here tonight; he called earlier to say he can't make it.

5 You never know, English ________ not always be a global language.

6 My brother ________ become a rich man if his latest business deal succeeds.

7 You're ________ going to get the job; I heard the manager telling her assistant that she's chosen you.

8 We're ________ going to buy a hybrid car just yet; our old one still has some life in it.

C Correct the mistakes in each sentence

1 Hannah probably will get the job.

________.

2 It depends how busy Lisa and Alan are, but they definitely will come tonight.

________.

3 The weather probably might be good this weekend.

________.

4 My neighbors could to at least try to keep the noise down a little!

________.

5 The local soccer club won't definitely win the league this season.

________.

D Complete the predictions so that they are true for you.

1 This year I'll definitely ________.

2 Next month I definitely won't ________.

3 Next year I might ________.

4 In five years, I'll probably ________.

5 Next weekend, I probably won't ________.

4.2 Change

Social change

PRONUNCIATION

'll: contraction of *will*

A Listen to five sentences and underline which phrase you hear.

4.2

1 a We work b We'll work
2 a I make b I'll make
3 a It cost b It'll cost
4 a You quit b You'll quit
5 a She let b She'll let

Linking words: final consonant sound and first vowel sound

B Listen and complete the sentences with a missing phrase.

4.3

1 You won't find ______ a self-help book.
2 ______ things can we do to help?
3 I think she ______.
4 ______ terrific plan!
5 You ______ what I'm saying!

C Practice saying the sentences in Exercise B. Make the links between the final consonants and the first vowel sounds.

D Listen again to check your pronunciation.

4.3

VOCABULARY

Prefixes: *dis-*, *mis-*, *over-*, *re-*, *under-*

A Circle the correct answer, a, b or c.

1 Oh, I thought you said you were a *lifestyle* expert. Sorry, I ___understood you.
a over b dis c mis

2 I wanted to move to the country, but I've had to ___think my plans.
a re b over c mis

3 I can't seem to find my wallet; I must have ___placed it.
a re b dis c mis

4 If ocean levels keep rising, many low-lying islands will ___appear.
a over b dis c re

5 This town used to be a nice place to live, but it's becoming ___populated.
a under b over c re

6 Working as a teacher is very difficult, and on top of that, you're generally ___paid.
a over b dis c under

7 Is it better to fix up an old building or knock it down and ___build it?
a re b dis c over

8 If you ___agree with your boss too many times, you might find yourself out of a job!
a mis b over c dis

B Complete the text with the correct form of the words given in capital letters.

The sea is rising

Urban areas all over the world are [1] *rethinking* their city planning as a result of rising sea levels. Officials must consider whether they should [2] ______ housing to better withstand the changing environment or erect high concrete walls. Of course, wealthier cities can manage climate change much better. **THINK** **BUILD**

Experts may [3] ______ over the best approach, but they are at least able to implement a solution when they come up with one. Bangladesh, for example, is at sea level and its capital was already [4] ______ before thousands of *climate refugees* began arriving. Many came to the capital because they were already experiencing changes in the environment – leaving behind coastal towns that will probably have [5] ______ in a few years' time. **AGREE** **POPULATE** **APPEAR**

Ultimately, it will take a global effort to find a solution to climate change, particularly by policymakers who [6] ______ the problem and heavy polluters who don't even want to admit there is one. **UNDERSTAND**

Indian Summer School at 9 pm on Channel 4

Challenge and change are the keywords to describe the experience of a group of teenagers in *Indian Summer School*, broadcast on Channel 4 in three episodes. This documentary follows the progress of five working-class British boys who are preparing to retake their high school exams at the Doon School in India. Having failed their exams in the UK, they hope that the famous Indian boarding school with the world-class reputation will help them to improve their academic performance and achieve the grades that they need.

The Doon School in Uttarakhand is one of India's finest, and most expensive, private boarding schools. Set in 70 acres of beautiful gardens and open spaces, the school was founded in 1935 by Satish Ranjan Das, a lawyer from Calcutta. The school has an exam pass rate of 100 percent and a zero-tolerance approach to any kind of misbehavior. Staff at the school encourage hard work, personal development and respect for others – there's no room here for somebody who is not prepared to accept the school's ethos.

However, this communal philosophy is not one that the British boys are used to. On their arrival, they are expected to have their hair cut short and are required to hand over their smartphones and tablets. The principal, Matthew Raggett, believes that up to 80 percent of problems in the classroom are caused by the distractions of electronic devices. One of the boys, Ethan, refuses to have his hair cut and none of the boys are happy about having their smartphones taken from them.

As the show progresses, we see a clash of two cultures, as the British boys find it extremely hard to adhere to the strict rules and traditional values of the Indian school. Ethan finds it difficult to socialize with the other students and usually skips classes. Alfie and Jack do better and become interested in the Hindu religion, as well as working hard to contribute to class discussions and homework projects.

As viewers, we all want the boys to do well, but we are possibly frustrated by their refusal to make an effort and gain from their experience. Will the boys manage to complete their six-month course? Are they up for the challenge? Will this be a life-changing experience or another academic failure? Watch the full series to find out!

READING

A **Look at the title of the text and read the first paragraph. Answer the questions.**

1 Is this a magazine article, a review or a letter to a newspaper?

2 Is it about fictional or real people?

3 Which countries are mentioned?

B **READ FOR DETAIL** **Read the rest of the review and check (✓) the information that is mentioned.**

1 the number of classes ☐

2 where the school is ☐

3 the people in the program ☐

4 when the school started ☐

5 the idea of the TV show ☐

6 the students' hobbies ☐

7 the size of the school campus ☐

8 why the boys are there ☐

9 what kind of program it is ☐

C **SUMMARIZE** **Which of the points you checked in Exercise B should be included in a summary? Why should the other points NOT be included?**

D **SUMMARIZE** **Complete the summary with a word or phrase from the box.**

British boys | deal with the challenge | documentary | failed | India

In this TV [1]________, five [2]________ who have [3]________ their exams are given a second chance when they take part in a study program at the world-famous Doon School in [4]________. In this three-part Channel 4 series, we see how the boys [5]________ and changes in their lives when they have to adapt to a very different way of life and learning.

E **REFLECT** **Think about the answers to these questions.**

1 Would you like to watch this documentary? Why/Why not?

2 How easy or difficult do you think it would be to adapt to life in a different country?

Glossary

boarding school (n) school that students live at
clash (n) conflict between different ideas/systems/etc
ethos (n) set of beliefs
zero-tolerance approach (n phrase) a system where no rule-breaking of any kind is accepted

LISTENING

A **What changes would you like to make in your life? Think about:**

- your health and fitness.
- your work, career or school.
- your free time.

B 4.4 **LISTEN FOR GIST** **You will hear Doctor Maria Davos, a psychologist, talking about how people can achieve their personal goals. Listen and check (✓) the statements you think Doctor Davos would agree with.**

a It's easy to achieve your goals. ☐

b Changing your life takes time. ☐

c Setting smaller goals is more realistic than setting one big goal. ☐

d People are happy when they can measure the results of their efforts. ☐

e Everybody should try to improve their diet. ☐

f Make changes one step at a time. ☐

Glossary

overdo (v) do too much, do more than is possible
transform (v) change completely

C **PARAPHRASING** **Read the sentences and circle the answer, a or b, which has a similar meaning.**

1 She failed to stick to her resolution.
  a She made a resolution but didn't keep it.
  b She didn't make a resolution.

2 You can only achieve long-term goals.
  a Your goals must be challenging.
  b You can't change your life overnight.

3 Track your progress by taking photos.
  a Use photos to keep a visual record.
  b Use photos to improve your appearance.

4 I want to cut down on sugar in my diet.
  a I have too much sugar in my diet.
  b I don't have enough sugar in my diet.

D 4.4 **LISTEN FOR DETAIL** **Listen and circle the correct answer, a, b or c.**

1 Many people
  a stick to their resolutions.
  b make resolutions but don't keep them.
  c don't make good plans.

2 You will succeed in changing your life if you
  a set difficult challenges for yourself.
  b act quickly and decisively.
  c set long-term goals.

3 A good way of achieving your goal is to
  a break it into smaller steps.
  b make a list.
  c concentrate.

4 Why does Doctor Davos suggest taking photos?
  a So you can admire your nails.
  b So that you have a visual record of your progress.
  c Because it will keep your hands busy.

5 Keeping a food diary can help you to
  a cut down on something.
  b feel more positive.
  c have more strength.

6 Doctor Davos says we should
  a try to achieve several goals.
  b achieve our goals one by one.
  c only ever make one change.

E **REFLECT** **Think about the answers to these questions.**

1 Are you good at achieving your goals?

2 Have you ever used any of the techniques that were suggested in the interview?

FUNCTIONAL LANGUAGE

Clarifying and asking for clarification

Complete the conversation with the words in the box.

catch going leave lost up what

Adele: Hi, Hector. What's [1] ____________? How's your first day of college [2] ____________?

Hector: Umm … it's OK but I'm having a little trouble with the layout.

Adele: With the … [3] ____________ did you say? Sorry I didn't [4] ____________ that.

Hector: With the layout … of the building.

Adele: You've [5] ____________ me.

Hector: Actually, it's me that's lost! I mean I can't find my way around. The college is really big and I've been late for all my classes because I can't find the rooms!

Adele: Oh, I see. [6] ____________ it to me. I have a map somewhere … of the college. Here you go. It shows the different rooms, the gym, the cafeteria. That should be a help.

Hector: Thanks, Adele.

 Write a short essay

Enter our competition and win a guided tour of our laboratories where we design and build robots for top science-fiction movies *and* for use in the real world.

Here, science fiction becomes science fact!

Robotics has already changed our lives in many ways and will continue to do so. We want to know how you think robots will change everyday life in the home over the next 50 years.

Write a short essay describing two changes you think robots will make to our home lives. Explain why you think these changes will happen and any consequences they may have.

The winning entries will be published in this magazine and on our website roboworld.com.

WRITING

A Read the ad for a competition above. Would you like to visit Roboworld? Why/Why not?

B **ORGANIZATION** Read a competition essay entry. Put the paragraphs (a–d) in the correct order.

a ___ Second, I believe that in the future, people will demand more free time to develop their personal interests, **and so** we will want machines to do more work. Robots will take over all of the housework **because** we will be busy with more useful and creative tasks.

b ___ To sum up, it is probable that robots will play a bigger part in our lives in the future. **Consequently**, we must decide how we will deal with those changes if robots are there to do everything for us.

c ___ One way in which they will be useful is in helping older people. **Because** people are living longer, the population has more elderly people, and **as a result** they need more care and practical help. The robots of the future will do household chores as well as keeping their 'owners' company with conversation and entertainment. In addition, they will be able to call for help in an emergency.

d ___ We already have a lot of machines in our homes which could be classified as robots, for example, washing machines and dishwashers. I believe that **because of** advances in robotics, we will soon have walking, talking machines which will live and work in our homes.

C Read the essay again and answer the questions.

1 What sort of machines in the home can be considered as robots?
2 What is the consequence of people living longer?
3 Why will humans want machines to do even more household chores?

D **USING LINKING WORDS** Complete the sentences with the words and phrases in bold from Exercise B. In two sentences, more than one answer is possible.

1 Robots will do all of the household chores, ___ we will have more free time.
2 We all have more free time ___ all the gadgets we have in our homes.
3 Almost every home now has a washing machine; ___, we no longer waste time washing clothes by hand.
4 There was an increase in unemployment ___ more and more machines were used.
5 Older people will need more care ___ people are living longer and longer.
6 Some elderly people do not have access to the internet and ___ they cannot benefit from modern technology.

WRITING PRACTICE

A **PREPARE** You are going to write an essay about what effect robots and machines will have on work and jobs in the future. Think about the answers to these questions and write notes.

1 What effect have recent developments in technology had on people's jobs?
2 How will technology affect work and jobs in the future? Think of two ideas.
3 What are the reasons for these possible changes?
4 What consequences do you think these developments will have?

B **WRITE** Write your essay in 150–200 words.

- Use your notes and ideas from Exercise A.
- Remember to use linking words to describe reasons and consequences.

5.1 Work and business

VOCABULARY
Employment skills and qualities

A Complete the text with the words and phrases in the box.

communication skills creative people
pressure reliable teamwork time management

TIPS FOR A SUCCESSFUL INTERVIEW

I've interviewed hundreds of people over the years. So, what do I look for when I'm hiring new staff?

Well, first, I'm looking for people who can get their ideas across to others effectively; in other words, people who have good [1] __________. Of course, to be able to do this, they also need to come up with good ideas and that means having [2] __________ thinking skills as well.

Anyone with both of these qualities will probably work well with others and be good at [3] __________, which is very important. Of course, all companies want their employees to have [4] __________ skills, not only with colleagues, but with clients, too.

Finally, if people aren't [5] __________ or aren't able to work well under [6] __________, then they don't make good employees. To be good at [7] __________ is as much a skill as anything else.

Verbs of influence

B Find and correct the mistakes in the sentences.

1 I was pleased that the manager let me to use my digital technology skills.

____

2 Did you encourage him looking for a new job?

____

3 She's tired because her boss made she come to work at 7 am today!

____

4 Our company allows us work from home one day a week.

____

5 She persuaded them that they cancel the meeting at the last minute.

____

6 Mrs. Carter told to me to improve my time management skills.

____

7 I advised my colleague for speaking to our manager about the problem.

____

8 Mr. Jones doesn't want that I give the presentation today.

____

C Choose the correct verb for each sentence.

1 My parents used to ***let / allow*** me to stay up late on the weekend.

2 Fans are supposed to ***encourage / persuade*** their team not *boo* them.

3 No one is ***making / wanting*** Jonathan quit college. It's his decision.

4 You really need to stop ***advising / telling*** me what to do!

5 Natasha's sister sometimes ***lets / allows*** her borrow her clothes.

6 Bill couldn't be ***persuaded / encouraged*** to come to the party.

7 Harry's friend Charlotte ***wants / makes*** him to teach her how to speak English.

8 I ***advise / tell*** you to leave early because the traffic can be terrible.

PRONUNCIATION
Intonation and rhythm: holding your turn

A 5.1 **Listen to eight sentences. Check (✓) the sentences where the speaker makes words longer or uses rising intonation to show they want to continue speaking.**

1 I think that my people skills are excellent. ☐

2 In the end, I realized that it wasn't the job I wanted. ☐

3 I left because I was overworked and underpaid. ☐

4 Job satisfaction makes employees more productive. ☐

5 The perks in my last job were really great. ☐

6 It wasn't just the pay that attracted me to the job. ☐

7 My work doesn't offer enough challenges. ☐

8 You can't imagine what kind of people work there. ☐

B Practice saying the sentences in Exercise A using rising intonation to show that you want to continue speaking.

C Practice saying the sentences from Exercise A using falling intonation to show that you have finished speaking.

5.1 Work and business

GRAMMAR

Past habits and states

A Complete the article with *used to* or *would* and the correct form of the verbs in parentheses. In some sentences, more than one answer is possible.

It [1] ______ (*be*) very difficult for women in the United States to get good jobs and be financially independent. Very few women [2] ______ (*work*) in professions such as medicine or law. For one thing, they [3] ______ (*not have*) access to a college education in order to be able to train for a profession.

It was even harder for working-class women. My grandmother [4] ______ (*work*) in a factory until she got married. She [5] ______ (*leave*) the house at dawn and return late in the evening. The workers [6] ______ (*rarely/get*) vacations, except for once a year, when the factories all closed down for a week. Then, everyone [7] ______ (*leave*) to spend time with family in the country.

B Complete the second sentence so that it has a similar meaning to the first sentence, using the word given. Write between two and five words.

1 Were you a career advisor?
______ be a career advisor? (*use*)

2 We didn't go on vacation when I was young.
We ______ go on vacation when I was young. (*never*)

3 She enjoyed their trips to the beach as a child.
She ______ their trips to the beach as a child. (*used*)

4 The whole team used to meet to discuss the day's business.
The whole team ______ to discuss the day's business. (*would*)

5 Darren didn't have good communication skills back then.
Darren ______ good communication skills. (*to*)

6 Sonja worked at a vacation resort when she was a student.
Sonja ______ at a vacation resort when she was a student. (*work*)

GRAMMAR
The passive voice

A Complete the sentences about the company *Aethaer* with the correct passive voice of the verbs in the box.

not prove | usually/buy | order | sell | set up | train

1 The project ______________ by De Watts after he read an article about bottled air.
2 Since the company started, 200 jars ______________ to customers in China.
3 The jars of air ______________ as gifts for wealthy customers' friends.
4 Jars of *Aethaer* can ______________ online.
5 Right now, new 'air-gricultural' workers ______________ to collect and bottle the product.
6 So far the health benefits of *Aethaer* ______________ by scientists.

B Rewrite these sentences using the passive voice.

1 Someone robbed Christopher's house last night.
____
2 Some people can learn the correct technique.
____
3 Someone has stolen the necklace.
____
4 Usain Bolt broke the 100-meter record.
____
5 The artist's assistant had completed the painting.
____

C Rewrite these passive voice sentences so they are active.

1 The alarm had been set off by Sheila.
____
2 The building was designed by Zaha Hadid.
____
3 The championship was held in Russia.
____
4 The Oscar for Best Picture was won by *Moonlight*.
____
5 Communities are being destroyed by the government's policies.
____

D Complete the extracts from a business magazine with the active or passive form of the verbs in parentheses.

He sells seawater

This year, a Scottish businessman 1 ______________ (*start*) selling his country's cheapest natural resource – seawater. The water 2 ______________ (*collect*) from the clear northern seas, and then it 3 ______________ (*use*) in restaurants for cooking. Since the New Year, 20 orders 4 ______________ (*receive*) from all over Europe.

Plastic Revolution in Ghana

Plastic trash is a serious problem, but now, in Ghana, trash 5 ______________ (*turn into*) handbags. The process is simple. Plastic water containers 6 ______________ (*pick up*) from the streets. After they 7 ______________ (*clean*), they 8 ______________ (*can/make*) into the bags.

The rock millionaire

Gary Dahl, the inventor of the *Pet Rock*, 9 ______________ (*die*) recently at the age of 78. He 10 ______________ (*run*) his *Pet Rock* business for one year in 1975 and he 11 ______________ (*make*) $1 million. The small rocks and stones 12 ______________ (*take*) from Mexican beaches, and they 13 ______________ (*sell*) as novelty gifts.

VOCABULARY
Business collocations

A Match words 1–5 to a–e to make collocations.

1	launch	a	a profit
2	run	b	a business
3	make	c	a brand
4	build	d	a campaign
5	attract	e	new customers

B Complete the sentences with the correct form of the collocations from Exercise A.

1 A lot of people dream of ________ their own ________, but they don't realize how hard it is to set one up.

2 Our company has just ________ to make more people aware of our products.

3 Some people are only in business to make money fast, but it's important to provide quality so that your satisfied customers can help you ________.

4 Sales figures are poor; if the company's going to survive, we need to ________ – preferably ones with spending power.

5 We lost money in the first two years of running the company, but I'm happy to say we have just started to ________.

PRONUNCIATION
Silent consonants

A Underline the silent consonants in each sentence.

1 Who launched this campaign to protect the environment?

2 We should talk on Wednesday.

3 The sign on the door said knock, so I did, but there was no answer.

4 I can't eat a whole sandwich – do you want half?

5 He's written a lot but I doubt that he knows everything.

6 We listened for an hour but his foreign accent made it hard.

7 When they gave the design prize, it went to the wrong person.

8 To be honest, I'd say that psychology would not be a good subject for you.

5.2 **B Listen to the sentences from Exercise A and check your answers. Practice saying the words and the sentences.**

5.3 Work and business

READING

A Read the first paragraph of the text and underline the best title for the article.

1. All about the money
2. Not just a job
3. Modern working conditions

B PREDICT What do you think the article will be about?

C REFERENCE LINKS Read the rest of the article quickly. Circle the correct person, place or thing that each numbered word or phrase in bold refers to.

1. company owners / employees
2. an employee's diet goals / tech firms' work environment
3. people at the recruiting agency / employees in general
4. the game developer's website / the amount of benefits
5. employees / dogs
6. at the beach / at the clothing company
7. make a difference / help the environment

D READ FOR DETAIL Read again and circle the correct answer, a or b.

1. Which of these do tech firms not offer their employees?
   a a diet plan **b** transportation
2. According to the article, what motivates many young people when looking for a job?
   a a high salary **b** job satisfaction
3. Working at the game development company mentioned in the text is unusual because you can
   a take your dog to work. **b** have free medical treatment.
4. What effect does the game development company's unusual policy have on its employees?
   a They work more. **b** They become more active.
5. How do working conditions at the clothing company reflect its products?
   a They are both related to the ocean. **b** They both promote fitness.

Glossary

boost (v) to help something increase
motivated (adj) enthusiastic and wanting to succeed
productive (adj) achieving good results

E REFLECT Think about the answers to these questions.

1. Which do you think is more important – a high salary or job satisfaction?
2. Which of the benefits mentioned in the text would be important for you?

Company owners and entrepreneurs all know that employee satisfaction is essential to a company's success, so it's very important that [1]**they** offer a working environment that nurtures and supports the staff. So what can a company do to keep employees motivated, loyal and productive?

Tech companies, such as Google and Apple, are now famous for their trendy office spaces with perks like free transportation to and from work, weekly massage sessions and, of course, free food and drinks. One employee at a well-known tech firm told us, 'It saves me time and money, and helps me stick to my diet goals.' But which other companies are following [2]**this** example? Hilary works for a large recruiting agency. 'We want and require the best – bright and intelligent young people who want to contribute to the development of the company they work for, and who really want to make a difference. A good salary is important, but [3]**they** are not only motivated by money. There are other ways to reward your staff.'

Take a leading developer of online games as an example. The games are played by millions of people around the world. The company website lists a large number of benefits: [4]**it** includes medical and dental care, paid parental leave, free gym membership and an on-site dry-cleaning service. But maybe the most unusual item on the list is this: 'Every day is bring your dog to work day.' Pet-friendly services include a rooftop park for dogs to play in, pet insurance and special treats for employees' pets. You probably won't be surprised to learn that in a survey carried out by *Business Options* magazine, employees who take their furry friends to work with them say that they are more satisfied with their working life than [5]**those** who can't. In addition, pets can help people to improve their physical and psychological well-being, and this in turn boosts productivity because fewer days are lost to illness.

Other types of companies which are known to care about the health and well-being of their employees are those which sell outdoor clothing and equipment for adventure sports. To help promote their brand they want their employees to stay in shape. What better example to its customers than to have an active staff? Employees are encouraged to use the company bikes, volleyball courts and on-site yoga classes. An example is a well-known American clothing company that has its offices right on the beachfront. Staff members can go surfing on their lunch breaks. In addition, the company runs campaigns to raise awareness of issues such as climate change, environmental protection and fair trade. 'The staff [6]**there** is motivated by more than just good pay', says Hilary. 'Employees believe that in their own small way they can make a difference. Working for an ethically sound company allows them to do [7]**that**.'

LISTENING

A PREDICT **What kinds of problems do you think school teachers have in the course of their work? Put the problems in order (1 = most important, 4 = least important).**

a difficult students ___
b heavy workload ___
c too much paperwork ___
d stress ___

5.3 **B LISTEN FOR EXAMPLES** **You are going to listen to a report about problems which teachers face. Check (✓) the phrases for introducing examples which you hear.**

1 To be more specific … ☐
2 For example, … ☐
3 What's most important is … ☐
4 … as the survey results show … ☐
5 That brings me to … ☐
6 For instance, … ☐
7 … such as … ☐
8 … like … ☐
9 … a more specific idea … ☐
10 Let's take a look at … ☐

Glossary

exodus (n) a situation in which a lot of people leave a place at the same time
qualify (v) earn the certificate, degree, etc which you need to do a certain job
vacancy (n) a job that is available for somebody to do
workload (n) the amount of work you have to do

5.4 **C LISTEN FOR EXAMPLES** **Listen to three extracts from the report and complete the sentences with one word in each space.**

1 For example, toward the end of my time in the teaching profession, I was grading up to ______ notebooks every ______.
2 That's what's important to students, and teachers, not just things like … ______ and ______.
3 For instance, government figures for this year show that there are 10,000 ______ for ______ school teachers.

5.3 **D LISTEN FOR DETAIL** **Listen again and answer the questions.**

1 According to the survey, how many newly certified teachers quit their jobs after less than five years?
2 Do more language teachers or science teachers leave the profession every year?
3 What did 80% of teachers consider doing?
4 How many teachers are missing from high schools this year?
5 How many types of assessments does Amal mention?
6 What did Amal have to do every week which took up all her time?
7 What does Amal believe is *not* so important, compared to a student's personal development?
8 When did Amal's heavy workload increase even more?

E REFLECT **Think about the answers to these questions.**

1 Is a teacher's job stressful in your country?
2 Would you like to become a teacher? Why/Why not?

FUNCTIONAL LANGUAGE
Structuring a presentation

Circle the best options to complete the talk given by a speaker on the topic of 'Interview Skills'.

Good morning and thank you [1]***for coming / that you came*** to today's workshop. The [2]***purpose / reason*** of today's [3]***interaction / presentation*** is to teach you how to succeed in a job interview. So [4]***first of all / at first***, I'd like to talk about introductions. Offer the interviewer a firm handshake, stand straight and look him or her in the eye. Confidence is the key here. Let's [5]***throw a glance / take a look*** at the first slide – this diagram shows the *dos and don'ts* of personal appearance. We'll talk more about these later.

Let's [6]***continue on / move on*** now to think about what you're going to say in the interview. Give thoughtful answers but … don't talk too much! [7]***From / Within*** our research we know that a candidate who talks a lot without interacting with the interviewer can leave a negative impression.

That [8]***carries / brings*** me to the final part of this *introduction to interview skills*. Try to use language which is suitable for the occasion – you should avoid slang words and any references to sensitive topics; and avoid humor if possible, it doesn't always go over well!

So the next [9]***theme / question*** is how to put these ideas into action. In pairs, you're going to role-play an imaginary interview. Now, [10]***do you have / will you make*** any questions before we move on?

WRITING

A Read the job ad and answer the questions.

1 What do you think the job involves?

2 Is having previous experience in the travel business essential?

3 What are the most important skills you need for this job?

Eurojobs.com: Travel Consultant

(Ref: 2713)

An amazing opportunity has become available to work for a dynamic, award-winning travel company.

Responsibilities include: being the first point of contact with customers, both face to face and on social media; creating and planning tailor-made travel arrangements; keeping up to date with offers, promotions and new products; providing advice and solutions to travel problems; providing first-class customer service; and attracting new customers.

The skills we are looking for:

- one year's travel agent experience or sales experience or relevant degree plus work experience
- a real passion for travel and interest in other countries and cultures
- confident, polite and reliable, with a can-do approach and a good work ethic
- comfortable dealing with people at all levels
- ambitious and capable of working well under pressure in a tough sales environment

To apply, email a cover letter and résumé to Carl Dennis: C.Dennis@wdtravel.nett

B ORGANIZATION Read Edward Browning's cover letter. What is the main topic of each paragraph? Write brief notes.

Paragraph 1 ______

Paragraph 2 ______

Paragraph 3 ______

Paragraph 4 ______

Dear Mr. Dennis,

I am writing to apply for the position of Travel Consultant currently advertised on Eurojobs.com (Ref: 2713). I have attached my résumé. I recently graduated with a BA in Tourism Management and am interested in starting a career in the tourism industry.

[a]The course included hands-on experience as well as insight into how different countries approach tourism. [b]This required organizational ability, good communication skills and the ability to work with others. [c]As well as being an active member of student societies, I organized the annual Meeting of Minds event, which gathers tourism graduates from all over the world. [d]I believe that the skills and experience I gained in college make me the ideal candidate for this position.

Working for your company would be a great opportunity for me to share my passion for travel. I am interested in working for a company which offers such excellent customer service. A role at one of the top companies in the travel industry would fulfill my ambition to work in the tourism industry.

Thank you for considering my application. I am available for interview at any time, and look forward to hearing from you.

Sincerely yours,

Edward Browning

C PARAGRAPH STRUCTURE The sentences (a–d) in the second paragraph are in the wrong order. Put them in the correct order to make a better-organized paragraph. Find the topic sentence first.

1 ___

2 ___

3 ___

4 ___

WRITING PRACTICE

A PREPARE You are going to write a cover letter for a job. Find an advertisement online or in a newspaper for a job you would like to apply for. Think about the answers to these questions and write notes.

1 Which phrases will you use to open and close this formal letter?

2 What is the job title and where did you see it advertised?

3 Why are you interested in this company and the job opening?

4 What skills and experience do you have which make you suitable for the role? Think of examples.

B WRITE Write your cover letter for the advertisement you found in Exercise A. Write your letter in 150–200 words.

- Use your notes and ideas from Exercise A.
- Remember to use standard phrases suitable for a formal letter.
- Don't forget to begin each paragraph with a topic sentence and give examples where necessary.

Irregular Verbs

Base form	Simple past	Past participle
be	was/were	been
become	became	become
begin	began	begun
break	broke	broken
bring	brought	brought
build	built	built
buy	bought	bought
can	could	been able to
catch	caught	caught
choose	chose	chosen
come	came	come
cost	cost	cost
cut	cut	cut
drink	drank	drunk
eat	ate	eaten
fall	fell	fallen
feel	felt	felt
find	found	found
forget	forgot	forgotten
get	got	got
give	gave	given
go	went	gone/been
grow	grew	grown
have	had	had
hear	heard	heard
hit	hit	hit
hold	held	held
hurt	hurt	hurt
keep	kept	kept
know	knew	known
leave	left	left
lend	lent	lent
let	let	let

Base form	Simple past	Past participle
lose	lost	lost
make	made	made
mean	meant	meant
meet	met	met
must	had to	had to
pay	paid	paid
put	put	put
read	read	read
ride	rode	ridden
run	ran	run
say	said	said
see	saw	seen
sell	sold	sold
send	sent	sent
set	set	set
shut	shut	shut
sing	sang	sung
sit	sat	sat
sleep	slept	slept
speak	spoke	spoken
spell	spelled	spelled
spend	spent	spent
stand	stood	stood
steal	stole	stolen
take	took	taken
teach	taught	taught
tell	told	told
think	thought	thought
throw	threw	thrown
understand	understood	understood
wear	wore	worn
win	won	won
write	wrote	written

PHONETIC SYMBOLS											
Single vowels			Diphthongs			Consonants					
/ɪ/	fish	/fɪʃ/	/uw/	news	/nuw/	/p/	pen	/pen/	/s/	snake	/sneɪk/
/iː/	bean	/biːn/	/eɪ/	face	/feɪs/	/b/	bag	/bæg/	/z/	zoo	/zuː/
/ʊ/	foot	/fʊt/	/ɔɪ/	boy	/bɔɪ/	/t/	tea	/tiː/	/ʃ/	shop	/ʃɒp/
/uː/	shoe	/ʃuː/	/oʊ/	nose	/noʊz/	/d/	dog	/dɒg/	/ʒ/	television	/'telɪvɪʒən/
/e/	egg	/eg/	/ju/	use	/juz/	/ʧ/	chip	/ʧɪp/	/m/	map	/mæp/
/ə/	mother	/'mʌðər/	/aɪ/	eye	/aɪ/	/ʤ/	jazz	/ʤæz/	/n/	name	/neɪm/
/ɜː/	word	/wɜːrd/	/aʊ/	mouth	/maʊθ/	/k/	cake	/keɪk/	/ŋ/	ring	/rɪŋ/
/ɔː/	talk	/tɔːk/				/g/	girl	/gɜːrl/	/h/	house	/haʊs/
/æ/	back	/bæk/				/f/	film	/fɪlm/	/l/	leg	/leg/
/ʌ/	bus	/bʌs/				/v/	verb	/vɜːrb/	/r/	road	/roʊd/
/ɑː/	arm	/ɑːrm/				/θ/	thing	/θɪŋ/	/w/	want	/wɒnt/
/ɒ/	top	/tɒp/				/ð/	these	/ðiːz/	/j/	yes	/jes/

UNIT 1

Lesson 1.4, Listening, Exercise A
1.3 **J = John K = Karen**

J: Coming up on today's show, a discussion on selfie addiction and an interview with an expert on the history of selfies. But first of all, we're going to talk to Karen Harris about the Chinese phenomenon of *Meitu*. Karen, what exactly is *Meitu*?

K: Well, John, it's a new Chinese photo-editing and sharing app. I say it's new, but in fact, it was launched in 2014 and is super-popular in China and throughout Asia.

Lesson 1.4, Listening, Exercise B
1.4 **J = John K = Karen**

J: Coming up on today's show, a discussion on selfie addiction and an interview with an expert on the history of selfies. But first of all, we're going to talk to Karen Harris about the Chinese phenomenon of *Meitu*. Karen, what exactly is *Meitu*?

K: Well, John, it's a new Chinese photo-editing and sharing app. I say it's new, but in fact, it was launched in 2014 and is super-popular in China and throughout Asia. It was only recently launched here in the US though. Just to give you an idea of its popularity … the app has been installed more than a billion times and has more than 450 million unique users throughout the world.

J: That's incredible! OK. So tell us a little more about it, Karen.

K: Well, *Meitu* means *beautiful picture* in Chinese and it's an app available on iOS and Android platforms which helps you to look more beautiful in selfies. For example, you can retouch your skin to make it appear smoother and younger, or remove spots or dark circles from under your eyes. You end up with an idealized version of yourself.

J: But don't most photo apps allow you to do that kind of thing anyway?

K: Yes, they do, but *Meitu* goes much further. After you've chosen one of seven filters …

J: What kind of filters?

K: Well, they have names like *Angelic*, *Blossoms*, *Mermaid* … so you can probably imagine the style. It creates a soft focus for your picture and makes you look kind of dreamy as well as giving you the option of adding effects like stars, flowers and tears.

J: And then?

K: And then … well, the best part … the most unusual aspect of this app is that it has an incredible hand-drawn mode that allows you to change your eye color, whiten your teeth, make your nose smaller, change the shape of your face …

J: Umm … a little like plastic surgery without the surgery!

K: Yes, exactly!

J: So how does it work?

K: *Meitu* uses facial recognition technology – you know – the kind of thing they use at airport security – to map your face using 171 different points. Then it puts make-up, effects and so on over the top of the image.

J: So have you tried it yourself, Karen?

K: Yes, I have. It took me about forty minutes to create the perfect me. The problem is …

J: Yes, …?

K: Well, some tech experts have warned that the app is collecting people's personal information. Every time you use it to create the perfect selfie, it accesses your phone's location, your app history, your photos, wi-fi connection information …

J: OK … that's a little scary.

K: Well, it is, but so many phone apps do that these days. I think the threat has been exaggerated a little.

J: Thanks, Karen, for sharing all that with us. Now, moving on to other aspects of selfies …

UNIT 2

Lesson 2.4, Listening, Exercise B
2.3 **M = Megan G = Gareth**

M: One difficult aspect of growing up is decision-making. You learn, as you get older, that there are tough choices to be made – life-changing decisions. Now, Gareth, you're a guidance counselor – what kind of support can you offer young people?

G: Well, it's important to note that there are a range of problems affecting young adults today – family troubles for one thing, exam stress, career choices. And, as you say, they need to make tough choices. And that can be hard. To give you an example – a lot of young people who come to see me have just left school and they don't know how to go on from there. They ask me things like, *Should I go to college, or should I get a job?* or they tell me that they're worried about living on their own for the first time in their lives.

M: So how do you help the young people who come to you?

G: The first thing we do in a counseling session is a classic technique. *Write it down*, is what I tell them. I get them to write a list of advantages and disadvantages. This seems like an obvious thing to do, but a lot of people don't actually think of it, and it's amazing how just seeing something written down in black and white can help to clear your thoughts.

M: Can't family members help with difficult decisions like these, Gareth? Why do young people feel they need to talk to a stranger – to you?

G: Family can be an issue. Even if the young person's problem isn't related to their family specifically, their families don't always support them in the way that, maybe, they would like. There's usually a lot of pressure.

Parents don't always agree with their children's choices. I regularly talk to people who know what they want to do, but their parents don't agree. And then you have issues of family loyalty, you know – not wanting to disappoint your parents, and so on. It's difficult to put a plan into action if you don't have support from your family.

M: So what do you tell them, Gareth?

G: Well I always stress the importance of thinking long term. *Think in years, not days*, is what I tell them. Consider the consequences of your decision. Set long-term goals. Think – will there be a positive outcome for me in five years, ten years?

M: How else can you help somebody to make a decision?

G: Something which a lot of people find very useful is the idea of having 'an imaginary friend'.

M: What do you mean?

G: Well, it's very easy to get absorbed in your own problem, to only see a very narrow, personal view. I tell them to imagine that it's somebody else's problem. If this was your friend, what advice would you give them?

M: I see – it's easier to come up with a solution when you're on the outside?

G: Exactly. And finally, just stop thinking for a while! Experts talk about 'decision fatigue' where you spend so much time and energy worrying about the problem that you just can't deal with it any more. Take some time off. Do something else. Get away for a few hours or days.

UNIT 3

Lesson 3.4, Listening, Exercise B

3.3 Good morning and welcome to today's lecture about young drivers and road safety. I want to start by giving you a few facts. You are probably aware that young drivers, that is to say, young adults between the ages of 17 and 24, are at a much higher risk of being involved in a fatal traffic accident than older drivers. Numbers from the National Highway Traffic Safety Administration show that young drivers are a third more likely to die in a crash than drivers who are over the age of 40. That's a pretty terrifying number and it's extremely important that we do something to change that.

First, I want to talk about some of the causes of the problem. Younger drivers have less experience, and this means that they're not as good at spotting hazards as older drivers. But more important is the fact that they are risk takers. They are far more likely to drive without a seat belt, pass dangerously or drive too fast. Speeding is a real killer.

Many young people feel very proud that they have mastered how to drive a car – and … I'm sure you know the feeling yourselves … it's so exciting … sitting at the wheel for the first time – they feel very confident. Too confident. And this is another problem. They think they're in control, but in fact, they're actually driving too fast and dangerously.

It's absolutely vital that we see a combined effort on the part of schools, healthcare professionals, social workers and the police, of course, to deal with this problem.

Now, let's turn to the solutions to some of these problems. The first thing we need to do is to improve driver training and testing. One suggestion is for us to introduce 'graduated' driver learning and licensing. What does that mean? Well, I'll explain this idea in more detail. We want to see a driving test which is divided into stages – smaller steps if you like. This offers a more structured approach and would include a minimum number of driving lessons followed by a trial period before young adults are actually issued with full licenses. For example, during the trial period, they wouldn't be allowed to drive at night, or to carry passengers.

In addition, studies have shown that raising the age at which young people can take their driving test would have a major impact on road fatalities. Parents especially should discourage the idea of learning to drive as soon as possible. If local authorities provide realistic transportation alternatives for young people – for example, regular buses and better bike paths, free train travel – then they might be more likely to delay getting their first car.

Now, that's all I want to say on the subject of solutions to this problem. Do we have any questions from …

UNIT 4

Lesson 4.4, Listening, Exercise B

4.4 **H = Henry M = Maria**

H: How many times have you said to yourself, *I'm going to exercise more* or *I want to stop wasting time and organize my life*? You make a plan and then … you fail to stick to it! Today, I've asked psychologist, Doctor Maria Davos, to come onto the show and talk to us about how we can not only set goals, but actually achieve them. Good morning, Doctor Davos.

M: Good morning. Thank you for inviting me onto the show.

H: Why do we find it so difficult to keep our resolutions?

M: I think the main reason is that we try to do too much, too soon. People think that they're going to transform their lives overnight. But it doesn't work like that. Making a lifestyle change is challenging, and it's part of a process that takes time and a lot of patience.

H: So how do you suggest we go about making changes that will stick?

M: A lot of people make a list of their goals, but these are usually fairly general. If you write down, 'Exercise more', that's not very specific, is it? Yes, you want to exercise more, but how and when? Be more focused in your goals. Write a note about which days you're going to exercise and for how long. You need to be realistic.

H: Yes, but, those kinds of goals are achievable because you can measure them. You can exercise for ten minutes every day, for example. But what if you want to quit a bad habit? For example, I bite my nails. I hate it, but I just can't stop doing it.

M: Again, you need to measure the progress you're making so try this idea – use your phone to take a photo of your nails every day and then you'll be able to track your progress as your nails grow back. Each time you reach your fingers to your mouth, take out your phone and look at the 'before and after' pictures. You'll be really happy when you see how good they look now!

H: That certainly sounds like very good advice.

M: Another idea is to keep a food diary. If you eat too much chocolate, for example, or drink too much coffee – write down how much you have each day. Then you can actually see, in your diary, the progress that you're making. It can be a really positive process and will keep you strong – help you to stick to your resolution. And remember – this is so important – don't try to do everything at once. Don't overdo it. Focus on one goal or change at a time. When you have succeeded in making one change in your life, you can move on to another goal.

H: How can our family and friends help us, Maria?

M: That's a good question, Henry. I believe that the support of family and friends is …

UNIT 5

Lesson 5.4, Listening, Exercise B

5.3 **J = John T = Tony A = Amal**

J: Today on *Education Matters*, we have a report from Tony Mills, our education correspondent. Tony – you're going to be telling us about a crisis in our high schools, is that right?

T: Yes, that's right, John. New statistics from a recent survey show that an increasing number of teachers are leaving schools. To be more specific, of all the young people who were certified as teachers in 2011, 30% had left the profession within five years. A different study found that this figure was even worse for teachers of core subjects. For example, 10.4% of science teachers and 10.2% of those teaching languages leave each year.

And maybe even more revealing is the fact that, as the survey results show, an astonishing 80% of teachers have actually thought about leaving their jobs over the last 12 months. Now of course, many young graduates qualify to become teachers every year, but the trend is definitely for declining teacher numbers – more people are leaving than entering. For instance, government figures for this year show that there are 10,000 vacancies for high school teachers. In college, the numbers are even worse, with a shortage of 20,000.

So what's the reason for this mass exodus? When asked, almost all teachers talk about the increase in their workload and the stress this brings with it. I asked Amal Hussain, a math teacher from New York about her experience.

Amal, you quit your job several months ago. How long had you been teaching?

A: I got my certification 11 years ago and, well, to be honest with you, I'd just had enough. I resigned in June last year and now I'm retraining as a career advisor.

T: So why did you leave the job?

A: My workload was just … well … it was overwhelming. The new government standards mean that the students are constantly being tested … assessed … through means such as coursework, oral exams, written exams, and we have to create those exams, grade them and complete endless paperwork … data collection they call it. For example, toward the end of my time in the teaching profession, I was grading up to 200 notebooks every week – I didn't have time for anything else! It's not teaching you know … it's just … well … it's not how I imagined the job when I first started.

T: And how does all of this affect the students?

A: Well, that's just it. Because the only important thing is getting good grades – teachers are forced to focus only on preparing students for exams. That's not why I became a teacher. I believe education is an ongoing process which is about learning, developing. I wanted to make a difference in students' lives – and I wasn't. That's what's important to students, and teachers, not just things like … exams and grades.

T: How many hours were you working on average? Can you give us a more specific idea of your workload?

A: Umm … about 60 hours most weeks, maybe more if we had end-of-year exams. The workload is what most of my colleagues complain about. I loved my job. I loved working with young people, helping them to grow. But … well, it was just too much.

T: So … an insider's view from Amal there. So what exactly, is the government planning to do …

Answer key

1.1 Communication today

GRAMMAR

A

1 do you speak
2 take
3 is learning
4 seems
5 am looking
6 are becoming
7 doesn't contain
8 is thinking

B

Stative	Dynamic
believe, belong, cost, include, know, mean, need, own, prefer, seem, understand, want	bring, complain, get, relax, show, take, watch, write

C

1 am/'m relaxing
2 need
3 have
4 don't think
5 travel
6 love
7 am/'m smiling
8 snows

VOCABULARY

A

1 looks
2 listen
3 hear
4 see
5 am/'m watching
6 are/'re looking
7 sounds
8 look

B

1 b 2 c 3 a 4 b 5 c

PRONUNCIATION

A

1 We speak a lot of English at home.
2 The Spanish exam was difficult, but I think I passed.
3 I don't usually listen to podcasts.
4 A photo doesn't always show the real you.
5 I met up with an old friend at the park.
6 That's me in the photograph with my family.

1.2 Who owns English?

GRAMMAR

A

1 ~~What do~~ **Did** you guys go out the other night?
2 ~~Which~~ **What** do you want, an ice-cream cone?
3 ~~What Jack~~ **What does Jack** want to do for his birthday next week?
4 ~~How much~~ **How long** did she have to wait at the bank?
5 ~~Who~~ **Whose** shoes are these?
6 ~~How~~ **Why** doesn't Laura come to the party with us?

B

2 Where did Danny learn Spanish?
3 When is the language lab open?
4 How can I improve my English?
5 Should we ask the teacher what this word means?
6 Who is considered the greatest writer of modern English?
7 What are you studying this semester?
8 What language do you speak at home?

C

2 Can you understand
3 Which/What
4 Is it difficult
5 how is it
6 How do you make
7 Will you teach
8 why are you

VOCABULARY

A

1 e 2 d 3 g 4 a 5 c 6 b 7 f

B

1 phrase
2 idiom
3 fluently
4 monolingual
5 accent
6 accurately
7 bilingual

PRONUNCIATION

A

1 b 2 a 3 b 4 a 5 a

1.3 Reading

READING

A

1 In many African countries, hundreds of languages are spoken.
2 Some people, known as *hyperglots*, are capable of learning 50 or 60 languages.
3 Learning new languages increases the size of the brain.

C

1 c 2 e 3 a

1.4 Listening; Functional Language

LISTENING

A

1 part of a radio show
2 a new selfie app

B

1 b 2 b

C

1 F (It's new in the US, but it was originally launched in 2014.)
2 F (It's available throughout the world.)
3 T
4 T
5 F (The technology is similar to that used by airport security companies.)
6 F (Many apps access and collect personal information.)

FUNCTIONAL LANGUAGE

A

1 mind giving
2 to (help)
3 to do
4 would be
5 you wouldn't/don't
6 go

B

1 hand **2** help **3** easy **4** amazing **5** favor

1.5 Write a report about trends

WRITING

B

Introduction: a and c
Paragraph 1: g
Paragraph 2: d
Paragraph 3: e and f
Conclusion: b

C

1 f **2** e **3** b

D

1 conducted
2 Many claimed
3 a lack of interest in
4 due to the fact that
5 It seems that

WRITING PRACTICE

B

Model answer

Report about trends in the use of technology for education

This report examines how people are using technology as part of the educational process. We asked one hundred young people about their experiences of technology in education and what they believe its advantages are.

Individual learning

Not everybody is successful at learning using traditional methods of study, and digital tools such as computers, iPads and digital whiteboards. This means that both teaching and learning can be adapted to suit individual students' various styles of learning.

Distance learning

Access to online learning allows teachers to reach students in different places at the same time. It also allows people who work to pursue educational goals in their free time. In this way, learning has become available to anyone and everyone.

Motivation

Most of the people we asked said that with computer-based courses they felt more in control of their learning. Digital methods make learning more fun, and students are less afraid of making mistakes.

Conclusion

No one suggested that technology should replace teachers, but it seems that the trend toward computer-based and distance learning has made educational opportunities available to more people and students can learn more by engaging in motivating educational activities.

2.1 Important decisions

PRONUNCIATION

A

1 We
2 I've
3 They've
4 I
5 He's
6 They
7 She
8 We've

GRAMMAR

A

1 have (you ever) made
2 wrote
3 haven't done
4 have (you) done
5 went
6 was
7 have/'ve (never) made
8 has/'s written
9 has/'s learned
10 went

B

1 still
2 went
3 have ever been
4 just
5 has been
6 never
7 went
8 yet

VOCABULARY

A

1 take
2 put
3 turn
4 set
5 lose
6 make
7 work
8 stay
9 make

B

1 lose heart
2 motivated
3 into action
4 the break
5 the next step
6 a decision
7 his/a goal
8 into reality
9 short-term goals

2.2 You can do it!

VOCABULARY

A

1 c
2 g
3 a
4 f
5 e
6 b
7 d
8 h

B

1 aware of
2 suitable for
3 typical of
4 looking for
5 working for
6 proud of
7 asked for
8 preparing for

C

1 deal
2 causing
3 suggest
4 coming
5 solve
6 analyze
7 agree

PRONUNCIATION

A

Verbs with stress on first syllable: focus, manage, study
Verbs with stress on second syllable: achieve, regret, suggest

GRAMMAR

A

1 couldn't
2 am able to
3 managed to
4 Was she able to
5 are able to
6 managed to
7 can
8 couldn't

B

1 does Kate manage to
2 being able to work
3 not able to prepare
4 able to spend
5 Could you speak
6 didn't manage to find
7 imagine being able

2.3 Reading

READING

A

1 want a simpler life
2 a TV announcer
3 for some people

B

1 c (without an internet connection, without electricity, without a car)
2 f (the security of a nine-to-five routine, left … behind in order to find a way of life that is simpler)
3 a (by helicopter)
4 b (food, fuel, clothing and bedding)
5 d (Things are regularly broken or damaged by the wind and rain.)
6 e (They are able to deal with change on a daily basis, ability to accept new situations.)

C

1 T
2 F (They have left the 'rat race' behind.)
3 F (The island is only accessible by helicopter.)
4 T
5 T
6 T

2.4 Listening; Functional Language

LISTENING

A

Answers will vary, but 1, 3 and 4 are the most likely.

B

1 adults
2 support
3 dealing
4 pressure
5 solve
6 decisions

C

1 life-changing decisions
2 family troubles
3 list
4 don't agree
5 long-term goals
6 advice
7 time, energy

FUNCTIONAL LANGUAGE

1 must be
2 can call
3 if I ask
4 Can we start
5 I'm sorry
6 Would it be
7 I'm afraid
8 I'd like

2.5 Write an informal email

WRITING

A

Sentences 2, 4, 5, 7 and 8

B

1 Sorry I haven't written / didn't write sooner.
2 Thanks for the advice.
3 I hope you're well. / How are you?
4 I didn't go because I was sick.
5 I haven't found anywhere (nice/cheap/etc) to live yet.

C

1 regularly 2 good 3 not sure 4 will

D

1 Hi Adriana; Love to you & Dave & the baby
2 So what to do?; Great new café near me
3 !!!; –; …
4 What's; It's been; a lot of stuff's been happening; I'd made; I've been; don't know; They're both; The other one's; I'll be far away; I'll have to find; it's a great opportunity
5 What's up?; stuff; magazines; Woo-hoo; cool; get it?; lol
6 ☺

WRITING PRACTICE

B

Model answer

Hiya Lottie,

Thanks for the birthday present. *The Necks*! You know me so well! It's their best so far. Thanks again ☺!! The card was great, too. Really funny!

Guess what? You know how you're always trying to persuade me to go skydiving? Well, … ta-da … Pete got me a ride in a hot-air balloon for my birthday! Trouble is, I have a thing about heights – really scared of them actually! I *so* want to go but at the same time I'm really frightened – terrified! I know that it will be an amazing experience but … will I have the courage to do it? Plus, I don't want to hurt Pete's feelings by refusing his gift. What should I do? Help!

BTW, when do you next get a break? Maybe I can come to Germany for a visit, or you can come over here – you know you're always welcome. Anyway … give me a call if you get the chance. Tell me what I should do about the whole hot-air balloon thing!

That's all for now, but write and tell me all your news.

Hugs and kisses,
Tonia

3.1 Travel experiences

GRAMMAR

A

1 a
2 b
3 c
4 b
5 c
6 b
7 c
8 a

B

2 hadn't seen
3 had been
4 decided
5 left
6 suddenly found
7 saw
8 had never noticed

VOCABULARY

A

1 f
2 c
3 g
4 d
5 h
6 b
7 a
8 e

B

1 connection
2 decision
3 pollution
4 action
5 reaction
6 situation

C

1 decision
2 connection
3 pollution
4 situation
5 reaction
6 action

PRONUNCIATION

A

2 Speaker B
3 Speaker B
4 Speaker A
5 Speaker B
6 Speaker B

3.2 Travel smart

GRAMMAR

A

1 a
2 the
3 –
4 an
5 –
6 a
7 the
8 –

B

1 much
2 enough
3 little
4 plenty of
5 a little
6 a lot of
7 Few
8 too much

C

1 a lot
2 much
3 enough
4 little/no
5 A lot
6 very

PRONUNCIATION

A

Students underline these phrases:
1 a lot of
2 a few
3 many
4 too much
5 enough
6 little

VOCABULARY

A

1 really
2 a little
3 very
4 furious
5 extremely
6 very funny

B

1 ✗ 2 ✗ 3 ✓ 4 ✗ 5 ✗ 6 ✗ 7 ✓ 8 ✓

C

1 impossible
2 brilliant
3 enormous
4 furious
5 filthy
6 hilarious

3.3 Reading

READING

A

Suggested answers
1 Maybe it will be about the use of technological advances in road transportation.
2 Probably positive.

B

1 d 2 c 3 a 4 e 5 b

C

1 a 2 b 3 c 4 b

3.4 Listening; Functional Language

LISTENING

B

1, 2, 4 and 5.

C

1 less
2 Older
3 live dangerously
4 confident
5 Different groups of people
6 different stages
7 wait until they are older

FUNCTIONAL LANGUAGE

1 guess 2 had/'d 3 thing 4 while 5 happened
6 best 7 kidding 8 end

3.5 Write an email of complaint

WRITING

A

a 3 **b** 4 **c** 2 **d** 1

B

1 extremely
2 regularly
3 totally
4 unnecessarily
5 seriously
6 definitely

WRITING PRACTICE

C

Model answer

Dear Sir or Madam,

I am writing to complain about the disastrous vacation package to Majorca we booked with your company. It is the worst vacation we have ever had.

First of all, there was no bus to meet us at the airport to take us to the hotel. We had to wait five hours for one to arrive, and when we arrived at the hotel, the kitchen was closed so we went to bed without having dinner.

The extremely loud noise of building work woke us up very early since the hotel is having an extension built. This went on for our whole stay, making it totally impossible to relax by the hotel pool or beach.

The service was completely unacceptable, too – beds not made or changed, rooms not cleaned – and the staff was very rude. Also, the planned trips to sites of interest either didn't happen or we had to pay extra for them.

This is to inform you that I am seeking compensation for a ruined vacation, because what was promised by your representative at the travel agency was nothing like the reality.

I hope to hear from you soon regarding this matter.
Harold Purly

4.1 Personal change

GRAMMAR

A

1 I am / I'm meeting Sarah
2 We are / We're having or We are / We're going to have
3 she is / she's going to run
4 I am / I'm going to try or I will / I'll try
5 I will / I'll do
6 What are you doing
7 he is / he's going to buy
8 I will / I'll turn

B

1 am/'m going to learn
2 will/'ll make sure
3 will/'ll lend
4 am/'m starting
5 Are you going to learn / Are you learning
6 are going
7 will not / won't be
8 Are you doing

C

1 a **2** b **3** a **4** a **5** b

PRONUNCIATION

A

1 not interested
2 excited
3 determined
4 positive
5 sarcastic
6 thoughtful
7 curious
8 ironic

VOCABULARY

A

1 cut
2 make/break/keep
3 reach
4 keep/make/break
5 quit
6 break/make/keep

B

1 quit a bad habit
2 break a resolution
3 make a resolution
4 reach a target
5 cut down on something
6 keep a resolution

C

1 down
2 quit/stop
3 keep
4 reach
5 resolution
6 achieve
7 set
8 stick

4.2 Social change

GRAMMAR

A

1 is going to
2 may
3 definitely
4 will
5 could
6 are going to
7 might not
8 will probably

B

1 will
2 going
3 probably
4 won't
5 might/may
6 could/will
7 definitely
8 not

C

1 Hannah ~~probably~~ will **probably** get the job.
2 It depends how busy Lisa and Alan are, but they ~~definitely~~ will **probably** come tonight.
3 The weather ~~probably~~ might be good this weekend.
4 My neighbors could ~~to~~ at least try to keep the noise down a little!
5 The local soccer club ~~won't~~ definitely **won't** win the league this season.

PRONUNCIATION

A

1 b **2** a **3** a **4** b **5** b

B

1 that in **2** What other **3** is overpaid **4** That's a
5 don't understand

VOCABULARY

A

1 c
2 a
3 c
4 b
5 b
6 c
7 a
8 c

B

2 rebuild
3 disagree
4 overpopulated
5 disappeared
6 misunderstand

4.3 Reading

READING

A

1 a review **2** real people **3** India and the UK

B

2, 3, 4, 5, 7, 8 and 9.

C

Suggested answers

2, 3, 5, 8 and 9 should be included.
4 and 7 are not relevant to the main idea of the program.

D

1 documentary
2 British boys
3 failed
4 India
5 deal with the challenge

4.4 Listening; Functional Language

LISTENING

B

b, c, d and f.

C

1 a **2** b **3** a **4** a

D

1 b
2 c
3 a
4 b
5 a
6 b

FUNCTIONAL LANGUAGE

1 up
2 going
3 what
4 catch
5 lost
6 Leave

4.5 Write a short essay

WRITING

B

a 3 **b** 4 **c** 2 **d** 1

C

1 Washing machines and dishwashers.
2 The elderly will need more help in the home.
3 Because we will want more free time to develop personal interests.

D

1 and so
2 because of
3 as a result / consequently
4 because
5 because
6 as a result / consequently

WRITING PRACTICE

B

Model answer

For some time now, robots have been used to build products such as cars and medical equipment, but how long will it be before they do the jobs we think only humans can do? Computers are becoming more intelligent, and as a result they regularly beat humans at chess. What else could they be taught to do?

Medicine is one area in which robots will be used much more. You can already see a doctor online, which is an important development, because people in remote areas can easily speak to a doctor. Consequently, healthcare will improve greatly. Robots can even be used to perform difficult operations, which will allow a surgeon in Germany to operate on a patient in Japan.

Another area where robots will change traditional ways of working is farming. Farm workers will not be needed any more because driverless tractors, GPS devices and robotic fruit pickers will do their jobs. However, some people worry that this kind of development will cause unemployment.

To sum up, because of new developments in robotics and technology, there will be both positive and negative consequences, and we humans will have to find new ways to live in the new world of machines.

5.1 At work

VOCABULARY

A

1 communication skills
2 creative
3 teamwork
4 people
5 reliable
6 pressure
7 time management

B

1 I was pleased that the manager let me ~~to~~ use my digital technology skills.
2 Did you encourage him **to look** ~~looking~~ for a new job?
3 She's tired because her boss made **her** ~~she~~ come to work at 7 am today!
4 Our company allows us **to** work from home one day a week.
5 She persuaded them **to** ~~that they~~ cancel the meeting at the last minute.
6 Mrs. Carter told ~~to~~ me to improve my time management skills.
7 I advised my colleague **to speak** ~~for speaking~~ to our manager about the problem.
8 Mr. Jones doesn't want **me to** ~~that I~~ give the presentation today.

C
1 allow
2 encourage
3 making
4 telling
5 lets
6 persuaded
7 wants
8 advise

PRONUNCIATION

A
1 ✓
2 –
3 –
4 ✓
5 ✓
6 ✓
7 –
8 ✓

GRAMMAR

A
1 used to be
2 used to work
3 didn't use to have
4 used to work
5 would leave / used to leave
6 would rarely get
7 would leave / used to leave

B
1 Did you use to
2 never used to
3 used to enjoy
4 would meet
5 didn't use to have
6 used to work

5.2 In business

GRAMMAR

A
1 was set up
2 have been sold
3 are usually bought
4 be ordered
5 are being trained
6 have not been proven

B
1 Christopher's house was robbed last night.
2 The correct technique can be learned.
3 The necklace has been stolen.
4 The 100-meter record was broken by Usain Bolt.
5 The painting had been completed by the artist's assistant.

C
1 Sheila had set off the alarm.
2 Zaha Hadid designed the building.
3 Russia held the championship.
4 *Moonlight* won the Oscar for Best Picture.
5 The government's policies are destroying communities.

D
1 started
2 is collected
3 is used
4 have been received
5 is being turned into
6 are picked up
7 are cleaned / have been cleaned
8 can be made
9 died
10 ran
11 made
12 were taken
13 were sold

VOCABULARY

A
1 d 2 b 3 a 4 c 5 e

B
1 running, business
2 launched a campaign
3 build a brand
4 attract new customers
5 make a profit

PRONUNCIATION

B
1 Who launched this campaign to protect the environment?
2 We should talk on Wednesday.
3 The sign on the door said knock, so I did, but there was no answer.
4 I can't eat a whole sandwich – do you want half?
5 He's written a lot but I doubt that he knows everything.
6 We listened for an hour but his foreign accent made it hard.
7 When they gave the design prize, it went to the wrong person.
8 To be honest, I'd say that psychology would not be a good subject for you.

5.3 Reading

READING

A
Not just a job

B
Suggested answers
Perks and benefits of working for a modern firm and how these affect employees' well-being and productivity.

C
1 company owners
2 tech firms' work environment
3 employees in general
4 the game developer's website
5 employees
6 at the clothing company
7 make a difference

D
1 a 2 b 3 a 4 a 5 b

5.4 Listening; Functional Language

LISTENING

B

1, 2, 4, 6, 7, 8 and 9.

C

1 200, week
2 exams, grades
3 vacancies, high

D

1 30% / thirty percent
2 science teachers
3 leaving their jobs
4 10,000 / ten thousand
5 3/three (coursework, oral exams, written exams)
6 grade 200 notebooks every week
7 exams and grades
8 when there were end-of-year exams

FUNCTIONAL LANGUAGE

1 for coming
2 purpose
3 presentation
4 first of all
5 take a look
6 move on
7 From
8 brings
9 question
10 do you have

5.5 Write a cover letter for a job application

WRITING

A

Suggested answers

1 Customer service, dealing with people, selling vacations, working in an office.
2 No – a degree and some work experience is enough.
3 Good people skills, being persuasive, knowledge of the travel business.

B

Suggested answers

Paragraph 1: Which job he is applying for and why (including where he saw the job ad and its reference number)
Paragraph 2: His suitability for the role
Paragraph 3: Why he is applying for this job in particular
Paragraph 4: When he is available for an interview

C

1 d
2 a
3 c
4 b

WRITING PRACTICE

B

Model answer

Dear Ms. McMahon,

I am writing to apply for the position of Assistant Manager which is currently advertised on jobsforu.com (Ref: 273A). I have attached my résumé. I recently graduated with a degree in Sports Marketing and Management and wish to start a career in the health and fitness industry.

I believe my experience and skills, gained both in college and working at health clubs during the vacations, make me an ideal candidate for the job. While in college I was chairman of the Athletics Committee and oversaw inter-university sports competitions, which required great organizational and leadership skills. Working at health clubs gave me an insight into how they were run.

Working for your company would be a great opportunity for me to share my passion for health and fitness and to put my skills and knowledge in sales and marketing into practice in an industry I have always had an ambition to work in.

Thank you for considering my application. I am available for interview at any time and look forward to hearing from you.

Sincerely yours,
Philip Stevens

Notes

Notes

Notes

Notes